A STORE ALMOST IN SIGHT

IOWA AND THE
MIDWEST EXPERIENCE

SERIES EDITOR
William B. Friedricks,
Iowa History Center
at Simpson College

The University of Iowa Press gratefully acknowledges Humanities Iowa for its generous support of the Iowa and the Midwest Experience series.

A Store Almost in Sight

THE ECONOMIC TRANSFORMATION OF MISSOURI FROM THE LOUISIANA PURCHASE TO THE CIVIL WAR

JEFF BREMER

University of Iowa Press, Iowa City

University of Iowa Press, Iowa City 52242

www.uiowapress.org
Printed in the United States of America

Design by Ashley Muehlbauer

The University of Iowa Press is a member of Green Press Initiative and is committed to preserving natural resources.

Printed on acid-free paper

ISBN: 978-1-60938-226-1, 1-60938-226-9 (pbk)
ISBN: 978-1-60938-247-6, 1-60938-247-1 (ebk)
LCCN: 2013953624

For Yana Reid, beloved wife,

and

in memory of Henry George Welcome, 1916–2003

CONTENTS

A STORE ALMOST IN SIGHT

1

AN ENTERPRISING AND INDUSTRIOUS POPULATION

At the start of the nineteenth century, the United States was a rural, agricultural nation, where the seasons and weather regulated life and work. The vast majority of its 5,300,000 people lived on farms and plantations in the original thirteen states or along rivers such as the Ohio or Mississippi. Less than 10 percent of its population lived west of the Appalachian Mountains, and its cities were small, with Boston having fewer than 25,000 people. America was a poor, preindustrial society, and was undeveloped compared to its European rivals, Britain and France. Steamboats and railroads had yet to be invented. The world usually moved at only a few miles an hour. It took weeks for news of the death of George Washington in December 1799 to reach most parts of the country.[1]

By time the Civil War began, steamboats, railroads, and canals had tied the nation together. Steamboats moved people and goods quickly and cheaply across the vast interior of the country in days rather than weeks, traveling on thousands of miles of rivers. Railroads linked Missouri with cities such as New Orleans, Chicago, and Philadelphia; travel time between St. Louis and New York was less than three days. In 1860, people were no longer concentrated on the Atlantic seaboard. Half of the population lived west of the Appalachian Mountains, and from east to west the country spanned a continent. New York City had more than one million inhabitants, about the same as the entire state of Missouri. Population growth, territorial expansion, and transportation improvements had allowed the country to become the world's second greatest industrial power.[2]

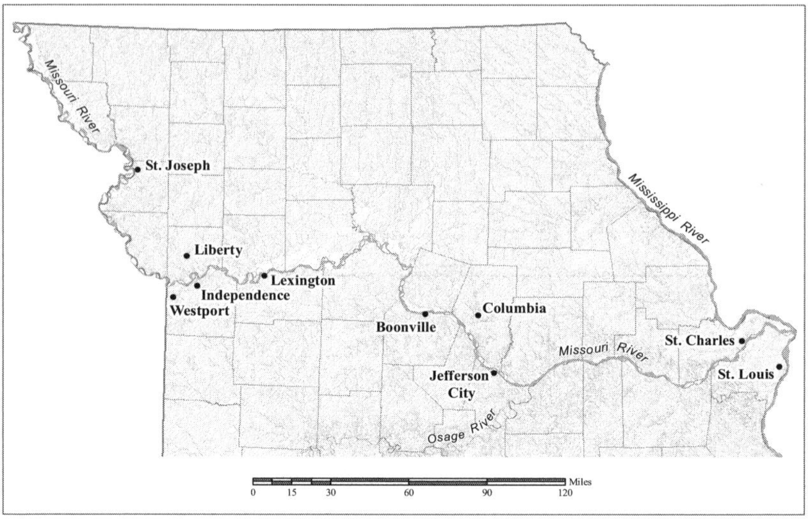

1. Map of Missouri © James Harlan, Geography Department, University of Missouri.

This book details a small part of the story of America's great antebellum economic transformation. By examining white farm families in Missouri and their economic pursuits, its main goal is to determine the market orientation of that state's rural residents. It provides a history of commercial development in central Missouri from the Louisiana Purchase to the Civil War, focusing on those counties near or adjacent to the Missouri River, which was the region most changed by settlement (fig. 1). Historians, finding various degrees of market participation across the antebellum United States, have debated the timing of its emergence, as well as its acceptance, in the past several decades. Charles Sellers, for instance, argued that capitalism was a malign and amoral force where "competition undermined neighborly cooperation and family equality." In his interpretation, the market threatened the family farm economy, which promised opportunity and equality. It disrupted traditional ways, reduced the independence of families, and exploited urban workers. Sellers asserted that when capitalism emerged in the antebellum period and brought about drastic change, resistance to it was widespread.[3]

However, a consensus is emerging that details a commercial and acquisitive society in the early Republic. In this view, the nineteenth-century market economy built upon its foundations from the previous century, developing further and spreading across the United States. There was no great disruption in the countryside during this period. Most Americans viewed the spread of commercial markets and the opportunity to participate in them favorably. This book's conclusions are in agreement with these ideas.[4]

Most Missourians welcomed the opportunity to take part in the market economy. They often produced a surplus for sale to improve their family's economic position, especially as improved transportation increased the opportunities to do so. These people were commercially minded, rather than outright capitalistic. Indeed, most lacked the necessary financial capital to be capitalists, neatly defined by historian Beatrice Craig as using capital to make money and multiply investments. The transition to capitalism had already begun by the early nineteenth century, and most migrants to Missouri had developed an interest in market participation before they arrived. Families sought out a competency, or comfortable independence, buying fertile land with market access that would best reward their labor. They wanted to own land and pass property on to future generations. A mix of production for their households, as well as markets, preserved family welfare. Increased production for trade did not erode the bonds between friends and neighbors, and the neighborhood exchange of labor, livestock, tools, and foods continued throughout the antebellum era, supporting the mix of subsistence and market farming that developed in Missouri. There was relatively little resistance to the market economy. Those who wanted to avoid neighbors or markets simply kept moving west or went into the isolated Ozark Mountains of southern Missouri, remaining on the fringes of settlement.[5]

Americans transformed a mostly empty region into a thriving, commercial society full of people out to get land and make money. By the mid-nineteenth century, American settlement had created a society that was much more influenced by market values than had existed earlier in the state. This commercial society was also far larger in terms of population. Americans pursued their own economic goals, as Simpson Kensinger wrote to his brother Lewis in Ohio. Missouri was a "rich country," he boasted. "Go way with your old poor land their you cant make the money their you could here." Restless people flooded in, searching for opportunities that were disappearing east of the Mississippi River as land prices increased or game for hunters diminished. They also came looking for new chances to make money from land speculation, family farming, or trade. Migrants from both the North and South found the region along the Missouri River to be a "land of promise," as William Davis Jr. boasted. Preacher Charles Peabody, traveling in Iowa, Missouri, and Illinois in 1846, described the St. Louis area as a "busy stirring country, too full of noise and tumult to suit my quiet spirit." He also noted in his diary, near Lexington, Missouri, "every man is most deeply intent upon doing his own business, and looking after his own affairs."[6]

Slavery was part of Missouri's business, though this story will not focus upon it. Several recent histories have detailed its role in the state. The newest of these is Diana Mutti Burke's *On Slavery's Border: Missouri's Small Slaveholding Households, 1815–1865*, the first comprehensive history of the peculiar institution in the state in nearly a century. She argues that the owners of a small number of slaves, who dominated Missouri, created a society very different from other Southern states. They built a system founded on family farms, not larger plantations, where white owners and black slaves worked and lived more intimately than elsewhere. This system did not require large numbers of slaves to practice the small-scale, diversified agriculture of Missouri. Families focused not on staple crops or capital accumulation, but on providing land or education for children. They also took advantage of river transport to take part in commercial markets. Another fine work, limited to the center region of the state, is R. Douglas Hurt's *Agriculture and Slavery in Missouri's Little Dixie*. Hurt's study of seven central Missouri counties where slavery was most widespread focused on the importance of bondage to the social and economic development of the region. He found a small planter class in these counties, with a far larger group of small farmers who produced a diverse mix of crops and livestock. Migrants brought Southern cultural ideals with them, but neither slavery nor Southern culture precluded the rapid development of commercial agriculture.[7]

This is a story about people, the economic choices they made, and their struggles to build their lives. The rural population of Missouri made millions of small decisions—ranging from how much of a certain crop to plant to how many eggs to take to the local store—that influenced the development of their state and contributed to the larger changes documented in this study. Thousands found economic independence, improved their families' lives, or realized their dreams. Many achieved their goals, but many failed. In total, they utterly changed Missouri. The life of ordinary people was tough, often short, and full of difficulty. Family, friends, and optimism about the future moderated such burdens. However, despite their travails, most Missourians accepted the market economy and its crucial role in their lives, even if they may not have always directly benefited from it.

Previous inhabitants, including the Osage and French settlers, had been linked to international markets long before any Americans arrived. The Osage played a dominant role in the region for more than a century and built an empire in the middle of the continent that remained the region's power until the arrival of the Americans. Living in the area between the Mississippi, Missouri, and Arkansas Rivers, by the late 1700s the Osage dominated the fur trade of St. Louis and used their vast hunting territory to bring in hundreds of deerskins each year. They operated as middlemen for the fur trade of the entire Missouri basin, controlling access to tribes farther west and denying their rivals the chance to gain weapons from trade. However, competition for animal resources reduced the availability of game and led to increased warfare among the area's tribes. These pressures splintered the Osage into three separate and independent bands in the last decades of the eighteenth century. In the early 1800s, smallpox, measles, and cholera repeatedly weakened them, as they struggled against incoming tribes for the diminishing resources in the Ozarks. By the time they surrendered their remaining lands in Missouri and Arkansas to the United States in 1825, incessant warfare, political division, and the destruction of their economy had devastated them.[8]

The French were the other influential power in the region before the arrival of Americans. They moved into the Mississippi River valley, lured by dreams of riches in the form of furs and precious metals, as well as by the hope of the conversion of natives to Christianity. Between 1699 and 1720, France built trading posts and settlements along the Mississippi River and Great Lakes. They ranged from Detroit to Mobile and Biloxi along the Gulf of Mexico, east of New Orleans. The French founded the villages of Cahokia and Kaskaskia along the Mississippi River, south of the Missouri River. They also built Fort Des Chartes, which served as the capital of Upper Louisiana, which included the future states of Arkansas and Missouri. By the middle of the century, France only had a few scattered settlements in the middle of the continent to support its claim to possession of the vast region between Canada and Spanish Mexico.[9]

French settlement in the Mississippi valley resembled that of northern France, but land distribution was more equitable. Settlement adopted a configuration of small, compact villages, surrounded by a fenced field of strips of privately owned land. Another field of commonly owned pastureland lay outside the enclosed field. French farmers devoted themselves to producing a mix of grain and livestock and produced considerable surpluses. Fertile soils and good growing conditions resulted in harvests that could be sent downriver to feed settlements along the lower Mississippi River. Exports grew so much that large boats had to be built to move foods south. With only a few small villages along the Mississippi River, the French could not develop the region or transform these settlements into a productive colony. Little changed when France gave Louisiana to Spain in exchange for its assistance in the Seven Years War.[10]

Even as the region was being transferred to Spain, the city of St. Louis was founded in 1763. St. Louis sat in the middle of a vast wilderness, at the meeting point of two of the greatest rivers on the continent. The town operated as a free-trade zone, outside the boundaries of French restrictions and Indian alliances. Osage, Sac, Fox (Meskwaki), and Missouri tribal members all came to trade and barter goods. French settlers, traders, and missionaries flocked to St. Louis in 1764 when the eastern bank of the Mississippi was transferred to England. They embraced the lucrative fur trade and also some production of corn, wheat, tobacco, oats, and beans. The new French settlement "quickly became a boomtown" and the center of a trading-post frontier. Most settlers devoted themselves full time to the fur trade, but some were also part-time farmers.[11]

St. Louis was the base of operations for the fur trade, and nearly everyone in the town was involved in some way. Trapping parties were organized and equipped in St. Louis, and most traders lived in the town. Warehouses and mercantile firms provided the necessary goods and services for the trade; they also purchased and stored the annual accumulation of furs and pelts. Merchants supplied the necessary Indian presents and trading goods, which included tobacco, guns, alcohol, thread, and tools. They could sometimes make a profit that exceeded 300 percent. In the spring, hunters and traders headed up the Missouri River. Hunters—mostly French and Indian—took beaver pelts in the spring, when the fur was thick after a long winter, and in the fall, after beaver coats recovered from the summer molting. Most commerce linked with the trade occurred in these seasons. Trappers and Indians were tied into international markets for furs and goods, but there was no self-sustaining domestic market in the region.[12]

This mix of agriculture and commerce did not change when Spain took possession of the province. The Spanish gladly accepted Louisiana from France, as it acted as a buffer against English and, later, American encroachment into

Spain's valuable Mexican colonies. However, like France, Spain suffered from an inability to adequately guard or people the vast region. When the first Spanish governor arrived, he had only ninety soldiers with him. During the thirty-eight years that Spain ruled Louisiana, less than twenty Spanish families settled there. Only a small number of top officials, clerics, and merchants moved to the province. Spanish Louisiana was chronically underfunded, and Spain never spent enough money to gain the loyalty of the Indian tribes in the region. Thus, many tribes traded directly with the English, who were much more generous with their gifts. Operating from a series of posts and forts near the Great Lakes and along the upper Mississippi, English traders continually challenged Spanish trade and authority. Customs, manners, and language remained French. From the start, Spanish authority was weak and its influence light. What control it had would be completely undermined by the arrival of the Americans.[13]

After the United States gained independence from England, American settlers surged westward over the Appalachian Mountains. At first, Spain attempted to choke off this migration by closing the Mississippi River to American commerce in 1784. Spanish authorities hoped that shutting off the only outlet for American exports would bring a halt to American settlement in the Ohio valley. Frustrated Americans threatened to open the river to trade by force, if necessary. Access to the Mississippi River was crucial, because New Orleans provided the most inexpensive trade route for Americans west of the Appalachian Mountains. Overland transport to east coast markets was prohibitively costly, and local markets were limited. Development beyond subsistence farming would have been very difficult without a market in New Orleans, and many farmers would have had little reason to move to Kentucky, Tennessee, or Ohio.[14]

The Spanish, realizing that angry, rifle-wielding American frontiersmen posed a serious threat to their weakly defended lands, decided to change their policies. Since the Americans could not be halted, Spain decided to allow them to move into Louisiana. Spain hoped that western settlers could be convinced to abandon their loyalty to the United States and embrace Spanish rule. Lieutenant Governor Zenon Trudeau contended that many Catholics, French, and Germans, as well as those who were "disgusted with their government," could be lured into Spanish Louisiana. The Americans who had migrated to Upper Louisiana, he noted, "have found lands superior to those of the Ohio, they are earnestly beginning to improve them." The newcomers built new flour mills and sawmills, cultivated hemp, and lived in houses better than those of the French inhabitants, he wrote. The administration in Louisiana believed that American pioneers were not strongly attached to the United States and that they could be convinced to accept Spanish culture, religion, and language. Unfortunately for Spain, this did not occur.[15]

Much to the concern of Spain and France, American commerce and settlement began to dominate the Mississippi River valley in the 1790s. Kentucky and Tennessee became states in this decade, and by 1800 cities such as Nashville, Cincinnati, Pittsburgh, and Lexington had been founded. Tens of thousands of Americans moved west every year. The Spanish governor of Louisiana, Baron de Carondelet, expressed concern about the newcomers. The advantages of the province were "counterbalanced by the unmeasured ambition of a new people, who are vigorous, hostile to all subjection, and who have been uniting and multiplying in the silence of peace, and almost ignored, with a remarkable rapidity." He believed, quite rightly, that the ambitions of this "vast and restless" population were not limited to the region east of the Mississippi River. If they lived on the banks of the Mississippi and Missouri Rivers, Spain could not halt an invasion of its provinces.[16]

Carondelet's fears were justifiable. The region from the Great Lakes to the Gulf of Mexico rapidly became an American sphere of influence, as land-hungry Northern and Southern families pressed west. One hundred and fifty thousand Americans lived west of the Appalachian Mountains in 1795; this number reached more than one million by 1810. The newcomers migrated in search of land, market access, and opportunity. They exported wheat, cattle, and lumber from western New York soon after settlement and sold whiskey and beef to Quebec. Americans also sent wheat from western Pennsylvania to New Orleans during the Revolutionary War. Farmers in the Ohio and Mississippi River valleys shipped hundreds of flatboats full of flour, whiskey, and other agricultural products downriver to New Orleans. In 1801, nearly 600 vessels passed Natchez, Mississippi, on their way to New Orleans from Kentucky, Tennessee, Ohio, and Upper Louisiana. These ships took lead, salt, tobacco, and other goods south to the port and demonstrated the economic power of the expanding United States.[17]

The Spanish tried to lure American settlers into Louisiana with a number of generous policies. Beginning in 1786, Spain opened the Mississippi River to U.S. trade and allowed some religious freedom. The chief inducement to American emigration was the opportunity to benefit from large land grants. A common technique involved offering settlement contracts to individuals, guaranteeing them extensive tracts of free land in exchange for establishing a new community. The Spanish called such people *pobladors*—"populators"—whose desire to develop the region via private enterprise was highly rewarded. Spanish commandants sent notices to western American settlements glorifying the many virtues of Louisiana in the late 1790s. Emigrants could claim land as individuals or families or organize larger settlement groups as *pobladors*.[18]

Thousands of Americans moved into Upper Louisiana in the 1780s and 1790s, including the famous American frontiersman Daniel Boone. He moved with his extended family to central Missouri in 1799 at the invitation of the Spanish lieutenant governor, who offered him 1,000 arpents of land (about 850 acres). Boone accepted, in large part because of his frustration with land disputes and lawsuits in his home state of Kentucky. "Little by little his wealth had melted away before these constant claims for damages, and when he finally left Kentucky in 1799 he was poor," recalled his son, Nathan. Boone suffered from serious legal and financial difficulties, which left him embittered and exhausted. He had capitalized on his fame after the Revolutionary War and became involved in land speculation, trade, and surveying. The old war hero was often a sloppy surveyor who left a confusing maze of overlapping plats behind. This imprecise and messy system cost him dearly, when his own claims were denied or disputed. Boone's trust in others was misplaced, as his loans to friends went unpaid or others cheated him of his land claims. He did not have the ruthlessness that land speculation required, noted historian John Mack Faragher.[19]

By the late 1780s, legal matters consumed Boone's life in Kentucky. He was sued for faulty surveys, breach of contract, personal debts, and the debts of others he had pledged to support. Opponents threatened his life, and he even feared assassination. "He often said he could not travel with safety. Even in time of peace he felt his own Kentucky was as dangerous to him as in the time of Indian wars," his son noted. Bad luck also struck, when a cargo of fifteen tons of ginseng for export to China was ruined by a collision. Nathan Boone sadly observed, "when I was married, it grieved the old colonel that he had nothing to give me and my wife with to start our new life." Daniel Boone moved to Missouri, pulled by the opportunity to find new lands across the

Mississippi and pushed out by financial troubles. Thousands followed him in the decades before the Civil War.[20]

When Upper Louisiana became part of the United States, 6,000 Americans lived in the region. They outnumbered everyone except the native Indians. American immigration led to the increased development of agriculture and industry in the province, contributing to salt making, lead mining, and farming. The French had begun to exploit the resources of the region, and the flood of incoming Americans accelerated this process. This progress came with a price, though. While Spain's immigration policies had encouraged the settlement of Louisiana and made the region a vital buffer for Mexico, Spain had practically handed the region to the Americans. Thus, the United States had enacted a "peaceful conquest" of the region even before it officially took it over.[21]

A French engineer working for the Spanish explained how the region was changing. Nicolas de Finiels wrote *An Account of Upper Louisiana* in 1803. St. Louis and the settlements around it depended almost wholly upon their own food production, he noted. The city contained about 1,000 inhabitants, and its citizens cultivated all sorts of agricultural products. He reported that the people of St. Louis grew many vegetables and fruits, including apples, pears, and grapes, as well as thousands of bushels of corn and wheat. In the woods, they found hazelnuts, cherries, pecans, blackberries, and walnuts. Other villages, such as St. Charles, just west of St. Louis, did not yet "believe that they need creature comforts and therefore disdain the arts and crafts." Scattered families and settlements produced almost all they needed, from carts and plows to shoes and clothing. People went to St. Louis for foodstuffs, luxuries, or items that they could not produce.[22]

Finiels argued that American migration to Upper Louisiana had begun to transform this region. He contrasted what he considered to be the idleness of the French inhabitants with the "industry" and drive of the newcomers. The Americans grasped at advantages that the region presented, and they pursued new avenues of business. Sawmills worked by Americans supplied more wood at lower prices, and more iron was also available and less expensive. Masonry, carpentry, cabinetry, and furniture were cheaper, too. Finiels, in fact, argued that Americans had changed the entire economic atmosphere of the St. Louis area. Before they had arrived, "you had to wait four to six years for windows, doors and furniture, which grew old in the workshops before they were completed. Vegetables, eggs, poultry, milk, butter and grain are more readily available, and thanks to the Americans' industry subsistence is generally more secure than before."[23]

Another Frenchman, Pierre-Charles de Hault de Lassus de Luzieres, also had favorable comments about the immigration of Americans. Speaking of Kaskaskia, a village about fifty miles southeast of St. Louis, he called the American migration "advantageous." Their arrival "provided skilled farmers," as well as masons, blacksmiths, carpenters, weavers, and "other useful artisans that we are lacking," he wrote in 1797. "This immigration is already stimulating distinct and beneficial improvements in agriculture, handicrafts, and industry." The newcomers also built flour mills and sawmills. Overall, he was very pleased that the majority of farmers were now increasingly devoted to agriculture.[24]

Amos Stoddard and John Bradbury made similar observations about Americans in Missouri. Stoddard noted that the distance from "ready markets in their neighborhood" was the greatest problem for the development of the region. Despite the problems of isolation and distance, Americans were exporting significant quantities of corn, tobacco, beef, pork, and even butter. "A spirit of industry prevails among settlers," Stoddard declared—ignoring the decades of French commercial pursuits—as the newcomers focused on agricultural production. American migration "gave a spring to agriculture and commerce; a spirit of foreign intercourse was diffused among all classes of the people; exertion was made to prepare raw materials for the West India and other markets." John Bradbury, an Englishman sent by the Botanical Society of Liverpool to investigate plant life in the United States, echoed the comments of Stoddard, de Luzieres, and Finiels. He wrote that French settlers were attached to the less productive traditional agricultural practices of their ancestors. He contrasted them with their American neighbors, who used improved tools and techniques and cultivated twice as much land. Bradbury also wrongly thought that the French lacked "industry." But he noted that their villages still had "an appearance of comfort and independence."[25]

The economy of Upper Louisiana was predominantly agrarian at the end of the eighteenth century, but it rapidly grew and diversified with American migration. Most agricultural production went to feed the local population, but an increasing surplus was sent to New Orleans. Americans settled around New Madrid, in the southeast corner of the state, and they increased the area's production of corn by ten times within five years of migration. Near Cape Girardeau, the newcomers grew large quantities of wheat, corn, and tobacco.

Incoming Americans were responsible for most of the new surpluses and their export. Boats carried ever-larger amounts of flour, corn, salt, pork, whiskey, and other products from the settlements along the Missouri and Mississippi Rivers to Illinois, up the Ohio River, or south to New Orleans. Americans also established flour mills, distilleries, salt works, and new farms. They produced a greater abundance and variety of farm goods and livestock for export and local consumption than ever before.[26]

After the Louisiana Purchase, thousands began to move into the region in search of cheap land. When people discovered that Upper Louisiana was to be transferred to the United States, the value of all property in the province skyrocketed, since almost any land, even that which was wild and uncultivated, had future value. Timothy Flint, a missionary from New England who lived in Missouri for four years between 1816 and 1822, argued that the scramble for land introduced "that restless spirit of speculation and improvement which characterize the people of the United States. The tide of emigration once more swept by the dwelling of Daniel Boone, driving off the game and monopolizing the rich hunting grounds." But the rush to make an easy fortune, where speculators purchased land that often was not legally held, seriously complicated life for migrants who wanted to buy land and settle in the territory. A horribly tangled mess of competing French, Spanish, and American land claims further complicated the situation. A series of severe earthquakes also rocked the Mississippi River region in late 1811 and 1812.[27]

Missouri was a sideshow in the greater story of the War of 1812 and suffered from no serious invasion during the war. However, it experienced many skirmishes, raids, and minor attacks that disrupted settlement and terrorized residents of the territory. The violence began in 1809, and the center of the state, the northwest edge of American settlement, bore the brunt of attacks. The Osage remained allied to the United States during the war, due to their dependence on trade goods and weapons. Other tribes—including elements of the Winnebago, Kickapoo, Sac, and Fox tribes—went to war to push settlers out of hunting lands and gain plunder. Local militia patrolled the countryside in an effort to deter attacks, while farm families took shelter in forts and local blockhouses when threatened. Violence peaked in 1813 and 1814, and terrified families rarely left their cabins or cornfields. Tribes made peace by the summer of 1816.[28]

The end of the war encouraged large-scale American migration. More than 40,000 people flooded into Missouri in search of land and economic opportunity between 1815 and 1820. This migration did more than anything else to help ensure the security of Missouri, and sheer numbers overwhelmed the Indian population. Timothy Flint observed, "the immigration from the western and southern states to this country poured in a flood." Watching the incoming settlers from St. Charles, he counted over 100 people passing through the village in one day, and "the number was said to have equaled that for many days together." The ferry near the village was continually busy, and he observed one wagon train of settlers, children, slaves, and hundreds of animals that was three-quarters of a mile long. Flint wrote that there was a "rage for speculating" after the War of 1812 ended and that the greed for profit dominated all conversations. Minister John Mason Peck commented that the "new-comers, like a mountain torrent, poured into the country faster than it was possible to provide corn for breadstuff."[29]

The territory's population nearly tripled between 1815 and 1820, and Missouri applied for statehood in 1819. Even before the war concluded, Henry Marie Brackenridge reported American settlements had appeared on the Missouri River 200 miles above St. Louis. Towns materialized almost overnight, and farms dotted the lands along the river in increasing numbers. The town of Chariton contained about 500 inhabitants, Stephen H. Long's expedition reported in 1819. It existed "on a spot where two years previous, no permanent habitation had been established. Such is the rapidity, with which the forests of Missouri are becoming filled with an enterprising and industrious population." The first steamboat, the *Zebulon Pike*, docked at St. Louis in 1817 and heralded a new age of rapid transportation in the West that promoted migration, settlement, and commerce. The government sold almost 900,000 acres of public land in Missouri before the Panic of 1819 brought migration, and the demand for land, to a sudden halt. Missouri turned a corner in the years after the end of the war. In the middle of the continent and straddling the major western waterway, as the focus of the fur trade, the Santa Fe trade, and overland western migration, Missouri became an economic center for the antebellum trans-Mississippi West. Cheap, fertile land encouraged settlement, and thousands of families moved into Missouri after the War of 1812, eagerly participating in the growing American market economy.[30]

The decline of European and Indian rivals allowed the United States to control Missouri and surrounding areas by the end of the War of 1812. Disease, overhunting, and warfare overwhelmed the Osage and ended their hegemony of the region. They were forced out of the Missouri River valley before most Americans arrived. The French were unable to exert much control over the area, due to a limited population. However, Upper Louisiana enjoyed strong economic ties to outside markets, exporting skins, fur, and grains. The Spanish brought the first Americans into Louisiana in an attempt to populate the vast region and maintain their hold on it. But American settlement only led to the more rapid social and economic conquest by the newcomers. The transfer of the territory to American control set off a rush by thousands into central Missouri that overwhelmed any possible resistance. The "industry" of the Americans in Upper Louisiana, as explained by Nicolas de Finiels, John Bradbury, and others, led to increasing economic development. Settlers produced greater amounts and an increased diversity of farm goods and sent their surpluses downriver. The greatest challenge to the new American administration was the tangled mess of competing land claims, which helped to delay settlement. The conclusion of the War of 1812 denoted the end of the first stage of Missouri's frontier history. The large-scale migration reported by Timothy Flint and John Mason Peck marked the beginning of widespread American settlement along the Missouri River.

2

A NEW AND BETTER LIFE

Antebellum Americans were driven and ambitious people who were out to make the best possible lives for themselves and their families. "Americans enjoyed more opportunity to pursue their ambitions, by foul means or fair, than any other people in history," noted historian Walter McDougall. After the American Revolution, millions flooded west in search of land, seeking opportunity and security. They were less constrained by their historical and geographical circumstances than any other people, and a resource-rich land without major continental rivals awaited their conquest. Americans also benefited from the new commercial society that emerged in the late eighteenth and early nineteenth centuries. The Revolution had unleashed entrepreneurial and commercial energies that transformed the country between independence and the Civil War. It weakened the hierarchal, paternalistic society inherited from the English and broke down barriers to the pursuit of individual economic gain. The antebellum United States was, as historian Gordon Wood has argued, "a very democratic and egalitarian society, dominated as it was by common, ordinary people with very vulgar and pecuniary interests."[1]

America became a "scrambling, acquisitive, individualistic" society. By the 1820s, it was "perhaps the most thoroughly commercialized nation in the world," Wood wrote. Nicholas Hesse, a German immigrant who lived in the town of Westphalia, Missouri, confirmed what Wood observed, noting, "Nearly everywhere that I visited an American farmer, his property was offered to me for sale. Everyone paints in lively colors the heralded advantages of his possession." He further wrote that Americans did not hesitate to "move on again from a good place, frequently for a great distance if [they] can sell [their] property advantageously." Another German immigrant in Missouri, Eduard Zimmerman, echoed this, writing that Americans "never become attached to a given region. If they can sell their property to any sort of advantage, they are certain to do so."[2]

Americans pursued their own economic self-interest whenever possible. They benefited from their English heritage of capitalism, which stressed such positive economic traits as creativity and ambition, as well as more negative aspects such as impatience and corruption. In Europe and elsewhere, wrote McDougall, "the privilege to manipulate the system to one's advantage was either reserved to elites or severely constrained: the wily peasant could not go far." In the United States, by contrast, white males enjoyed greater opportunity to pursue their own desires for economic gain. Common and ordinary people did not accept the hierarchal and aristocratic societies that existed in Europe. Their "separate and strenuous pursuits of happiness," as Gordon Wood declared, "directed and shaped the values and contours of life to an extent never before or since seen in modern history."[3]

Alexis de Tocqueville echoed these comments in his classic study *Democracy in America*. He wrote that he was "more struck by the innumerable multitude of little undertakings than by the extraordinary size of some of their industrial enterprises." Almost every farmer combined "some trade with agriculture; most of them have made agriculture itself a trade." Americans saw settlement as temporary, he wrote, especially in the western states. The continual increase in population usually led to an increase in the price of land and the opportunity for profit. Like Nicholas de Finiels, Tocqueville saw Americans as having a "passion for industry" that viewed farming as a trading venture. In fact, he claimed, "I know of no other country where love of money has such a grip on men's hearts."[4]

Missouri provided opportunity for these ambitious and mobile people, who brought an acceptance of the market economy west with them. Most of these people came from the upper South—Kentucky, Tennessee, Virginia, and North Carolina. Migrants usually settled near rivers, as soils were more fertile and waterways provided easy transportation and market access. They also brought slavery westward with them. But the peculiar institution did not impede involvement in the growing market economy. Small slave owners and farmers populated Missouri, owning modest amounts of land and a few slaves. They produced a diverse mix of crops and operated more like small farmers than planters. Southerners had shown an interest in commerce since they had crossed the Appalachian Mountains in the late 1700s. Most Missouri residents did not resist markets. Of course, not everyone wanted to be part of this emerging market society. Some chose to live more isolated lives on the edges of settlement, due to an inability to buy land or a preference for such a life. Many still took advantage of the chance to enjoy the material opportunities provided by trade, as Henry Schoolcraft witnessed in the Ozark Mountains of southern Missouri.

Historians have long debated the importance of market participation before the Civil War. Some have argued that the *mentalité*, or worldview, of preindustrial Americans was opposed to individual gain and market participation. These historians believed that farmers and rural artisans produced mostly for a local market and that communal ideas and institutions constrained their actions. Meeting household needs and maintaining established social relationships were far more important than profit maximization, and economic gain was not a dominant value. The barter of goods and services and the exchange of labor between neighboring farmers did not provide evidence for the existence of capitalism. Personal relationships and tradition trumped commercial interests.[5]

However, families did not have to focus on short-term profits to take part in commercial markets and did not have to violate communal bonds to do so. They could simply use a household surplus for exchange in local towns for goods they desired. Massachusetts farmers traveled surprisingly long distances to market their farm produce in 1750. This only increased in the following decades. In the late eighteenth and early nineteenth centuries, farmers were not isolated from markets and chose to participate in them. Some historians have even argued for a society that accepted capitalism in New England in the 1600s.[6]

The United States was caught between two economic systems from the Constitution to the Civil War—a barter system and a market system. Farm households had to take part in commercial markets to earn money to buy and cultivate their lands, but subsistence production continued, even as commercial production increased. Farmwomen continued to make clothing, for example. Families practiced "safety-first" agriculture and sought communal self-sufficiency, based upon household food production, female labor, and the assistance of neighbors. The success of the farm household required market participation. It also required subsistence production and community exchange. Historian Richard Bushman has called this mix of economic pursuits "composite farming," where sharp distinctions between market production and household use do not exist. Robert A. Gross observed that households in Concord, Massachusetts, had been producing a surplus—albeit a small one—for their neighborhoods and trade since the 1700s. These historians argue that market participation assisted families in meeting their needs and did not seriously displace traditional farm production. The situation in Missouri reflected this. There was little conflict between the market and subsistence modes of production.[7]

Families in Missouri accepted the necessity and importance of the market economy to improve their economic situation, even as they produced a substantial amount of their basic needs themselves. Migrants from both the North and South showed a willingness to produce a surplus for market use. This gave them access to items that improved their lives, such as tools, spices, and cloth. A farmer might take a cart of corn and potatoes five or ten miles to a local town once a month to buy flour or glass. Indeed, people migrated to central Missouri seeking such opportunities and took part in the market economy because it benefited their lives.[8]

Missouri settlers showed an interest in market participation. J. Clemens, who lived near St. Louis, wrote home to his family in Kentucky in 1816. He praised the virtues of the countryside around the city, writing that those who acquired lands could not fail to enjoy a "rich harvest if they purchase in a speculation point of view." Farming, he added, would also be successful. Hemp and wheat were marketable, granted enough labor. Thomas Duggins wrote to his family in Virginia that property in Buchanan County, in the northwest corner of the state, "would be called immensely rich by a Virginian," despite the fact that these lands were inferior to other sections of the area. "I believe as to property you would do much better than Virginia with the same industry and economy." Another Virginian, S. E. Slater, similarly informed his family back home that land in northwest Missouri was cheap, and grazing range for livestock was excellent. It was easy to market goods to the flourishing town of St. Joseph, which also offered "fine inducement for speculation." He told his family that they could "make more money" through agriculture or slave hiring than in Virginia. Frances Fackler wrote to her sister-in-law, also in Virginia, to say "we sell everything we make here at our door and could sell a great deal more if we had it." She noted that local farmers brought cherries to sell for $2 a bushel. Mary Hardin also reported that her father had "fine crops this year" and had sold 120 head of hogs to another Kentuckian.[9]

The story of German immigrant Frederick Steines is an example of the opportunities and challenges available for those who settled in Missouri. In June 1834, Steines arrived in Baltimore, having left his hometown of Neu Loehdorf, in present-day northwest Germany, for a new life in the United States. Steines and his extended family traveled across the Appalachian Mountains and down the Ohio River to Missouri. They then purchased farms along the Missouri River about thirty miles west of St. Louis, joining other family members and friends around the town of Washington. Steines bought a 115-acre farm, complete with livestock, orchards, tools, and other necessary farm equipment, for $1,000. Though he lost his wife and children to cholera in his first summer in America—he told his family that he had been "robbed of everything"—he survived his devastating losses and prospered over time. He wrote home a year after he arrived, saying, "I am fine and very satisfied with my destiny of being in agriculture in free America." He found the people "extremely friendly" but noted they "are speculators and if in commerce they can offer more which may be cheap, they will seldom fail."[10]

Steines had been very unhappy in Prussia and enjoyed his new home. He could live peacefully on his farm, undisturbed by military service, high taxes, or political oppression. Steines wrote in his letters home, "we have all been resurrected to a new and better life, and it seems to me that I must especially pity the dead that they were not permitted to enjoy their life here for a time. Especially am I one who feels happy here!" He was "constantly" glad to live in a republic where "by the law all are equal and the rights of the offended are protected." He was not forced to serve in the army, and he could elect his own political representatives, who "cost us little or nothing." Furthermore, America offered far greater opportunity for social and economic advancement. "Diligence and industry find their full reward here; the state makes few demands on the citizens." He proudly told his family, "I can assure you, a German who has been here for a time feels as if he has escaped from prison to freedom." In America, "a human being is a human being," and the lowest person was equal to anyone else. He could work in moderation and live well on his farm with his new wife and children, his family settled around him, his fortunes constantly improving. He purchased more land; sold eggs, butter, poultry, livestock, and crops; and made 10 percent interest on loans to fellow farmers. Steines told his friends and family to come to America, for work was a delight and "yields abundant fruit."[11]

In 1840, after six years of living in the United States, Frederick Steines provided a clear summary of the market interests of Missourians. He observed in his letters, "to make money is the only ambition of the typical American. Money is the motive of his action; it is the axis around which the whole world turns." He told the story of an American schoolmaster who lived in the town of New Washington on the Missouri River. This teacher wrote in the copybook of one of his students this instruction: "God made bees and bees make honey. God made men and men make money." Steines complained that Americans—and "unfortunately the already sufficiently Americanized Germans"—usually asked each other the question what they were worth and judged themselves according to their wealth. In this way, "he knows how he should value the man." He enjoyed his new life, but Steines harshly judged his fellow Americans and crudely cursed them as a people ranked only second to the Jews in their "deeds and drive." He criticized Americans for their continual interest in making money and wrote, "a person just vegetates here," presumably due to a lack of culture on the American frontier. In Germany, he noted, people "lived."[12]

More than one million people came to Missouri between the War of 1812 and the Civil War. The War of 1812 had been decisive in the West because Native American opposition to American settlement had been mostly defeated. The war had broken the stubborn resistance of tribes around the Great Lakes and opened the upper Mississippi valley to Americans. Millions of acres of newly available lands and rising prices for staple crops drew settlers westward. American nationalism, confidence, and optimism spurred people west. Historian Malcolm Rohrbough declared, "Never had the land been richer; never was there so much of it; never was the future brighter."[13]

Most of those who came to Missouri before the Civil War migrated from the upper South, with a large majority coming from Kentucky, Tennessee, Virginia, and North Carolina. Missouri was an important destination for both small slave owners—who usually only owned a few slaves—and those who did not own slaves. Families from the upper South were attracted to the fertile soil of the region and the opportunity to grow crops similar to those in regions they had left. They followed migration patterns that ran along parallel latitudes and moved to areas that allowed them to replicate social and economic systems back east. Most planters, those who owned more than twenty slaves, chose to remain in the lower South, moving to states such as Mississippi and Texas. Planters were attracted to these areas because of their ability to grow cotton. They also feared that Missouri, surrounded by free territory, might not be safe for large numbers of slaves.[14]

"Emigration was a central fact of life in Southern states," wrote historian James Miller. Southerners moved in search of economic advancement, as migration was often necessary for success. Westward movement frequently produced upward mobility by providing access to new and better farmland. Rejecting migration often meant rejecting the chance for advancement. A perceived lack of opportunity, or the inability to purchase land, also forced Americans west. Many thousands departed the Southeast for greater opportunity elsewhere in the nineteenth century. In the 1790s, two-thirds of landless white men left Virginia. This was for good reason, as the top 10 percent of landowners in the state, according to one estimate, controlled 70 percent of Virginia's real estate. Half of all whites born in South Carolina after 1800 also departed their state; one-quarter of Georgians similarly left their homes by 1850. In Kentucky, slave owners, speculators, and commercial growth reduced economic opportunity for poorer residents by monopolizing land ownership and bidding up land prices. In 1792, only one-third of adult men owned any land, and most of them had their land titles contested. Daniel Boone was a victim of this system. In the 1790s and the first decades of the 1800s, thousands of families fled westward to Illinois, Alabama, and Missouri in search of greater opportunity and economic independence.[15]

Southern men moved west to achieve independence for themselves and their households. They left their homes to establish their own families or to escape dependence on their parents. Property ownership provided small landowners with power over their lives and was a badge of independence and citizenship. It also gave them control over the labor of dependent members of their households, from children to spouses to slaves. Autonomy was directly tied to control over productive resources, such as land and labor. Southern men were committed to landowning because it allowed them to avoid the terrible fate of dependency and subordination to others. Such farmers understood the evils of dependency well, as they lived in a society based on the control of slave labor. The perpetual control of blacks reminded them of the horrors of subordination, which they desperately wanted to avoid.[16]

Southerners emigrated for economic advancement, usually based on the acquisition of inexpensive and fertile land. In Mississippi, Louisiana, and Texas, newcomers sought land and slaves, emphasizing cotton production, land speculation, and slave ownership. In Missouri, where cotton production was not possible due to colder weather and shorter growing seasons, emigrants looked to obtain land as the foundation for personal and household independence. Southerners left their homes because of a lack of affordable or productive land. Soil exhaustion, overcrowding, or high prices for property pushed ambitious men west. They left for the chance to get ahead, gain status, or make money. John Tannor noted that the land in Missouri was "rich beyond richness," compared to Virginia. When he returned to Dinwiddie County near the Atlantic coast on a trip back home, he wrote, "I was not aware how poor the dirt was in 'Ole Virginny' and thank my stars that our land in Missouri is worth having." Tannor observed that a plantation in Virginia would surely lead to poverty for its owner and his children.[17]

Soil exhaustion contributed to the migration out of states such as Virginia, where a focus on immediate profit pushed Virginians to overwork their land. Farmers grew crops, especially tobacco, on the same piece of land for six or seven years until the soil was worn out. Then they abandoned the property. Another field would be planted and exhausted in turn. "Soil exhaustion and tobacco production went hand in hand," wrote historian Avery Odelle Craven. It was often easier and cheaper—for those who could afford it—to purchase more land than to improve property already owned. By the late 1790s, much of Virginia's farmland had been devastated. Exhausted soils required more organic matter and fertilizer than were available. Planters avoided attempts at more efficient practices, as slave labor and large fields reduced incentives for more rational agriculture. George Washington, for example, was appalled by the terrible state of his fields after he retired from the presidency. By the 1830s, a glut of property was for sale, as desperate debtors tried to meet their costs. This pushed down prices. Land values fell even farther, pulled down by abundant and more fertile tracts in the West. Insects and diseases, such as weevils and wheat rust, added to the agricultural crisis in the state. Many who left Virginia came to Missouri.[18]

The first centers of European and American settlement along the Missouri River were near St. Louis and in the center of the territory, known as the Boonslick. A famous settler gave his name to the area, and salt licks attracted animals.

Its extraordinary fertility made it the most desirable farmland in Missouri. In the early nineteenth century, settlement had leapfrogged west more than 100 miles from the St. Louis area to the Boonslick. Plenty of game could be found, unlike many places east of the Mississippi River that had been overrun by settlement. The alluvial soils were well watered, and the river bottoms contained rich and virgin soil that far surpassed the older farming regions east of the Mississippi. For millennia, glaciated topsoil from the upper Midwest had been washed downstream. Rivers and floods deposited this soil deeply in places such as Tennessee, Missouri, and Mississippi. In the center of the state, the woodland and prairie met, and newcomers considered this mix of open land and timber ideal. Farmers selected land that they could easily clear of trees and ready for cultivation. They avoided heavily timbered areas that took excessive amounts of time to clear, as well as the prairie that they believed contained inferior soil. Settlers also had difficulty breaking the thick prairie sod. Pioneers settled on less forested lands near the edge of plains, where they had access to wood for construction and heating, as well as open grazing land for their livestock.[19]

Henry Marie Brackenridge wrote a travel account that helped to popularize the Boonslick region. He had traveled up the Missouri River in 1811 and reported his observations in *Views of Louisiana*, published just before the end of the War of 1812. Brackenridge described the area as a "garden spot" that "must one day yield nourishment to a multitude of beings." He wrote that the bottomlands along the Missouri River in the Boonslick were "of the finest kinds for three hundred miles." It was well watered and had good streams, too. He compared the land to Kentucky but considered the Boonslick superior since it did not have "a forest so dark and heavy." Brackenridge rhapsodized about the area, writing, "There is an extensive strip of land along this side of the Missouri, of nearly thirty miles in width and about one hundred and fifty in length, altogether woods, and excellent soil." While surveying central Missouri, he stood on a hill 100 feet above the surrounding countryside and described an ocean of prairie covered with waving grasses. Occasionally a solitary cottonwood or walnut tree stood out like an island. He saw 50,000 acres of the finest land, "and yet on all this open space, there is but one little cultivated spot to be seen." He wrote that his mind naturally adorned the landscape with "happy dwellings and richly cultivated fields."[20]

Americans quickly settled the region. The population of Missouri almost doubled in the seven years after the Louisiana Purchase, and more than 20,000 people lived in the territory by 1810. Another 40,000 flooded into Missouri in the following decade, almost tripling the population between 1810 and 1820. They brought with them almost 10,000 slaves, who made up about one-sixth of the total population by statehood. About one-third of the population, including more than 3,000 slaves, lived in the Boonslick region by 1820. By statehood, the banks of the Missouri River west of St. Louis, where the growing towns of Franklin, Columbia, and Boonville had been founded, were dotted with villages and farms. Franklin, located on the north bank of the Missouri River, was established in 1816 and quickly grew to be one of the largest settlements in the state. The town became the seat of Howard County and by 1820 had more than 1,000 inhabitants. It was a thriving settlement, with a number of stores, a post office, a bank, a courthouse, a newspaper, and a jail. It also benefited from one of the territory's federal land offices. Other towns, such as Boonville (just across the river), Arrow Rock, and Rocheport, also grew rapidly with the flood of immigrants. These booming towns later operated as market centers for the export of agricultural goods and the sale of merchandise to rural areas.[21]

Geography played an important role for immigrants. Most preferred to live near rivers for ease of transportation and because riverside farmland was more productive than eastern lands. Even the least fertile farmland produced more than eastern farms. Such good soil allowed settlers to grow large quantities of crops, to both feed their family and also provide a surplus for neighborhood or market exchange. American settlers across much of the country, as well as central Missouri, demonstrated this geographical interest. In southwest Illinois, three-quarters of the farmers settled within twenty miles of Fort St. Louis, the maximum distance considered profitable to transport goods for sale. In Iowa, lands near the Mississippi River in the southeast corner of the state sold first, followed by interior areas that usually paralleled rivers. Farther south, migrants to Arkansas settled mostly along rivers for ease of transport and market access. The same pattern occurred along the Missouri River and other waterways, as settlement was closely linked to market access and soil fertility.[22]

Most farm families were comfortable living in a more developed area with market potential, but some chose to live isolated from other people. People who wanted to live a more primitive, mostly subsistence lifestyle resided in places away from larger rivers or in the hilly Ozark Mountains of southern Missouri. Plenty of fish and game were available, and a combination of corn and hogs helped feed families who preferred a more self-sufficient life (fig. 2). Driving

2. Missouri settlers relied on hunting birds and animals to help feed themselves during their first years in the state. *Frank Leslie's Illustrated Newspaper* (December 18, 1858).

livestock to towns or steamboat docks was the best chance for commercial participation. Those who chose to live in isolated or frontier areas, according to Henry Marie Brackenridge, lived a life "truly free . . . beyond the sphere of that larger society." Such people lived as Daniel Boone did, moving farther west as civilization edged closer. Stephen H. Long quoted Boone in 1819, "I think it is time to remove when I can no longer fall a tree for fuel, so that its top will lie within a few yards of the door of my cabin." Another settler on the Missouri frontier told Long that he did not want to spend all his life in one place. Long quoted him as saying that "he had learned from experience that a man might live in greater ease and freedom, where his neighbors were not very numerous."[23]

The frontier preacher John Mason Peck noted the austere life of one family who chose to live away from more settled areas (fig. 3). Peck, a Baptist minister from Connecticut, moved west to work as a missionary after the War of 1812. He kept a series of diaries recording his experiences in the Midwest over four decades. On a tour through eastern Missouri, he found a family living in very basic conditions. He described one family, south of St. Louis, as living in a single log cabin "of the most primitive structure." It sat in the middle of the

3. Baptist preacher John Mason Peck spent decades as a missionary in the Mississippi River valley. His diaries are important sources on Missouri history in the early nineteenth century. Rufus Babcock, ed., *Forty Years of Pioneer Life: Memoir of John Mason Peck* (Philadelphia: American Baptist Publication Society, 1864), frontispiece.

family's cornfield. Two middle-aged parents, four children, two spouses, and three or four grandchildren lived there. This extended family had migrated from Virginia to Kentucky to Tennessee and then to Missouri. Peck wrote, with some surprise, that they had not seen a Baptist preacher in eight to ten years. He judged that there was "evidence of backwardness" before him. They cooked breakfast outside on a table built of logs. Hunting knives served as utensils, and the group used broken or melted pewter as plates. "Not a table, chair, or any article of furniture could be seen. These deficiencies were common on the frontiers; for emigrations from 'the settlements' were often made on pack-horses, and no domestic conveniences could be transported except the most indispensable cooking utensils, bedding, and a change or two of clothing." Peck stated that this portrait of frontier life represented "hundreds of families" that he found scattered at the extreme edges of settlement in Missouri in 1818 and 1819.[24]

Peck's travels across Missouri brought him into contact with other families who lived on the edge of American society. In January 1819, he saw many frontier squatters scattered throughout the region. They lived in "single log-cabins of the most inferior quality, and made a cornfield of half-a-dozen acres, and a 'truck-patch,' on which they raised cabbages, turnips, cucumbers, and melons." He said that he visited families who had not heard a preacher for twenty years. He described one remote cabin as twelve feet square, built of rough poles with a wooden and dirt chimney. Peck noted with disdain that the spaces between the logs were not properly filled and did not provide any protection from the winter winds. He was shocked at its inhabitants and interior. "The floor was the earth, and filthy in the extreme." Eight people lived inside, the youngest almost an adult. "Soon as we entered, the youngsters rushed out with an expression that probably was a mixture of wonder and fear." He could not understand why the family was so dirty, as there was a spring nearby for washing. They were dressed in deerskins and covered in grease and dirt. There was "not a particle of cloth" of any kind on them.[25]

In undeveloped or isolated regions, farm families had to produce most of their needs from within their neighborhood, as they were distant from markets or transportation, and they were often unable to purchase goods. This family had lived in Missouri for three or four years and had migrated west from North Carolina, after the War of 1812 had ended. They had continuously moved westward—"beyond the settlements"—any time others lived too close. Peck wrote that the family "supposed they would have to move again soon; they had heard the 'settlements' were getting into the Boone's Lick country, and the land was to be sold." During prayer, the children would not come in the cabin. Their mother said, "they had never heard a *human* pray in all their borndays." This family was one example of those who chose to remove themselves from American society and scratch a living from the wilderness.[26]

In the Ozark Mountains, near the current border between Arkansas and Missouri, Henry Schoolcraft stumbled across another remote family farm. Schoolcraft would later become a noted ethnologist of Native Americans, but he had set out to explore the Ozarks without adequate preparation. He and his friend Levi Pettibone were tired, cold, and hungry, eating acorns for dinner. They were also lost. Finding a hunter's home, the two visitors asked for help. The one-room cabin had an interior, he wrote with disdain, that would disappoint anyone "beyond the civilized world." Dried meat, rifles, and animal horns adorned the wall, and deerskins made into containers for honey and "bear oil" hung next to the fireplace. The family fed Schoolcraft and his companion a large meal of corn bread, honey, butter, and milk. "The rude pursuits, and the coarse enjoyments of the hunter state, were all they knew." For a price, the hunter provided the two travelers with directions to more settled areas. Along the north fork of the White River, in southern Missouri, the two men found a keelboat that had made its way upriver from the Mississippi. The vessel, which Schoolcraft estimated could carry thirty tons of cargo, had brought flour, salt, and whiskey upriver, along with coffee, calico, and other items. Local farm families and hunters exchanged animal skins, pork, beef, and honey for the things they wanted. He concluded that the trading voyage would earn an "immense profit," selling goods in a remote area where stores did not exist.[27]

The most obvious aspect of the migration of Southerners to Missouri was the importation of slavery into the region. Slavery permeated society in Little Dixie, the region in central Missouri with the largest slave populations, declared historian R. Douglas Hurt. The institution strongly influenced life in the region, as slaves cleared land, cultivated crops, labored for their owners, and, of course, became status symbols. A small planter class arose along the banks of the Missouri River, based on a mix of diversified agriculture and livestock raising. Small farmers, who made up the large majority of Missouri's population, produced the same crops as their wealthier plantation transplants but in lesser amounts. Both groups raised corn and wheat, as well as hogs, cattle, and mules. Small farmers and slave owners also sold beef, pork, bacon, whiskey, or salt from the area's springs for profit. Tobacco and hemp became important commercial crops in Little Dixie. Flax for clothing and export was grown in smaller quantities. Slavery, Hurt argued, did not preclude commercial agriculture. Slavery and the market economy expanded together in Missouri.[28]

The vast majority of slaveholders in Missouri owned modest amounts of land and few slaves, operating like small farmers rather than owners of larger plantations. The Missouri countryside was full of thousands of moderately sized farms. Few plantations existed to produce large amounts of cash crops. Only about 10 percent of Missourians owned slaves by 1860, one of the smallest percentages in the South, and most slaveholding families had fewer than ten slaves. Only Delaware, which had a tiny slave population, had a greater percentage of slaves living on small farms. Families and their slaves focused on the production of a wide variety of agricultural foods and products. They produced goods for household consumption and market use, consuming grains, meats, and vegetables from their fields. These families practiced both diversified farming and also grew some staple crops for commercial use. Missouri slave-owning families employed the river system to market surplus tobacco, hemp, corn, and livestock to the lower South. This earned them cash and credit to provide for their families or to buy or improve land. Migrants from states such as Kentucky shared this commercial outlook, and the question for them was not whether to participate in commerce but how to take part.[29]

Enslaved Missourians helped create antebellum Missouri, as their labor cleared land, grew crops, and built farms. Their work allowed families and businesses to prosper, earning income for their owners and adding to their owners' wealth. Slave labor produced large quantities of corn, wheat, pork, and other crops for household use or market sale. Enslaved Missourians completed most of the agricultural work in some of the counties adjoining the Missouri River and provided crucial labor in an area with a shortage of free white workers and little labor-saving technology. In addition, slaves often did the hardest tasks, from clearing land to plowing. Owners hired out excess slaves, a lucrative practice that could earn owners up to one-seventh of a male slave's value each year.[30]

Slavery was the economic foundation for many counties along the Missouri River. It helped feed thousands of white families and allowed them to begin to produce farm goods for market soon after settlement. In 1850, ten Missouri counties had a slave population of at least 24 percent of their total; three counties had between 31 and 35 percent. Eight of these counties adjoined the Missouri River, including Howard, Boone, and Clay, stretching from Columbia westward almost to Kansas City. Areas away from the river had fewer slaves, except for counties adjacent to the Mississippi River north of St. Louis and in the southeast corner of the state. Counties with a larger number of slaves usually produced greater amounts of labor-intensive crops, such as tobacco or hemp. Slaves were almost totally responsible for growing and harvesting hemp in Callaway County, for example. These counties also produced larger amounts of goods for commercial sale. Sam Ralston, a slave owner who lived near Independence, boasted that his hemp crop would be "equal to cotton in its palmiest day." He wrote to a friend that slave labor could produce ten to fifteen barrels of corn per acre. Such production would have been impossible without slave labor.[31]

Slaves, of course, had value that could not be calculated financially. They nurtured and raised white children and cooked, cleaned, and washed clothing. Their labor made the lives of their owners easier. They gave the families that owned them additional leisure time to socialize, go to church, or spend time with friends and relatives. Slave ownership also allowed farmwomen and their daughters to avoid the hardship of field labor, tough work often completed by the women of nonslaveholding families. As family members aged, slave labor continued to support them. Those in bondage, and their children, were hired out to earn income to support widows, orphans, and the elderly. An example of this was the Lenoir family, who hired out six slaves in Boone County in 1851. Sarah Evalina Lenoir wrote, "the hire of my servants is a better business" than the profit from her farm.[32]

Southern migrants to Missouri brought an openness to market participation. From the beginning of settlement west of the Appalachian Mountains, there was some form of commercial activity, which accelerated over time. In 1775, when the first American pioneers had settled in Kentucky, a merchant operated a store at Fort Boonesborough. Even the most isolated farmers embraced some consumerism. Hundreds of merchants in the early Republic moved their businesses over the Appalachian Mountains, hoping to profit from western settlement. Itinerant peddlers and small-scale storekeepers helped to meet the appetites of residents for material goods. In the 1790s, the *Knoxville Gazette*, in eastern Tennessee, advertised a wide variety of goods from Richmond,

Baltimore, and Philadelphia. In Tennessee, farmers searched for a cash income almost from the start of settlement, and market participation increased over time. Some of the better-off Kentucky frontier families owned consumer goods that would not be expected so far west, such as pewter tableware and tea dishes. Other goods found in frontier Kentucky included imported gloves, hats, cloth, and tableware, as well as paper, spices, and shoes. Elizabeth Perkins's detailed analysis of Kentucky pioneers found that half of the families in her sample spent between one and fifteen pounds at the local store; one-quarter of the families spent more than twenty-five pounds. (Settlers often used English currency. In 1800, the English pound was worth $4.55.) This early economy was neither fully capitalistic nor subsistence, but situated somewhere between these two forms of production. This acceptance of markets moved west with Americans in the late eighteenth and early nineteenth centuries and spread across Missouri in the antebellum period.[33]

Many of the migrants to Missouri came from the Appalachian Mountains. These people were not low-yield, subsistence producers who were isolated from the larger commercial economy. In fact, historian Wilma Dunaway argues, the area was "born capitalist" and produced market surpluses and participated in commercial exchange. The region exported grain, livestock, tobacco, and cotton to nearby states; actively consumed imported foodstuffs; and bought commodities to meet farm needs. A large majority of households produced some crops for market sale. Most Appalachian farms actually produced at a level that exceeded the output of Southern farms in general. Ninety percent of all farms in the region used nonfamily labor and made some income from nonagricultural endeavors. "Overwhelmingly, the farmers of this region were producing for the market and were striving to become ever larger and wealthier in their holdings," she contended. John Inscoe came to similar conclusions in a study of western North Carolina, arguing that dependence on markets in this mountain region was pervasive. These Southern farmers—and thousands of others equally accepting of market participation—brought this outlook with them to their new homes in Missouri.[34]

Settlers, both slave owners and non-slave-owning families, could export surplus crops and livestock for market sale almost from the time they settled in central Missouri. The *Gazetteer of the State of Missouri* reported in 1837 that surplus production was so great that steamboats were unable to carry it out. This was after the "home market" for agriculture, created by the arrival of emigrants, "diminished exports." Farmers in Howard County furnished hemp, tobacco, wheat, corn, oats, and pork for "foreign markets." Markets were also close at hand in western Missouri, where emigrant Indians and soldiers in Fort Leavenworth provided a steady demand for farm goods. Migrants from the upper South took part in community and regional markets to earn a profit and better their standards of living. For these newcomers, there was no conflict between farming and commerce. Market involvement allowed those from Kentucky, North Carolina, or Tennessee to achieve their primary goal of economic improvement. Transportation provided by the Missouri River made commercial production possible almost from first arrival. "Opportunities, not limitations, shaped the agricultural development of Little Dixie," observed R. Douglas Hurt. This could also be said for the region all along the river. Most settlers eventually took advantage of the chance to take part in some market production.[35]

People came to Missouri seeking land and the opportunities that the expanding market economy could provide. They were part of a nation scrambling to get ahead, and Missouri provided a new place for Southerners to find success. They brought slavery with them, but the peculiar institution was not a barrier to market participation. Southerners had been long involved in commerce, as markets had moved west with settlement in the late 1700s and early 1800s. Most viewed their land as a way to make money, profiting from its eventual sale or the sale of their crops. Some immigrants, such as Frederick Steines, also departed their homes seeking greater opportunities and ended up criticizing their acquisitive American neighbors. Most of these incoming migrants settled near rivers, for the benefits of market access and soil fertility. However, some lived isolated from the more developed regions along the Missouri River. Many of these families eagerly took advantage of the chance for trade though, as shown by the people Henry Schoolcraft encountered in southern Missouri. Even while isolated from markets, they chose to pursue them when possible.

3

I CAN LIVE HERE BETTER

Families came to Missouri in search of a competency, or comfortable independence. They sought productive and affordable farmland that allowed them to buy property for future generations. They also wanted rich soil, which better rewarded their effort. This enabled them to produce more farm goods for market or to more easily provide for themselves. J. Davis, in a letter to his family in Massachusetts, claimed his chance to gain a "competency" was far greater in Missouri than in New England. He also noted that the soil of Missouri was "rich in the extreme" and produced almost any crop in "great profusion." People like Davis came west to achieve what they could not in more populated or expensive areas: settle their children nearby on their own land. Family welfare required land ownership and the continued acquisition of it. Parents needed to have property far beyond their own needs, so it could be passed on as they aged.[1]

Parents also did not want to be separated from their children. Nathan Haines made this clear in a letter to his siblings. "To think my son is so far from me that I cant se him no more it is almost more than i can bear." Stephen Goddard wrote to his children in Pennsylvania, asking them to come join him in Clay County, Missouri. He promised to give them ten acres of land and livestock each, including as "many hogs as you wish." Goddard added that he would also provide each child with grain and meat for a year, as well as additional improved land if they would come join him. Dr. John Sappington, who promoted the use of quinine to fight malaria in the antebellum United States, made a fortune from his medicine business. One of his goals was to provide for his children and less successful relatives.[2]

Cheap land offered the opportunity to start a new life or to add to a family's wealth. The ownership of land in antebellum America gave families economic independence and social status. Since most households lived in rural areas, people made their living from the soil. Thus, inexpensive and fertile land provided unparalleled opportunities to those who had access to it. Most migrants mentioned the possibilities that this provided, and they commented on it regularly. John Chauncey wrote to his friend Francis Dallam in Baltimore praising the opportunities that Missouri offered. He noted that the country was healthy and provided a "frontier market for all kinds of produce." Chauncey urged his friend to join him in the state, as it would benefit his family. Dallam would be able to secure his children's independence through investments in land or business. He suggested that his friend set up a store, as merchants had been making large profits. Waltus Watkins and his brothers left Kentucky in the 1830s, hoping to buy land at low prices in Missouri. They planned to sell property in their home state that was valued at $30 to $40 an acre and purchase land at $1.25 or $2 an acre in Clay and Clinton Counties in the western section of the state.[3]

Land shortages and soil exhaustion in Virginia forced thousands to leave in the late eighteenth and early nineteenth centuries, as young men in southeastern states faced diminishing economic prospects. Such men went west in search of the independence that they did not think they could find in Virginia, just as Davis had left Massachusetts. Younger sons and their families left the state, often leaving older family members behind. In October 1826, George Bingham wrote to his son, Wyatt, from his home in Stanardsville. He wished that he could see his son and his family again, but they were too distant. "I am now brought to be glad that so many of my children and grand Children have made their escape from this poor part of the world and have got to a safe fertile Country where they get to raise a plenty to support life comfortably." Wyatt's chance to find a competency had steep costs, though. "Well I know I cant live long and you my dear Children lay near my heart and as we cant expect to see each other in this life O my dear Children pray for me and let us try to meet in Heaven."[4]

Land ownership and market participation complemented one another and helped support family autonomy. Those who bought substantial amounts of land often found future gains. Not only did the value of their property increase over time, they could pass it on to future generations. Property could be divided among children, or families could often sell land for a profit. Then they could move west to repeat the process of farm building or provide children with cash to buy land. Missourians had the advantage of possessing soil that was fertile, as well as that which was close to transportation routes. Families had two mandates, served well in Missouri. These were providing for daily needs and earning income for additional land purchases. Market participation was a way to achieve family goals, by earning income for land purchases or to buy things that made a family's life easier.[5]

Missouri provided opportunity to migrants, but many struggled and some failed. Thousands of families found new and profitable lives in the state, securing inexpensive land and improving their lives. Newcomers spoke highly of the possibilities of the region, and the rich land rewarded many who were able to own it. Some wrote to their families about business opportunities, while others bragged of better weather or market opportunities. The rush to accumulate property often led to heartbreak, as deceit, fraud, and greed exacted their toll. Some gambled recklessly in speculation and were ruined. Others simply suffered from bad luck. This chapter surveys the motivations for migration, as well as the mixed record of success for those who planned a life in Missouri.

Americans and Europeans moved to Missouri for a number of reasons. Traditional historical explanations for migrations can be grouped into two broad categories: "push" and "pull" motivations. "Push" factors are those that forced people to leave their homes, such as unemployment, hunger, or political or religious repression. "Pull" factors are attractions that drew migrants to a new area, such as cheap land, higher wages, greater social and economic opportunity, or favorable reports from earlier migrants. Most of these "pull" factors acted on migrants to antebellum Missouri, especially the seductive lure of cheap land. Indeed, according to economic historians Jeremy Atack and Fred Bateman, there was a direct correlation between cheap land and migration in the Midwest. Inexpensive farmland was an "almost irresistible attraction to many," they wrote. Migrants, they argued, were "obvious optimists" who expected to improve their lives and those of their children. Land in antebellum America provided the most obvious route to wealth accumulation and upward mobility. Property was more abundant in the West, so social mobility usually required westward migration. This drive for economic improvement appears to have motivated most migrants and is clearly seen in the movement of Americans and Europeans to central Missouri.[6]

"Push" factors were also operating on migrants to Missouri, as the examples of Frederick Steines and Daniel Boone have shown. Negative circumstances often compelled people to abandon their homes. Famous examples of these situations included the Irish potato famine and the violent suppression of the revolutions of 1848 in Europe. Bernard Bailyn's study of European migration to the American colonies demonstrated that economic pressures such as poverty, high rents, or tyrannical landlords forced thousands out of their homelands. These immigrants left home to escape dire circumstances or for the opportunity to own property, gain independence, or find security. Once in the United States, many of these same factors continued to push people west.[7]

In the United States, a number of factors helped to drive Americans westward out of the Northeast. After two centuries of settlement, New England had become a crowded region, and there was simply not enough arable land to provide farms for every family's sons. Many moved west rather than abandon their dreams of farm-based economic independence. Those who remained in New England were people who inherited land or had close family ties that could provide stability. Comparatively high property taxes in New England townships also made the West seem attractive. Fearing a reduced standard of living or more modest lives than they had expected, migrants from Northern states left New England or New York. Older sons especially left the East, knowing that they might not inherit any property for many years. Those whose families had no recorded wealth were also more likely to leave, as were younger people.[8]

Northerners spoke highly of Missouri. J. Davis informed a friend living in Massachusetts that Missouri had greater "chances for speculation" than New England. Davis compared the lands of Missouri and Illinois to the most cultivated gardens back east: "A Yankee can make money just at farming if he will preserve his habits of industry." Joshua Belden, from Connecticut, informed his mother that there was almost no place in the country that provided him with "so great an opportunity of doing good." The Reverend Amasa Jones left New Hampshire for Missouri in 1821 to work as a missionary with the Osage. He suggested family members leave the "rocky and sterile regions which gave us birth" and abandon the long, cold Northern winters. Jones estimated he had earned $191 on his livestock in one year and wrote that corn and wheat were also profitable. "It would be much better for many of our brothers and sisters to emigrate as soon as arrangements can be made."[9]

Americans normally migrated in groups, usually related by blood, marriage, or adoption. Planters and less wealthy farm families moved west in extended family networks. Some kin groups migrated together, others sequentially. Individuals rarely moved alone, often migrating with family members for personal safety or economic advantage. Strong bonds provided emotional and personal ties that helped families survive and find success in their new homes. Siblings, adult children, or aged parents might follow an initial party. Others, from grandchildren to cousins and in-laws, might also emigrate. Daniel Boone moved to Missouri with more than two dozen members of his extended family. These included Boone, his wife, four children, his brother, assorted spouses, and seventeen grandchildren. One large group of twenty-five adults and fifty children, mostly related, came to central Illinois in 1835. In the 1850s, many related families migrated to Saline County, Arkansas, traveling about 400 miles from homes in Alabama to settle near each other. Kin loaned money, helped with farm tasks, acted as guardians in case of death, administered estates, and provided social, political, and economic support. Families also helped each other to obtain land and capital. In Sugar Creek, Illinois, a majority who stayed in the community were related, showing the importance of kinship ties in the settlement process.[10]

Some family members declined to move west, though. John McKown's mother chose to remain in New York, as she was used to "good and genteel" society and "an abundance of good things." McKown's brother, Joshua Bradley, wrote that she did not want to go to the barnyard and milk cows, or make candles or "play 'Rub a Dub' on the wash tub." Furthermore, Bradley noted, she refused to sleep on the floor of a drafty log cabin, where "the wind snow hail and rain came rattling in."[11]

Large numbers of German immigrants did come to Missouri before the Civil War, adding a new stream of people to those that moved internally from the American North and South. Many came because of the influence of one man, Gottfried Duden, whose writings convinced thousands of Germans that Missouri was a place of opportunity. Duden lived in the state for three years, and he published *Report on a Journey to the Western States of North America and A Stay of Several Years Along the Missouri* in 1829. His book was the most popular of the fifty such books published about America between 1815 and 1848. He wrote favorably of the good land, abundant game, mild climate, and political freedom. Duden also reported that land prices were "very low," that wages were high, and that residents had "moderate taxes." All of this stood in stark contrast with the difficulties ordinary Germans faced in Europe in the nineteenth century. High taxes, expensive land, and military service reduced the chance for many to improve their lives, as did the negative repercussions of failed revolutions in the 1830s and 1840s. Even the good years left many landless peasants with a marginal existence. Some also left seeking greater religious freedom, but most left for economic reasons. More than one million Germans left Europe for the United States between the 1820s and the Civil War. One-half of Missouri's foreign-born population before 1860 was German.[12]

German immigrants came to Missouri in two waves before the Civil War. The first of these surges was in the 1830s, following the publication of Duden's book. In the late 1840s and 1850s, a second wave followed. Many of these people fled German states after unsuccessful revolutions against autocratic governments. Emigration societies helped organize many in the first surge of settlement, while that of the later period was usually made up of individuals. St. Louis received many middle-class immigrants, such as teachers, clergy, and lawyers, and the city had more than 50,000 German residents in 1860. Those who lived in rural regions, mostly in east-central Missouri and south of St. Louis, often maintained the architecture, language, and customs of German-speaking areas for decades. These people usually lived in communities surrounded by other German immigrants.[13]

Not every family was successful, though. Despite Duden's promise of an agricultural paradise, farm life in Missouri was tough and often primitive. Frederick Gustorf commented in his diary about the Germans he met. "So many of them were unfit for the life here in the wilderness, and they regret the day and the hour when their eyes and their fancies were captivated by Duden's fallacious accounts of America." He found one struggling family who suffered from poverty and sickness living in a "shabby cabin." He described the owner of the property as "thin, pale and undernourished." A "poor shoemaker surrounded by his ragged children" lived in Duden's former home. The cabin was dark, the windows broken. "With no emotion whatsoever, he told me that one of his children had just died."[14]

The lure of good agricultural land was shown repeatedly in letters people sent back to their friends and family. Almost every individual commented on the rich and fertile earth and the availability of cheap land. Some may have exaggerated Missouri's advantages to convince family members to join them or to impress others with their success. Many declared that the land in Missouri was far better than that in states farther east. Ethelbert Lewis wrote to his brother in Virginia, "I am so much pleased that I am afraid to communicate for fear that you will accuse me of exaggeration." He then wrote: "This is the richest country that I have ever seen." J. R. Bohannon observed to a cousin that the land was "very rich by far richer than any I have ever seen in Virginia" and that corn, wheat, and tobacco crops were far more productive than in his home state. Archy Kasson, writing to family and friends in Albany, New York, proudly noted that in Missouri, "the fertility of its lands, it ought to be satisfactory to any person in search of good lands." Thomas C. Lannan moved from Maryland to Saline County to work as a teacher. He wrote to friends, "indeed, there is no poor land at all in the Saline as far as I know." Another immigrant, Samuel Sawyer, came to central Missouri to set up a law business.[15]

Sawyer provided his father with a detailed description of the agricultural paradise that he had found in Missouri in a July 7, 1838, letter. (He is probably one of those who overstate the benefits of his new home. In fact, Sawyer may be trying to convince his father to move west and join him.) "The country about the river after you have passed up nearly 200 miles is certainly the most beautiful I ever saw. The land is as rich as mud and has a bottom from fifteen to twenty five feet producing an abundance of every kind of grain and vegetable. . . . I have been about a little and certainly think I never saw land that would compare with this. And another advantage they have which is rare in new countries, first rate water. The people, particularly the farmers, are wealthy. Wheat is worth a dollar per bushel and then this in proportion." Sawyer observed that the land and crops were so good that he doubted his father would leave without buying some property.[16]

Settlers also reported that the land in Missouri was far better than the poorer lands in the East. A. A. Edwards wrote to his uncle, Lewis G. Harvey Sr., in Virginia, about the lousy farmlands in that state. "I can't imagine how I am to make a living by cultivating that poor Forrest land [back home]. You will say to yourself, will why did I not think of this before . . . but it never forced itself so heavily upon my mind until I came to compare the products of this fertile country with the poor barren forrest land of Old Va." Edwards wrote that farming in Missouri had once been "not so profitable, although the comparative yield in this country is so much greater than that of Virginia." William Powell also commented on the superior land that he found in Missouri. He wrote to his brother in North Carolina, "if you know as much about Missouri as I do you would leave them poor old worn out Ridges and Come forth with to Missouri." Powell called the land the most beautiful and richest that he had ever seen. He later reported that a neighbor, named Barsulla, "was well pleased with the Country." Powell reported that Barsulla had been "working poor land all of his days, but now he is don working of poor land."[17]

But the land was not just fertile. It was also inexpensive. Americans from both Northern and Southern states commented on this. Thomas Harvey wrote to Susan Harvey in Virginia from Saline County, "the land in this neighborhood is considered fully equal to any in the State. I do not own an acre of land that is not rich enough to raise tobacco plants and I can add to it any quantity at $1.25 an acre." He added that he was "delighted" with his farmland, as it was "level, dry and as rich as land can be." The lawyer Samuel Sawyer wrote home to his father that he could buy land for $1 an acre, far cheaper than what his family could find in New Hampshire. David Manchester, from New York, wrote to his sister in 1819 that land office sales "gave every man a chance of getting land at the moderate price of from $2 to 26 per acre, although the average price in this district is but $4.00 an acre."[18]

Wilson R. Smith, who came from Kentucky, expressed the belief that Missouri gave settlers greater chances for success than elsewhere. "Market at Boonsville 1 mile from here," he wrote. "I have heard a heap said about Missouri but it is much better than it was represented to me. There is the best boddy of land here that I ever saw in my life. Any person can do well to come here." Smith said that he would not be returning home. Jessie Mellon wrote home to his mother in Virginia that the land was "very rich" and that he had established a fine farm, with good springs and sugar trees. "I am in hopes you will rejoin to here that I have bettered my self and family so much by coming out here[.] I would like veary much to see you agane."[19]

Frederick Steines told his family how pleased he was to be living in America as a farmer. He questioned a friend about his future plans and indicated his pleasure with his new home and the opportunities that it provided. "And you, Dellman, do you wish to be here? That you would be pleased here? Do you think an American farmer's life would agree with you? Listen, if your circumstances do not please you any more, don't hesitate and come here confidently. In every case you will find it better here, as we have." Steines wrote in his letters four months after he arrived in Missouri, "a German who has been here for a time feels as if he has escaped from prison to freedom." He added that his extended family—who lived along the Missouri River just above St. Louis—had "all been resurrected to a new and better life."[20]

Missouri had such a reputation as a land of opportunity that William A. Shelton recalled that his father, who had been working in Kentucky on rented land, decided to leave immediately for the state after a farming mishap. "His mattock broke, which was about the third break. He pitched the mattock to one side and called to his brother to quit work, saying 'Bob, I am going to Missouri as soon as I can get ready.'"[21] Shelton's family left Kentucky after selling all the property that they could and trading a cider mill for a rifle. They found farming much better in their new home. Shelton remembered that the hunting, the hogs, and the water surpassed those in Kentucky. He said that he had "never known a better neighborhood" than where he settled in Putnam County, Missouri. Such stories and reports only encouraged further immigration, even if some may have been exaggerated. J. T. Walker wrote from Fayette, Kentucky, to his friend Charly Walker in Missouri that he would come as soon as he could. "I shall use all possible industry to get off as soone as possible for no one Ever wanted to move worse than I do here[.] I cannot stay." Walker did not explain what reasons pushed him to leave, but like thousands of others who fled Kentucky, he probably was unable to purchase the land he needed to gain a comfortable independence.[22]

Many were so impressed by Missouri that they wrote home to friends and family and asked them to "come out" and join them. Thomas Dresser instructed his parents in Vermont to move west, while Walter Lenoir told his brother William to send out his sons from Tennessee. Justus Post encouraged his brother to leave home, as Missouri was "the best country for an industrious and enterprising man to get rich that I ever saw." William Powell reported to his family in North Carolina that Missouri was "the finest country that was ever seen" and that his father said "he would not give it up for ten thousand acres of the best land in Caswell," in North Carolina. He encouraged his relatives to "Come on to Missouri." Wilson R. Smith wrote home to his nephew in Kentucky, Henry W. Smith, that the land was "as good as I ever saw in my life." He told his nephew: "Henry I must advise you come next spring with Roberson you can do better here than there. . . . Don't fail of coming and you must come also, sooner the better." In a letter two years later, R. G. Smith urged his family to move out. "Like to see you in this promised land where you have no need to work for the land is so rich you may plant crow bars at night and it will sprout 10 penny nails by morning." In letters to his family, William Woods echoed Smith's emphasis on the fertility of the soil and the opportunity for successful farming that it provided. "I have no right to complain of this country[.] it is a fine one indeed and I think if you were to come and see it it would wele repay your for your toil[.] crops look well wheat is good oats grow large and the people will rais as much corn a acre here as you would on two or three and can tend more ground."[23]

Newcomers often spoke of the highly productive farmland in Missouri. Wilson Smith praised a farm owned by a family member in Howard County in a letter to his nephew in Kentucky. Smith informed him that Missouri lands were better than those in Kentucky. William Powell sent a letter back to his brother about his new home. "It is the greatest Country for Corn Tobacco and hogs and horses that Ever was known." Ethelbert Lewis also had great praise for the region. He told his brother in Virginia that his farm produced "more than the average crop of corn per acre" and that he had heard of places where thirty, or even forty, bushels of wheat were grown per acre. (The average in eastern states was about ten bushels of wheat and fifteen bushels of corn per acre.) J. R. Bohannon bragged that his farm in Chariton County produced three times the wheat per acre as his old Virginia lands had. He added that he could grow one-third more tobacco per acre with half of the labor. Such reports described lands that people in the East could only envy.[24]

Other settlers also wrote home to tell their families about greater opportunities in Missouri. William Wood, who lived in Independence in the early 1830s, told his parents and siblings in White Plains, Tennessee, "I can live here better than thare for the land is esa cultavated and it is good." He boasted of the fine land and the good timber, as did most settlers. "You are working a mongst them rocks and hils killing up you and your boys so that tha wont be worth a sent in ten year[.] if you can get four hundred dollers in cash you can get you a 160 akers of land." The soil was so productive, he wrote, farmers could grow twenty-five to thirty bushels of corn or wheat per acre. If his family could clear fifteen or twenty acres of land, they could produce up to 600 bushels a year, with a surplus probably intended for market sale. Wood also wrote, "tobacco grose excellent and everything you put in the ground." Near the end of his letter he asked, "why not be her?"[25]

Settlers also commented on the moderate climate of their new homes. Those from New England spoke glowingly of the improved weather and the longer growing season. Justus Post teased his brother about the weather differences between Vermont, where his family lived, and Missouri. "In your letter of the 24 Sep you boast much that you had no frost—here we had no frost till the fore part of November—the last of October our garden afforded us plenty of green beans, what do you say to that?" Post expressed sorrow that any of his friends were "going to the North" because it was too cold a place for any man to live unless "he wishes to be eternally at work." Samuel Sawyer begged his parents to leave New England and come to Missouri. "I wish if you sell at Nashua you would come out here and look at the country." Sawyer argued that there was much less snow and frost in Missouri and that they would have greater opportunity, not to mention much better weather.[26]

Settlers arrived with commercial interests, and many grew surplus agricultural produce intended for market sale. Justus Post wrote in an 1817 letter to his brother John in Vermont that the land was so rich, "an industrious man might make his fortune in two or three years." Ethelbert Lewis, a farmer who settled near Jefferson City, wrote to his brother in 1837 that there was "more money to be made farming here than Virginia." He told his brother that he could make "$800 to $1000 here" and that he received good prices for crops and livestock. William Powell similarly informed his brother that his father's slave labor had produced an excellent crop. Powell wrote that "there is the finest Crops in Country I ever saw in my life[.] your father ses he don't wanter live in nobetter a Country than this." He reported that their farm yielded 25,000 pounds of tobacco and 300 barrels of corn one year. According to Powell, someone had offered $1,000 for the tobacco crop, but the elder Powell had turned it down, probably in hopes for a higher price. Thomas C. Lannan wrote of hemp "as high as your head." He noted that the crop could bring in up to $50 an acre. An industrious farmer, with two good slaves and several hundred dollars, would find "his fortune is at once secured."[27]

Migrants' letters often displayed their interest in market participation. Calvin Berry believed the Mississippi and Missouri Rivers provided fine transportation to markets downriver and that St. Louis provided a great domestic market for the region. Another settler, J. R. Bohannon, reported to friends in Virginia that the Missouri River and its tributaries provided excellent transportation for crops grown in the central section of the state. "I know that it is regarded by many Va.s [Virginians] that this country is too far from market. But none of the country of which I have been speaking is more than 20 miles from the river, where there is market for everything from an egg to a hhd [hogshead] of tobacco, but the fact is market is at every mans door. You can form no idea of the beauty of this country without you could see it. I consider it equal in point of soil to the Lexington country in Ky and it certainly has the advantage in promise of market convenience and equal to the world in beauty." Bohannon added that the railroad charters that the Missouri legislature was considering would "greatly add to the market convenience of the land and very much enhance the value of the country." R. G. Smith also commented on the eventual sale of the surplus foodstuffs that he grew. He echoed the commercial opportunities that Bohannon described. Smith informed his kin that "we have good market for all our produce" in Howard County. (He had ground his corn and sold it in Boonville for seventy-five cents a bushel.) Archy Kasson and J. Clemens also praised the navigable rivers and the opportunity for trade that they provided.[28]

Individuals took advantage of the opportunity to harvest timber, raise livestock for sale, produce maple sugar for market, or hire out slave labor. Wilson Smith told his nephew in Kentucky that the timber on his land would pay for itself twelve times over. J. R. Bohannon noted that Missouri was the "finest country for stock that I have ever seen" and that he saw a "drove of hogs" sold for $760. Bohannon was especially impressed by the fact that the owner had not needed to feed the livestock even one barrel of corn, but had allowed them to forage for food. He also remarked on the high prices of mules and the ease of raising them. Settlers also made money by buying and selling slaves or through hiring out their labor. Owners rented out their slaves to others and pocketed up to $50 a month, as Walter Lenoir reported in an 1835 letter. Slave owners and those who wished to own slaves often reported slave prices, purchases, and labor rental. Samuel Sawyer had bought slaves before he had even purchased a farm. Presumably, he hired his slaves out until he owned land for them to work.[29]

Many discussed profit-making opportunities. William A. Richards and J. Goodwin came to the region to go into business. Richards left Richmond, Virginia, to move to Missouri to become a merchant. He wrote to his brother, Charles, back home, "you think it Strange in me for so doing." Richards explained that he was "selling so few goods" that he could not make enough money in Virginia. "I never could have a better opportunity of making a fortune than I now have" in Missouri. Goodwin wrote from Jefferson City to a friend in Indiana that the town was a flourishing place and would benefit from its location as the seat of government. "Our Grocery bisness is a grait deal better then wee expected to find," he boasted. "We have as far prospect for a living as wee ever had thair."[30]

Others also wrote of the chance to make money, including land speculation. Archy Kasson spoke of a rash of speculation in St. Louis in 1831, where lots on a main street sold for $100 to $120 per front foot. Walter Lenoir wrote to a friend in North Carolina in 1834 that he was selling his own farm for $1,500 to $2,000 and that fifteen other tracts of land were for sale within four miles of his farm. Indeed, he suggested that his friend should come to the region and try and make money from the land frenzy. He wrote that if a "man of capital was to purchase a few lots and to establish a store extensively aported it would be the means" of securing a large profit. He informed his friend that one could make money not only as a merchant but also by drawing attention to his store's location, thus enhancing the value of his land; one could then sell the lots for a high price.[31]

The drive to make money or gain land fed the three great economic booms in the antebellum United States. These occurred in the late 1810s, from the mid-1820s to the mid-1830s, and from the mid-1840s to the late 1850s. Financial panics in 1819 and 1837 brought these expansions to a crashing halt. (The downturn after 1857 was less severe.) These flush times—and the mad rush to make money in any way possible, but especially in land—helped show the market interests of Americans. "Land was the nation's most sought-after commodity in the first half-century of the republic, and the effort of men to acquire it was one of the dominant forces of the period," wrote historian Malcolm Rohrbough. The lure of cheap and easily accessible land drew Europeans and Americans west and helped populate the states bordering the Ohio and Mississippi Rivers. In the immediate postwar years, a number of areas drew immigrants—"gardens of Eden," as Rohrbough called them—including the Kentucky Bluegrass region, the Shenandoah valley of Virginia, and the Boonslick region of central Missouri.[32]

In Missouri, the land boom and the migration of thousands after the War of 1812 fed the get-rich-quick mania. There were "few truly disinterested parties when it came to land claims in the Missouri Territory," noted historian William Foley. Thousands moved into the Boonslick, seeking the cheap land that would provide their subsistence, independence, or easy wealth. The St. Louis *Missouri Gazette* commented on this migration in October 1816: "A stranger to witness the scene would imagine that Virginia, Kentucky, Tennessee and the Carolinas had made an agreement to introduce us as soon as possible to the bosom of the American family. Every ferry on the river is daily occupied in passing families, carriages, wagons, negroes, carts &c, &c."[33]

During these three great speculative booms, a steadily increasing population pushed land values up, and seemingly everyone participated in the quest for easy wealth. Settlers rushed to buy before they lost the opportunity to someone else. Increasing prices for farm goods during these periods also encouraged the additional acquisition of property. Policies of the federal government further encouraged speculative activity, as millions of acres of land were opened for sale across the nation. Many in Missouri lived on unsold land until August 1818, when the federal government finally began to sell public land. Purchasers could buy property on easy credit over four years without interest. The federal government sold more than eleven million acres of land between 1815 and 1819, when the Panic of 1819 brought the economic expansion and westward migration to a sudden halt.[34]

Widespread speculation demonstrated that Americans were optimistic about the future and accepted risk-taking in search of economic gain. Purchasers did not need to pay the entire cost of land up front, but could put as little as one-fourth down, with three additional equal payments beginning after two years. The rise of land values turned normally prudent farmers or rational merchants into expectant millionaires who hoped to find overnight success. Everyone joined in the craze for profit, and "the poorest squatter and the wealthiest nonresident found this activity attractive," according to historian James Davis. Speculators also invested in towns, town lots, and imaginary towns. In Illinois, for example, boosters planned 500 new town sites in the mid-1830s. Timothy Flint, in his *Recollections of the Last Ten Years*, provided insight into the reckless, and often foolish, pursuit of easy money. Flint lived near St. Charles, just upriver from St. Louis. He wrote that settlers in Missouri were not yet a "reading people," for they were "too busy, too much occupied in making farms and speculations, to think of literature." Flint criticized the "swindling" and exaggeration—"one puffs up [an investment] and another down"—and the "vile pretensions" of the boom. He wrote that the same tract of land was often "offered for sale by two or even three claimants." The entire county of St. Charles, along with its inhabitants, was up for sale, he wrote. Someone paid $1,300 for it, "on the spot."[35]

Flint detailed the frenzied and gambling spirit of speculation in land and town sites. "Town-making introduces another species of puffing. Art and ingenuity have been exhausted in devising new ways of alluring purchases, to take lots and build in the new town." Promoters praised the fine rivers, healthy hills, mineral springs, and valuable forests of their potential towns. They also spoke of central locations, steamboat navigation, vast open fields, and fertile lands. "Last of all the cheerful and undoubting prediction of what the town must one day be. I have read more than 100 advertisements of this sort." The "rage for speculation" and the "zeal to purchase amounted to a fever." He noted unkindly, "no Jews were ever more greedy to accumulate money." Speculation was the dominant subject of discussion. It was "like the weather in other countries, standing and perpetual topics of conversation." David Manchester, who lived in Chariton and worked as a surveyor, commented on the massive migration and speculation in Missouri. He wrote to his sister in New York, "Our country has been over run with forenors and speculators."[36]

This furious pursuit of profit was not completely illogical or reckless, though. Those who were able to buy land early, before prices increased, had the opportunity to make large gains. Robert Swierenga estimated that speculators in Iowa in the 1850s earned at least 20 percent a year. In 1854 and 1859, gains exceeded 60 percent each year. After the Civil War, however, later migrants had to buy more expensive land that only appreciated in value in the single digits, if at all. Unfortunately, there are no such studies for Missouri, but these figures provide some idea of the possibilities for profit. Thomas Harrison serves as an example of this good fortune for early investors. He left Virginia in 1831 to join his brothers in Callaway County. In a letter to his children in Montgomery County, Virginia, he reported that his two brothers, John and James, had sold land that they had bought at $1.25 an acre for $7 an acre. "They helped themselves very much by the change," Harrison commented, though he did not provide an estimate of their total gain.[37]

However, many were not so fortunate. Those who moved into the region late missed the opportunity to buy cheap land or enjoy the profits of earlier settlers. An example of this was planter Walter Lenoir, who left North Carolina in 1834 and lived near Columbia. He wrote that all the land around the town had been purchased at public sale by the time he arrived and that almost as many purchasers lived in the area as there were quarter sections to be bought. "There is but few if any desirable situations west of this to be had at government price," he wrote. The best land, which had wood and water, had already been settled. Fifteen tracts of "first-quality" land were for sale nearby at prices between $6 and $8 an acre. But he did not want to pay such high prices and decided to look for property in the interior of the state that might have been bypassed by settlers and speculators, "without regard to its worth or locality." Lenoir rented forty acres and relied on the labor of his slaves to work his farm. A year after his arrival he had not yet purchased any land, as the "quantity quality situation" did not please him.[38]

Those who could buy a farm could not always keep it. James Riggs's family struggled in Missouri to keep their land. His father "commenced the unequal contest of fighting poverty and making a farm in the timber," when he first purchased property in Montgomery County, west of St. Louis, in the 1830s. The elder Riggs was able to improve his farm and stay out of debt until the 1840s, when his wife's health was broken by a difficult childbirth. It was "impossible for my father to work his farm, make a living, take care of his afflicted wife, pay doctor bills," and keep out of further debt. In the summer of 1844, the Missouri River overflowed its banks and flooded the family's lands. James's parents were sick, no crop was planted, and "everything went to waste." Bills and debts piled up "frightfully." The next year the family lost the farm, selling it for 20 percent of its value. The proceeds were divided up among creditors, but the family was still in debt more than $500. His father rented land and raised corn, oats, and tobacco, but could barely keep up with interest on his debts.[39]

They moved in with James's grandparents to cut costs, and the family slowly caught up on its bills. Riggs's parents lost two infant boys in the late 1840s. They purchased a new farm in 1850, but lost it a year later. The elder Riggs had made the mistake of providing security, or collateral, for another man for $300. He ended up even deeper in debt. "Everything around us seemed dark and gloomy," James remembered. The family could not afford to send their son to school. They plunged deeper into debt after new doctor's bills. A drought then reduced their corn crop; the family moved into an abandoned schoolhouse. They prospered in 1856—"a splendid crop year"—and planted all the wheat, corn, and tobacco "we could manage," hoping to pull themselves out of debt. Then the "cinchbug" appeared and wiped out their harvest. The next year was also nearly a total loss, and the Riggs family fell deeper into debt. "I found out how almost impossible it was for a poor man to make a living and make a farm at the same time," James Riggs recalled. By the end of the 1850s, the family was still in trouble. He noted, "that old security debt had hung over our head like a dark cloud for nearly ten years. It had caused us to lose one farm and we had paid more than double the principal in interest and cost yet the debt was as large as ever."[40]

Competition for land could be fierce, and dreams of riches pushed many to engage in shady behavior. Such competition also existed even where most people depended on each other for aid. Herbert S. Jones recounted in "Missouri—A Promised Land" just such a story. Jones wrote a brief history of his ancestors, William and Margaret Bays, and their settlement in Missouri in the 1840s. After hearing of the Platte Purchase, which opened up land in northwest Missouri, the family and their slaves left Virginia. They stayed in southern Illinois for a few months before moving to Caldwell County in 1844. They found an abandoned cabin and lived off wild game, fruits, nuts, and "provisions they could purchase in distant settlements." Then they finally moved to northwest Missouri. William Bays decided to settle there, as there was a good spring present, and the land was "similar to that which he had left in Virginia." They built a home and planted an orchard. However, Jones reported, William was "a very trustful man" who "trusted a man unwisely." A man who had not yet paid for his land lived nearby, and he asked Bays how he would pay for the land he wanted to buy. William showed him gold that he had saved, and the man "turned on all the charm he could muster." The neighbor told William how difficult his life had been and how he had always wanted to buy his own land. Bays felt sorry for him and loaned him enough money to buy forty acres. The man then purchased the same plot of land on which William Bays had lived.[41]

Another migrant to Missouri, twenty-year-old John Bidwell, also lost his farm. Bidwell had left Ohio and headed to Iowa with only his clothes and a pocket knife, he recalled in an autobiographical article fifty years later. He attempted farming in Iowa, but abandoned the state because everyone in his neighborhood suffered from malaria. Then he headed south to also look for land in Platte County, Missouri. "The imagination could not conceive a finer country—lovely, rolling, fertile, wonderfully productive, part prairie, part timber." There was not a poor acre in the county, he wrote. Bidwell and other families settled on land that had not been surveyed by the federal government or purchased by anyone. Though they did not own the land, these early settlers hoped to be able to buy it when it came up for sale. "On this attractive land I set my affections, intending to make it home." He worked as a teacher to earn money. Soon after he arrived, in June 1839, surveyors followed. Bidwell claimed some land and hoped to have his father move out from Ohio to join him. He left on a trip to St. Louis and returned a month later than expected only to find that another man had "jumped my land." Bidwell bitterly noted that this individual was a bully who had killed a man, leaving everyone in the countryside afraid of him. Unfortunately, Bidwell had no legal protections, since he was not old enough to enjoy preemption rights and had not lived on the land. "I lost about everything I had," he wrote. "Nearly all I had earned had been spent upon the land." He left for California shortly afterward to start anew.[42]

Small farmers, planters, and speculators came to Missouri with the intention of acquiring land and making money. A prime example of this last category was Vermont native Justus Post, who came west immediately after the end of the War of 1812. In November 1815, the former army officer arrived in St. Louis with his family to try to earn his fortune. He had quit the army after the war at the rank of colonel and moved west from New York, where he had been stationed. Post arrived in the Missouri Territory very wealthy already. He had $13,755 in cash and was ambitious to become even richer. The youngest of eight children, Post was highly educated—he had attended Middlebury College before graduating from West Point first in his class—and driven to carve out wealth and high social standing in his new home. Post wrote that his arrival in Missouri "commences a new era in my existence." He wrote to his brother, John, in Vermont that St. Louis was a city destined for "great importance." Post saw himself as a force in the development of the region, writing to his brother, "to promote my own interest [and] the good of the country must be the great object & the mark at which I must aim." He penned a long series of letters to his brother over the next six years that traced his fortunes in Missouri.[43]

Post bought and sold land at a rapid pace, attempting to make money off the appreciating land values along the Missouri and Mississippi Rivers. He was involved in large-scale property purchases, town and lead mine speculation, as well as the purchase of slaves. He began to buy large tracts of land as soon as he could, within a month of his arrival in St. Louis. Post bought land warrants for two square miles of land—1,280 acres. This land was equal to "*eight* good Vermont farms." He also examined a "small tract" of land bordering the

Missouri River about one mile above St. Louis. "In a very few years, the town will cover it," he boasted to his brother. Post planned to offer up to $5,000 for it, but his letters do not record if he ever purchased this piece of property. He told his brother that if anyone discovered that he was considering buying the land, "*ten thousand* would not fetch it, and even were it mine it would require that sum to take it from me." Post also purchased "floating claims" for 1,920 acres that could be used across the territory. However, he was burning through his capital quickly and asked his brother to send money in early 1816.[44]

Post justified his expenditures by explaining that the territory's population was increasing much faster than he could have expected and that the price of land "increases in proportion." Americans flooded into the region because the war had "done much toward settling this quarter of the world—the militia and rangers who have traversed the country after the Indians have been so pleased with the land that great numbers of them are now settling on it." He also tried to explain his speculation in land to his brother by arguing that his purchases should be governed by the "prospects of gain, that is, the greatest gain." If the value of one place would increase more than that of other lands, he should buy it. If one held on to land long enough, "you know it will be worth 10 or perhaps 20 dollars an acre."[45]

Within six months of arrival, Post owned nearly 19,000 acres of land. He reported that he bought most of the property at less than $2 an acre. More than half of this land was in St. Charles County. He also owned 6,000 acres of Missouri lead mines, 1,000 acres on the Ohio River in the Illinois Territory, and almost 2,000 acres of "floating claims." His lands in St. Charles County had been purchased for between sixty-five cents and $1.25 an acre. He probably paid for most of his land as he had paid for his Ohio investment, with a substantial down payment and a promise to pay off the remainder over several years. Like all speculators, he hoped to sell his land for a profit before his debts came due. A year after he arrived he wrote, "There is a constant motion here and land rapidly increases in value—what can now be gotten for two dollars soon sell for four." Post bragged that the "first high ground above the mouth of the Ohio is ours. It is the greatest speculation I ever made." He claimed that Andrew Jackson had informed the War Department that it was a prime location for "the great military depot of the western world."[46]

Post continued to buy land and make other investments. He was especially proud of his purchase of lead mines and wrote to his brother that they could produce "lead enough to kill all the kingdom of Great Britain." He also bought an interest in a copper mine in the Illinois Territory. Post purchased 6,000 acres of a former Spanish land grant near St. Louis that surrounded "the richest lead mines in the western country." He wrote to his brother in early 1816 that he had examined every paper relating to it and that he was convinced the government had to confirm his ownership. However, if it refused his claim he hoped to get other public lands, which he estimated he could sell for more than $30,000. He kept buying and selling land and bragged that he had six tenants on several thousand acres near his home in early 1818. In December 1818, he informed his brother that he had made almost a 600 percent profit in just two years on some property. "What a fortune I could make in land speculations if I had a capital to work with!" However, he was short on cash. But greed pushed him to acquire even more property. He asked his brother, again, to send money. Justus wrote that "money is a scarce article in this quarter." Just four years after his arrival, all of his grand plans came crashing down around him in the wake of the Panic of 1819.[47]

The speculative bubble of the late 1810s began to deflate in 1818, when European demand for American imports, especially cotton, fell. American agricultural prices had stayed high after the war ended, encouraging westward migration and massive land purchases that supported the boom. When demand fell, farm prices plummeted; a financial panic ensued, and scores of banks failed. The value of everything—from cotton to corn to inflated land prices—collapsed. The Bank of the United States made the crisis worse when it tightened credit. In the wake of the bust, many were ruined as the value of their assets collapsed, leaving them deeply in debt. Unemployment became widespread. Ten percent of New York City was on poor relief in 1820. Thousands went to jail for debt across the nation. Migration came to a halt, and in some places in Missouri land lost 95 percent of its value. Both banks in Missouri went bankrupt, and a shortage of currency plagued the region throughout the 1820s. Farmers were unable to sell their surpluses, merchants could not collect their debts, and speculators were left holding tremendously overpriced lands. Economic activity in Missouri virtually ground to a halt. Men like Justus Post, who had staked everything on their land speculations, lost everything. "The times are extremely hard here," he wrote. "Destruction is hurrying upon the people in all directions." There was not "half enough" money in the state to even pay the laborers for digging the graves of the dead, he noted. Near the end of a June 1821 letter, he forlornly penned that he owed $30,000 and that the loss would "really ruin me and throw me back to begin the world anew."[48]

Post lost everything in the aftermath of the panic. He lived until 1846, spending another decade in Missouri as a farmer, and was elected as a local judge and as a one-term state senator. Justus Post was an example of the frenzied rush for quick profits that gripped the nation after the War of 1812 and during other economic booms. His letters reveal a commercial interest shared among many Americans in antebellum America, as well an interest in risk-taking and profit-seeking. The lure of easy money, or the chance for economic advantage, captivated people across the country. Many who took part in such risky endeavors lost their investment. The aftermath of the Panic of 1819 was a harsh introduction to the negative repercussions of the commercial economy. Panics and economic downturns in later decades brought subsequent booms crashing down as well, ensnaring millions in hard times that they did not create but from which they nevertheless suffered.[49]

Families came to Missouri to achieve a competency, looking to secure their independence through the acquisition of rich land that could be passed on to children. Settlers in Missouri noted the fertility of the soil in their letters, contrasting it with poorer and more costly land in the East. They believed that Missouri provided them with a greater chance for success than states farther east. Southerners and Northerners saw it as a better place to make money than elsewhere, expressing an interest in selling surplus farm goods and taking part in local markets. They praised Missouri's market access, as well. Those who migrated to the state after the War of 1812 enjoyed a brief period of economic expansion before the boom collapsed with the Panic of 1819. Newcomers, including Justus Post, frantically scrambled to amass as much property as they could, looking to make a quick fortune off rapidly increasing land values. Those who arrived early often found success and cheap land, but good timing and luck did not favor everyone. Some, such as the family of James Riggs, found little success and much heartbreak. Others, such as John Bidwell and William Bays, were cheated out of their land. While Missouri seemed to be a place of opportunity, success was often fleeting or impossible to achieve for many.

Once migrants had arrived in Missouri, they had to carve a farm out of the wilderness. Most came with an acceptance of the market economy, but they were forced to live a tough few years, building a farm and focusing on mostly subsistence production. Farm families depended on hunting, corn, pork, and garden vegetables to feed themselves during their first few years in Missouri. They also relied on the assistance of neighbors to help them with labor-intensive tasks such as land clearing and harvesting. The next two chapters provide a bridge that connects early settlement with the development of a more commercially oriented economy. These chapters detail the farm-building process and the crucial role of neighborhood assistance in helping farm families survive and prosper.

4

VEXATIOUS AND HARD LABORS

Those who came to antebellum Missouri found a farmer's paradise, its riches limited by the hard work and many challenges required by family farming. The land was extraordinarily fertile, the alluvial floodplain soil nearly black. The banks of the Missouri River usually sloped gently away from the waterway, making the level countryside easier to work than the mountains of Appalachia from which many came. Plentiful natural resources were available. Streams and creeks crisscrossed the region, and fresh water was found on most farm sites. Settlers could easily find large quantities of wood in the thick forests near waterways; bottomlands with nutritious forage for livestock sat near rivers. The Boonslick was the far western extension of the continuous forest that most Americans knew east of the Mississippi River. So, it was familiar to newcomers. About 100 miles east of Kansas City, however, prairie grasses began to dominate the landscape.[1]

Missouri offered opportunities and challenges, both economic and environmental. The land provided almost everything a farm family could need, from animals for hunting and fishing to berries, beehives, and maple trees for foodstuffs and sweeteners. It was a fine place to grow corn, vegetables, or other crops, even if clearing land was an exhausting, frustrating task. But building a new farm took enormous effort, as well as some money. Many never had the chance to buy their own land or enjoy the security of a competency. Life was also often a struggle against a variety of opponents. The land hosted a number of life-threatening, or life-sapping, diseases that often made a tough life even more difficult. Cholera killed some shockingly quickly, while malaria usually took a less final, but more regular, toll on rural families. Insects, such as mosquitoes, bedbugs, lice, and ticks, lived everywhere and spread disease and misery as well.

Migrants to Missouri came in search of economic independence. Such autonomy required family agriculture and the ownership of property, as well as some market participation. In the early nineteenth century, most began their lives in Missouri by clearing a few acres of land for crops and housing, unless they could afford improved land. While families were forced into a primitive existence when they first arrived, few remained outside the market economy for any length of time. Many had no choice, as new migrants often had to purchase some food for themselves in their first year. Morris Birkbeck wrote that farmers in southern Indiana found a market for all their surplus production because of the influx of newcomers and the local growth of population. Even the most isolated people desired items that they did not produce, such as coffee or sugar. Pioneer farming was a difficult period of adjustment that rural families endured until they could make the transition to the production of some of their farm goods for market. Nearly everyone in rural areas consumed a large part of what they grew. However, until transportation and trade developed enough to encourage more market production, settlers had to establish a family farm, an arduous and labor-intensive task. Families anticipated a more comfortable life after a few years of hardship.[2]

New families usually purchased land from the federal government or from private owners, such as speculators. The government sold public land at auction to the highest bidder; private owners sold to those who paid the most. Men could also use land warrants, a promise of free land gained from military service in conflicts such as the War of 1812, to obtain public land. Not everyone could afford to purchase property, though. Often families simply lived on a plot of land without buying it; they were known as squatters and moved onto land years before government surveyors appeared. (The word "squatter" began as a negative description for those who claimed land they did not own.) Thousands of squatters had migrated across the Appalachian Mountains in the 1770s and had kept moving west after the American Revolution. Such families received title to their land—if they could afford to buy it—based on the right of preemption, a policy that originated in the early 1800s. Preemption gave families the opportunity to purchase a limited amount of public land that they had improved and inhabited at the minimum government price. If they could not purchase property, they often kept moving to the next frontier.[3]

This policy, as the Interior Department stated in 1860, rewarded "the adventurous pioneer who is found in advance of our settlements, encounters many hardships, and not unfrequently, dangers from savage incursions." Preemption laws existed in Illinois and Missouri in the 1810s, but not all states and territories had such rights. By 1830, preemption rights extended to all surveyed public land in the country. Since frontier settlers were usually poor and often landless, the law was established to reward their "enterprise." However, neither this law nor any other could ensure that everyone could afford to buy land. Preemptors had to file a claim with the nearest land office, usually within three to six months of a government survey of their property. Land surveys occurred across all public land before it went up for sale. Squatters who claimed land could not purchase more than 160 acres under the law. After 1840, they had to be a U.S. citizen or have filed a declaration of intent to be one; individuals also needed to be the head of a family, a widow, or a man over the age of twenty-one. To claim land, families had to inhabit and cultivate the land and build a home.[4]

John James Audubon, the naturalist famous for *The Birds of North America*, encountered many squatters during his travels across the antebellum United States. He wrote that such people moved from other parts of the country because land was too expensive or because their previous property had been exhausted by decades of use. They wanted to "provide for themselves" and moved west to find rich land that was full of game and good timber. Such families also migrated in hopes of market access along the Mississippi River, which Audubon noted served as a road to "all the markets in the world." River transportation gave these families the opportunity to sell or exchange the products of their farms. More important, families had the chance to live on land, possibly for many years, that they did not have to buy, rent, or pay taxes upon. "How many thousands of individuals in all parts of the globe would gladly try their fortune with such prospects?" Migration was difficult, though, and families moved with only the absolute necessities. They often left behind items too heavy or expensive to move, he wrote, taking animals, bedding, and tools on an arduous trek that could last for weeks or months.[5]

The Reverend Nicholas Patterson, who traveled extensively through Missouri after the War of 1812, helped explain the behavior of squatters. In a January 1819 letter, Patterson described the motivations of "pioneer" settlers, who lived off of hunting, a dozen acres of corn, and a garden patch. Such families usually moved together to a new area and lived within a few miles of each other. A few livestock, such as cows and pigs, helped feed them. These people moved on once the land was surveyed and ready for sale, or when neighbors crowded around. Tax collectors and the "machinery of government" oppressed them, and they quickly set out for newly opened territory, such as Arkansas. Massena McCormick echoed this explanation in a 1901 reminiscence. He recalled a neighbor of his family, George Cathey, who was "one of the kind set on living on the fringe of settlement." Such families lived ahead of others, searching for the best springs. They raised a cabin and cleared some land, planning to sell improvements once the land was surveyed and came up for sale. McCormick's father bought out Cathey, who then moved on to another water source to repeat the process. Selling improvements was one way to accumulate funds to buy land.[6]

Those who could not afford to buy land and outfit a farm often remained in Missouri. These families usually rented land, hoping to accumulate enough money to buy property after a few years of work. Normally, they tried to feed themselves and produce a surplus for market sale. However, low crop prices during economic downturns, such as those in the early 1820s and after the Panic of 1837, reduced opportunities to earn an income. Other misfortunes, from droughts to floods, could also make it difficult to pay off debts or save money. The costs to establish a farm were often steep. It cost money to migrate west, as well as to buy land and purchase needed tools, seed, wagons, and livestock. By 1860, these costs could range from $500 to $1,700, the larger figure an amount three times the average annual wage. Even a small forty-acre farm was too expensive for 40 percent of midwestern families in 1860, nor would this small amount of land provide property for children.[7]

It was financially challenging to establish a family farm. Minimum costs for migration, land, livestock, and expenses for the first year—when families were starting a new farm—could run into the hundreds of dollars. If a family could sell land in the East, this might cover their expenses. However, high start-up costs limited options for those without capital to invest in new farms. Such people had to rent land from others and hope for good fortune to get ahead. Others provided a share of their crops as tenants. Bad luck or unfortunate timing might leave a family with few good options. One estimate determined that those who did not own land worked 20.5 percent of Missouri farms in

1860. These people faced long-term dependence on others or had to move to a new region to try to start again, usually as squatters. Missouri provided opportunity, but the chance to gain a competency was not equally distributed. Hard work and sacrifice often went unrewarded.[8]

The pioneer family went into areas unsettled or unclaimed by whites with a small number of tools, basic supplies, and foodstuffs. The most essential elements of frontier agriculture were the ax, for clearing land and cutting logs, and the rifle, for hunting and self-defense. Historian Richard Bartlett observed of the early settler, "while the rifle gave him protection and fresh meat, the axe gave him his farm." Farmers also usually carried a mattock, a "grubbing" hoe with two blades, one for digging and one for cutting. Migrants also took hoes, spades, and plows, as well as seeds for such crops as corn, squash, pumpkins, and beans. They also carried their family Bible, clothing, pots and pans, furniture, poultry, and family pets—all packed into a wagon, normally drawn by oxen. Pigs, cattle, and sheep usually accompanied the family.[9]

The first few months, typically in late winter or spring, were full of the hard work of clearing land and planting crops. Shelter often initially consisted of a crude lean-to, open on one side, with a fire before it for heating and cooking. Families had to clear their land before planting. They usually cut a circular strip of bark from trees, a process known as "girdling," and this killed trees by cutting off the flow of nutrients through the bark. Within a few weeks the leaves fell off and let the sunlight reach the forest floor. A crucial task that continued for several years was to clear away brush and trees. Newcomers cut as much timber as possible so that it could be burned in the late summer or autumn. Land was continually cleared throughout the first winter to provide more space for the second year of planting. Historian Clarence Danhof estimated that ten to fifteen acres of land could be "roughly" cleared in the first year. However, other necessary farm chores, such as planting, harvesting, and hunting, could reduce this amount to only five to ten acres. A family with limited labor, such as young children, or one that lacked slaves, found clearing land even more challenging. Most cleared land as quickly as possible and usually left stumps to rot that could not be easily removed by a plow. Such methods often left obstacles in fields for a decade or more, but corn, beans, and squash grew well in just such a clearing. Using an ax and hoe, the family and any slaves cleared the ground of weeds and brush. Women and girls occasionally performed this work as well, if their labor was required. Then corn planting began in small mounds, with beans and squash usually intermixed. Any surplus of corn could be used to feed hogs or made into whiskey.[10]

Nicholas Hesse, a German immigrant who settled in Missouri in the late 1830s, wrote about the backbreaking labor required to start a farm. Hesse discouraged potential settlers, warning them of the exhausting work on the American frontier. "The greatest amount of activity is required in order to obtain a temporary and inadequate dwelling and a few acres of cultivated land," he explained. "Only a few German immigrants are able to stand the multitudinous, vexatious and hard labors." Clearing land involved cutting down and moving larger trees to open land for planting. Smaller trees, bushes, and shrubs needed to be cleared, the last being "an especially difficult task." Trees had to be cut into logs and hewn into shape for construction; logs also had to be split for fence rails. Branches and decayed trees had to be burned. Stones for chimneys needed to be quarried and hauled to where the home would be built. Farmers then had to dig up undergrowth, often using a large mattock. Hesse wrote that none of this work could "compare to the exertion of handling a grubbing hoe weighting twenty pounds." Plowing began once the trees, shrubs, and bushes were removed. The work was so arduous that "not enough time is left for ordinary, wicked cursing."[11]

Philander Draper, whose family settled in north-central Missouri in 1815 when he was a child, provided insight into the initial settlement process (fig. 4). Most of the people who came to the territory in the late 1810s had to become hunters to feed their families, he reported. Fortunately, hunting was easy, and wild turkeys could be shot from the doors of migrants' tents. "He who could not kill a deer by 9 o'clock any morning would have been laughed at," Draper wrote. Families who decided to establish a farm traveled a few miles into the woods in a heavy wagon full of their possessions and drawn by their horses. Such households were "fortunate if they had a few pounds of cornmeal and a little salt. For everything else they must rely on the trusty rifle." The family could not travel too far each day—maybe four or five miles—until they had to camp for the night near a creek or brook to "rest and wash up." They collected wood and made a shelter of an extra wagon cover and poles. The horses were turned loose to graze, and the "head of the family" went out to hunt. Often the first or second stopping place became a new residence, especially if it "offered sufficient inducements to make a home of it." Then a log hut was built, and the family began to clear land. Though such settlers were isolated, other

4. Philander Draper migrated to Missouri from Tennessee in 1815 at the age of four. He was a farmer and a merchant before the Civil War. State Historical Society of Missouri, Columbia, photo collection, gift of Art Draper.

families usually lived within a mile or two. Such neighbors often loaned tools to each other to help build homes. Draper reported that it was not unusual to see saws loaned to neighbors ten miles distant. Isolation made families dependent upon each other.[12]

Building shelter was as necessary as feeding a family, but log cabins only contained the "most necessary things," wrote Nicholas Hesse. During the first year, a family might survive in a three-sided structure, with the open end facing toward a large fire for warmth. Most families had a more permanent cabin by the second year. Hesse described how settlers built log cabins in a square, using young tree trunks between one and one-and-one-half feet in thickness. These structures were initially one large room, with a roof of clapboards resting on a latticework of poles. Families cut out doors, windows, and openings for chimneys and filled any open spaces between logs with split wood and clay. They then added a stone chimney. Dirt floors prevailed in the early years of farm building. People often built their own rude furniture, hewn with an ax and other tools. They made tables from a slab of lumber and built beds by setting wood on poles supported by posts. Small logs, hollowed out, became cradles for babies. Fences also needed to be built or repaired to protect cornfields and vegetable gardens. Fallen trees had to be removed and firewood cut for cooking. The annual cycle of plowing, planting, cultivating, and harvesting from spring to autumn dominated the life of male workers. "The settler has so much work to do that there is no time for the establishment of a more comfortable dwelling," Hesse noted.[13]

John Woods and Edmund Flagg, two travelers to the Mississippi valley, provided additional details on the architecture of frontier homes. Woods noted that settlers added chimneys to cabins by cutting out a section of a wall and inserting a rectangular segment. They walled it up with stones, laid in clay or loam. Above the stones, the interior walls were plastered to protect the wood from fire or sparks. Families then added a hearth made of stones and clay. A porch might parallel one side of the home. Flagg, traveling northeast of St. Louis near the Mississippi River, described a log house owned by an old Virginian settler. It was three times as long as its width, with a double layer of thin boards for a roof. Wood planks made up the improved floor of the home, and windows had been cut for ventilation. Behind the building a series of lesser structures stood, including a stable, a corncrib, and a meat house for the smoking and drying of pork and beef. A zigzag fence enclosed fields of corn, a garden, and orchards. Swine, cattle, poultry, and "naked" children populated this backcountry farm. A smokehouse, or meat house, was common. They were smaller than cabins, with Woods noting that his was eighteen feet to a side. Such structures dried meat or pork over coals that cooked the meat over many hours. He also wrote that his corncrib, built to allow the circulation of air to keep the crop dry, could hold more than 600 bushels of unshucked corn.[14]

Life on the Missouri frontier was not just isolated but also primitive. Jacob Lanius, a Methodist circuit preacher in the 1830s and 1840s, wrote that the frontier country was a place where the settlements were very sparse and "the condition of the pioneer not enviable." He wrote in his diary about a farm he found "TWO MILES FROM ANY OTHER place . . . Surrounded by hills and poor land." A little more than two weeks later he was back at an equally remote farm, where an old bachelor baked his corn bread in an iron oven and ground his own coffee beans by beating them in a mortar. He fried hog meat from one of his pigs in the oven with the corn bread. As the man had no table, and little furniture, they sat on logs piled near the fire and ate their dinner. While in southwest Missouri near Springfield, he recorded, "the country at present is in a very bad state of cultivation and improvement. People mostly live in log huts, with small farms and plenty of stock, such as horses, cattle and children." Lanius found a clear division between rough frontier life and the more developed sections of the state, where people "seemed to live comfortable. Have good farms and good log houses. How changed the aspect since I crossed the Osage River. I feel like I entered the old world again that is the north part of the state." Here, Lanius clearly demonstrates the striking difference between the more developed and commercial areas near the Osage River—which flowed into the Missouri River and thus was tied by water to the river-based market society—and the more remote, less market-oriented farming in the Ozark Mountains.[15]

Others also wrote of families and individuals on the margins of settlement. James Bumgardner Jr. explained how his family had lived in Clinton County in northwest Missouri in the early 1840s. His father bought land one-and-one-half miles south of the town of Plattsburg, after his mercantile business failed. Plattsburg, twenty miles north of Kansas City, was a small town of about 200 residents. The county surrounding it was "very sparsely settled," and its people lived mostly along the streams and the bottoms of the area. Bumgardner wrote that Clinton County was "then on the western edge of civilization." The land the family farmed "was entirely wild and father set out to work at once to fence, improve it and build upon it."[16]

Bumgardner's family lived a mostly subsistence existence, barely involved in the larger commercial economy. Their property and the land around it provided most of their sustenance. The rich soil, "under very simple tillage, yielded abundant harvests. A few acres of corn and of wheat and the garden furnished abundant supplies of bread and vegetables." The cows grazed on prairie grass, and "the whole country was alive with game." Bumgardner wrote that capturing 150 quail in one day was not unusual. He sometimes killed turkeys right outside the door of their house. As a boy, he would often catch prairie chickens in traps he set near corn shocks in the fields. Once, about 1845, he and his father killed a "splendid buck" in early winter near their farm, which he claimed provided 255 pounds of venison for the family. His mother and sister made the clothing for the family. He recalled that the ordinary clothing for everyone "was spun, dyed, woven, cut out and made at home." Bumgardner remembered, "I feel sure that I never had a suit of 'store clothes' until after we moved to Virginia."[17]

Lucy Blythe repeatedly mentioned the isolation and primitive life of her grandparents in her memoir of their migration from Kentucky to Missouri. They lived about fifty miles west of St. Louis in Montgomery County. "All of the early settlers went through a great many hardships in settling up the new States. There were no conveniences whatever for the farmers or their wives." Blythe wrote that water had to be hauled in from a nearby creek until a well could be built. For lighting, she reported that they killed a groundhog and rendered its fat. The family used an old cup with a cloth wick saturated in the oil to provide candlelight. They produced most clothing at home. Eliza Dyer Price also commented on the isolation of her father's farm. Like Lucy Blythe's family, they lived a mostly subsistence existence, aided by their slaves. In 1822, they settled about 100 miles west of St. Louis. Game was "most abundant and much was trapped." To capture turkeys, they built a square of fencing and baited it with corn and wheat; once enticed into the trap, the turkeys stayed until needed, content with food, water, and a "good roost." Quail could be driven into nets and captured. Deer also provided venison on a regular basis. Price wrote that since "there being no markets to supply, father would drive out every few days to see the progress of animals and vegetables so we could prepare for winter." If the family lived closer to Columbia, or another town, they would have sold surplus farm goods, such as bacon, eggs, or butter, to local stores. They visited shops in Columbia that supplied them with "absolute necessities" on occasion.[18]

A variety of diseases added to the physical toll of difficult and repetitive work and increased the burdens of life in Missouri. Malaria and cholera were the two greatest dangers, but residents also suffered from intestinal and infectious diseases such as dysentery, typhoid, and whooping cough, as well as biting insects, such as lice and bedbugs. Europeans brought malaria to North America when they arrived with the parasite in their bodies. The disease spread from infected humans to mosquitoes and then to new hosts. Unlike epidemic diseases, such as smallpox, malaria did not wipe out local populations. It continued to lurk in the bloodstreams and wetlands of the New World. The Mississippi River valley had a well-known reputation as an unhealthy place in nineteenth-century America, and malaria was widespread. The disease, often called ague, was the most common malady west of the Appalachian Mountains. Americans viewed it not so much as an epidemic disease, but an inevitable consequence of life. Malaria moved westward with migrants, and the Midwest and South proved to be ideal breeding grounds for the *Anopheles* mosquito. Each region hosted a handful of the *Anopheles* species. As humans migrated, the insects followed, through habitats and across vast areas, allowing the most effective parasite to evolve to penetrate human populations.[19]

Mosquitoes and malaria made life miserable. Settlers who cleared land often disrupted water drainage, which helped create stagnant pools of water in which mosquitoes could breed. The warm summer weather further encouraged breeding. An absence of roads, which increased the use of rivers for transportation, as well as settlement patterns along waterways created ideal conditions for malaria. Mosquitoes preferred environments that were damp, dark, and warm. Unfortunately for nineteenth-century Americans, these words perfectly described their housing. Most family members lived and worked in total exposure to hordes of mosquitoes, because homes lacked screens or glass for windows. John C. Bush, onboard a steamboat on the Missouri River in 1819, noted, "musketoes are so bad to nite that we cannot enjoy any satisfaction." He called the insects "outrageous" and wrote, "they had like to hav eten us up this evening." The Presbyterian minister Charles Peabody battled mosquitoes in 1846, complaining to his diary, "even now while I write I hear the hateful little varmits (mosquitos) ying, ying, ying, ying about my ears."

Furthermore, no one had any idea that insects transmitted disease. Missouri residents suffered from malaria regularly, enduring chills and fevers, combined with jaundice and listlessness. Malaria was not usually fatal in Missouri, but it could be debilitating. It helped to weaken infected persons and reduced their ability to fight off other diseases.[20]

Malaria brought about a cycle of high fevers and chills that could repeat daily, every other day, or less often. Serious listlessness often overcame victims. It could entirely drain a person's strength. One victim of such an attack, in St. Joseph, Missouri, in 1849, suffered from shivering, freezing chills, followed by fevers that left him feeling like a mass of "living fire." Settlers thought of the fevers, chills, and attendant "shakes" as a normal part of rural life, a necessary "seasoning" for new neighbors. Elizabeth Cooley, a teacher who emigrated from Virginia to Missouri with her husband, struggled with malaria during the two years she lived in the state. She reported fevers and headaches during the summers of 1846 and 1847, also noting the sickness of her friends and students. On September 23, 1846, she confessed to her diary, "I fear to stay here, I fear death." Two years after her arrival in Missouri, typhoid fever killed her at the age of twenty-two. Dr. John Tannor, who lived near St. Charles in the mid-1840s, wrote that he had to "smoke my room every night with tobacco and shut the windows and doors afterwards to keep out the Gallynippers and moschetoes—this is one of the pleasures of living in the West." He also noted that the "way folks shake hereabouts is curious. I have not had the first chill yet and hope I shall escape." Sewell Hepbron also commented on the effects of malaria in letters to his family from Madisonville, Missouri. "Some fever and chills but no one was so sick as to make it necessary to send for a doctor."[21]

Cholera was a terrifying disease that could bring everyday life to a standstill, as it could kill infected people very quickly, often in less than a day. Infections came from water contaminated by feces; soiled bedding or clothing could also spread it. The cholera bacteria replicated incredibly fast in the small intestine. It destroyed the intestinal lining, leaving those infected with it incapable of absorbing food or water. Victims suffered from twenty to thirty episodes of diarrhea a day. Such traumatic diarrhea helped deliver the bacterium into water supplies or contaminated the surroundings of victims, ensuring the disease's further transmission. High fevers, painful cramps and vomiting, as well as maddening thirst, swollen tongues, and delirium accompanied it. Strong adult men could be killed in less than forty-eight hours. Children often died in less than a day, since they dehydrated so much quicker.[22]

Cholera epidemics reached St. Louis in the 1840s, coming with immigrants from Europe, but were not such a threat to relatively dispersed rural populations. In June 1849, cholera killed 1,249 people in St. Louis alone. The city instituted a quarantine of infected people that summer. President Zachary Taylor proclaimed a day of prayer in August to plead for the end of the outbreak. The disease killed more than 4,000 in St. Louis, finally ending in late summer. It killed thousands in the Mississippi River valley, leading the German relatives of William Waye to write in concern: "As you had not written for a long time, we were afraid that you had died of cholera, a thought that made us very sad."[23]

Frederick Steines lost all four of his children and his first wife to a cholera outbreak in July 1834, shortly after their arrival in Missouri. His children took ill while he was away, and he rushed home, "so frightened that my whole body trembled," to find two very sick children. His daughter was "corpse pale." Medical help was useless, and his daughter and son both died, within half an hour of each other, later that day. Steines's sister-in-law died the next day, and his wife fell ill. Next, his youngest son, Lebrecht, passed away. His wife "went to bed, slept almost continuously, and died." Then two brothers became sick, his brother Peter suffering from severe diarrhea. "Oh, my dear ones, now followed horrible hours!" he wrote. "You should have seen what pains the two sick ones had to endure. Constant cramps, and the cries of the suffering resounded frightfully through the house and neighborhood." One brother survived. Steines lost his last child, Ida, on July 25. "No language is rich enough to express in words how the heart in its profoundest depths quivers with inexpressible sorrow," he wrote that autumn.[24]

Dysentery was similar to cholera because it caused serious diarrhea, fever, and cramps and endangered lives from dehydration due to fluid loss. It resulted from water contamination and a general lack of basic hygiene among nineteenth-century Americans. The disease peaked in warmer months, when high temperatures and humidity provided an ideal environment for the growth of bacteria. Few Americans paid much attention to the source of their drinking water, and human or animal wastes often contaminated creeks and rivers. Insects, gathering in stagnant water, could also transfer diseases to food that humans consumed. In addition, a lack of refrigeration led to the rapid spoilage of foods and the growth of further pathogens. Dysentery was a major cause of death among passengers crossing the Atlantic Ocean, and some towns had yearly outbreaks of the disease from contaminated waterways or wells. Since it brought about rapid dehydration from diarrhea, especially among the young, average mortality rates in some places could reach 5 to 10 percent.[25]

Typhus and whooping cough also afflicted residents of Missouri. Typhoid fever was another illness caused by contaminated water. A rash accompanied it. Whooping cough was a respiratory ailment that hit children the hardest but also infected adults. It could last up to six weeks. Sewell Hepbron wrote, "we are about through with the whooping cough. There has been no less than nine who have had it in our family this winter and it killed one of Hannah's children about a year ago and came on mighty in one or two cases." Five years later, he recalled how he had picked up a "slow kind of typhus fever which kept getting worse up to about the 25th of July. I had a doctor see me several times. I then began to mend about an inch at a time." He noted, "I was only confined to my bed about a week."[26]

The cause of death is sometimes unknown, as sources may not reveal enough information to determine the malady. Jonathan Harris wrote about a fever that his children suffered from in May 1843. "Something was the matter that I new nothing of." He begged the local doctor to help his daughter. His son was "out of his senses." His daughter died when "some blood vessel gave way and the blood gushed out of her mouth and she expired in about two hours." He confessed in a letter to family that the manner of her death was "more than I can bar." Nathan Haines wrote to his brothers and sisters that his daughter, Rebecca, had died in 1845. She had suffered from a serious cough and vomiting for several days. "She continued unwilling to die until the night before her departure when she called all of us around her bed and began to express the love she had for us all and how she hated leaving of her friends but told us She was not afraid to die. She felt confident she would meet her sisters that was gone before." Fourteen months later, his wife, Elizabeth, wrote another letter to their family informing them that Nathan's brother, Jonathan, had also died. He had suffered from "coughing and puking" and died May 23. "He had a great desire to live to the last," she wrote. "He said he could not make any thing of himself," she added mournfully.[27]

Preacher Charles Peabody did not fight a losing battle against death, but he did grapple with an array of insect enemies. Peabody traveled to Illinois, Iowa, and Missouri in mid-1846 and had his first encounter with bedbugs at a fellow pastor's house near Boonville on July 2. Bedbugs, attracted to body heat and carbon dioxide in the breath of humans, waited for their prey in dark locations. They often waited months for victims. The insects fed for only five to ten minutes, leaving a row of bite marks on their victims, as well as clusters of itchy red bumps and welts. Peabody humorously called his encounter "the greatest battle that I ever fought." He wrote that it seemed that the bedbugs "had been starved for a long time into a tolerably biting condition. They boarded me fore and aft and the battle waxed hotter and hotter until past 2 this morning, when the pirates left my vessel (blood vessel)" and departed for their "dark hiding places." Peabody wrote in exasperation that he was weak and weary after having slept only two hours.[28]

The next night, onboard a steamboat on the Missouri River, he "was boarded again as on the preceding night by an innumerable horde of bedbugs." He fought with them for more than two hours, and "neither quarter was asked nor given." The preacher eventually gave up and retreated, prompted by "cowardice," to the cabin floor, with a chair under his head as a pillow. When daybreak came, he returned to bed to find "the enemy had all left the field and not even carried off the dead and wounded." On July 6, he found not only bedbugs but also flies and mosquitoes. They continually harassed him while he stayed in a "miserable bunk." In a dining room, he met "ten hundred millions of flies." That night the bedbugs returned, and he ruefully complained to his diary that his two previous battles were "but skirmishes." He "never saw bedbugs so thick and ravenous," and they again forced him in disgrace from his bed to the floor. The next morning he found a huge bedbug floating in his coffee at breakfast. "Merciless creatures! Not satisfied with tormenting a man all night . . . but ready to pursue him to this table and blindly endeavor to take his coffee from his lips!!! That cup of coffee went down hard."[29]

Lice and ticks were also part of the antebellum world. Solomon Eby unkindly commented on "filthy" German immigrants he encountered on the steamboat *St. Joseph*, which was heading to Jefferson City in 1847. He described them as picking lice from each other's bodies and heads, then carefully breaking the legs of the insects by rolling them between their thumbs and fingers. Lice were then thrown into the river to be disposed of. Surveyor John Shriver found almost no problems with lice or bedbugs, but complained of another insect enemy, the tick. He wrote in the summer of 1829 that he killed fifty or sixty every day. "The itching which they produce is almost insupportable, indeed we are literally covered with sores by them." He hoped for an early frost, to reduce the torment, writing that "if ticks had existed at the time of Job, all his patience might have been overthrown." Ticks covered the ground and bushes in 1840, Joel Palmer reported. When picked off, the heads remained embedded in skin, causing many small painful wounds.[30]

While most sources do not detail the perils of disease or insects, many accounts of frontier settlement mention the necessity of hunting for food. In 1819, John Bush took part in one of the first steamboat voyages up the Missouri River, leaving a detailed diary of his year on the river. Near the Osage River, he saw more deer than "I ever before have seen." Bush also witnessed lakes full of swan, geese, and ducks and hunted a countryside occupied by herds of elk and deer and flocks of turkeys. In September 1819, he found a prairie full of elk, "alive with them, large gangs in every direction." Others also found passenger pigeons "by the thousands," where hunters killed as many as they could carry home, and turkeys "very tame in the woods." Jacob Lanius described how he was able to shoot a turkey from inside the house of one of the members of his congregation, the rifle resting on the dining room table. He wrote that he found game, particularly deer and turkey, plentiful along the streams in the sparsely populated areas he toured while preaching. Two weeks later, near Potosi in south-central Missouri, he came across a friend who had killed four panthers, a bear, and a number of "cats" over the winter. But Lanius praised the hunting abilities, not the religious dedication, of residents. He wrote of "few Christians and many religious speculators" in April 1840.[31]

Settlers used a number of different hunting techniques and strategies in the nineteenth century. Successful hunting demanded expertise, experience, and patience. Hunters had to know the habits of their prey, be able to recognize animal tracks, and know their ranges. The most basic form of hunting was "still" hunting, where individuals waited to ambush their prey along known game paths. Animals also might be lured into an ambush by imitating their calls, by leaving salt to attract deer, or by using decoys. "Trap" hunting, which involved using traps and snares, became much less common when the accurate rifle became widespread. Torch hunting occurred at night. One person used a light to shine in the eyes of animals, which illuminated the creature and made it remain motionless. A "drive" was completed on horseback along with packs of dogs, which flushed game from their hiding places. Animals such as deer or bear were pursued until cornered or exhausted and then killed. The final form of hunting was known as "encirclement." Here, as the name describes, animals were surrounded by groups of men who progressively moved toward the center of their dispersed circle, trapping animals. This technique could kill large numbers of game, but required more labor than most families had available. This method could also be used with fire, but proved dangerous, as some set blazes grew out of control.[32]

A humorous example of the use of several of these techniques is found in a memoir by John Lewis Peyton, who visited Missouri in 1848 on a tour of the country that took him through much of the Ohio and Mississippi River valleys. While visiting relatives south of Jefferson City, his friends invited him to go hunting. His hosts stationed him in a safe location, close to their home, at a creek where deer often passed when pursued. A group of hunters set out with a pack of dogs, hoping to drive some game toward him. After several dull hours of waiting, Peyton heard dogs approaching and found that they were chasing a deer and a very large bear. He shot and killed the deer, but missed the larger animal. The bear clambered over a fence and rushed toward a nearby couple. The man, seeing the onrushing bear, abandoned his fiancée and climbed a nearby tree "like a monkey." The screams of the young woman scared off the bear, which disappeared in a different direction, still pursued by a pack of dogs and men. Predictably, the woman's family broke off the engagement. Peyton did not comment on the fate of the bear.[33]

Hunting and fishing were an important part of life for adults and children, who could begin such activities as young as five or six. Even while he was improving his 115-acre farm, which was full of animals and crops, Frederick Steines hunted to supplement his diet. "There is no scarcity of wild animals here," he wrote, even as he complained of the difficulty of finding the smaller birds in the underbrush. Steines described wild ducks, geese, and turkeys as "delicious" and roast venison as a "real delicacy." He often found large flocks of turkeys near his home, usually numbering forty or fifty birds. He liked fried squirrels "very much" and detailed the fine fishing in Missouri. His favorite fish was catfish, which often weighed forty to fifty pounds, and had "so much fat that one could fry it without anything." David Graves found fishing and hunting so rewarding that he often skipped Sunday school as a boy to fish at one of his favorite creeks. He made primitive hooks from brass pins, twisted together his own lines from thread, and dug earthworms for bait. Hunting rabbits, quail, and prairie chickens provided some income, as he sold them to country stores or sent them to St. Louis when his father went to the city to sell livestock. He noted that he and his dog, Cape, caught many rabbits, the process only complicated by his dog's lack of interest in barking when chasing animals.[34]

Plenty of hazards existed for those who went in pursuit of game, especially young and inexperienced children. Henry Kelley, recalling his childhood in Indiana, wrote in his reminiscences that he and two other boys became lost as night fell. They had been pursuing a deer they had wounded. "So eager in the chase that we took no thought of direction, distance or time." They wandered in the darkness, filled with "anxiety and fear," guided by a compass. A pack of wolves startled them by howling nearby. "Our hearts leaped in our mouths and our hair was on end. I felt weak and nervous. The thought of being torn to pieces by wild beasts was anything but pleasant." They stumbled through the night, as quickly as possible, in deep snow. A barking dog led them to a neighbor, who pointed them home. Kelley hunted raccoons, hogs, and possums with his brothers and dogs, but never allowed himself to be caught in such a situation again. However, he did learn to leave skunks alone, once suffering badly from the "loud breath" of one after he tried to capture it.[35]

Wilson R. Smith, who lived in New Franklin, Missouri—old Franklin having been consumed by the Missouri River—wrote home to his brother about the excellent hunting, saying that it was "better than ever represented to me." He declared to his nephew, "game of description dear ducks gees fish and all other dumb things, rabbits possums squirrels thousands no danger of starving." Wilson's brother, R. G. Smith, also wrote to Henry: "We can work hard all the summer and in the fall shoot all kinds of game; squirrels, rabbits, coons, opossums, groundhogs, turkeys & deer, wild geese, Brants and ducks." The hunting was so good in central Missouri, reported Stephen H. Long in 1819, that one man was able to feed himself and his family for two years solely by hunting.[36]

This bounty did not last forever. In 1837, the *Gazetteer of the State of Missouri* noted that settlement had reduced the state's game, especially buffalo. By the 1830s and 1840s, large animals in Pettis County, in west-central Missouri, had become increasingly rare. Massena McCormick wrote in his memoir that bear, elk, and buffalo "were gone." A herd of elk was spotted one year, but never seen again. Deer, turkey, pheasants, and other fowl were still present, though. Hunters killed the last bear in the county when Massena was "too small to go along." They also wiped out flocks of green parakeets in the area. The passenger pigeon, according to D. W. Graves, once had been so numerous in Missouri that "the trees would bend beneath their weight. All I had to do to get all the pigeons I wanted, was to go down near the branch, point my gun upward, cock it, pull the trigger, and down the pigeons would come." Before he wrote his reminiscences the passenger pigeon was extinct in the wild. The last pigeons were wiped out around 1900. Wolves, which used to regularly kill livestock, were very rare by 1915, when Graves wrote his autobiography.[37]

Meat that people did not eat fresh—mainly pork, venison, and bear—had to be preserved for future consumption. Smoking or drying usually preserved it. Hog slaughtering normally took place after the first hard freeze of autumn, so high temperatures would not rot the meat. Pork and other meats could then be hung in the smokehouse for curing. In areas where maple trees were common, some settlers used sugar to cure meat, while those living near salt licks could use this. People packed pork in salt for about a month and then left it in the smokehouse until "well colored," according to Thomas Beckwith's recollections. Meat could also be jerked in warm weather by cutting it into strips and stringing it out on a scaffold a couple of feet off the ground. Coals then slowly cooked the meat for several hours to dry it. Such dried and jerked meats often appeared on the tables of Missouri families.[38]

Hunting supplied most food while families worked to clear land. Then they faced the task of plowing and planting their fields. A crooked tree branch with an iron prong (or share) operated as the most primitive type of plow. It cut the soil and turned the earth in preparation for planting. A more sophisticated plow with an iron share and curved board, known as a moldboard, pushed the plowed earth away from the furrow. After plowing, a farmer usually resorted to harrowing the ground to smooth out the field and break down the larger clumps of soil. Farmers often dragged a heavy log or a brushy tree limb across the field to accomplish this task. Then the planting and seeding began. Family members usually spread wheat by hand across a field; they planted corn in mounds.[39]

The most important crop on the frontier—corn—complemented hunting well, as it was a productive and easy-to-cultivate grain. One person could raise about ten acres. Corn was "the universal grain raised practically wherever there was farming," according to historian Paul W. Gates. It was a tough plant that yielded four times more food per acre than wheat. Corn was also relatively simple to grow and could be harvested at the convenience of the farmer. It required no tools for harvesting. Corn was the leading crop on the frontier, the "pioneer's subsistence," that provided food for both humans and animals. It required little plowing, demanded less labor than other crops, and was easily preserved. Corn pone, corn bread, grits, flapjacks, hominy, corn mush, and corn fritters were standard items in families' meals. Animals also ate corn to supplement their diet before slaughter or before they were driven to market.[40]

Planting corn was one of the first priorities for new settlers, as it provided much of a farm family's diet during their first few years. Indeed, it and pork provided much of people's diets for decades. Corn was planted by hand, sometimes with a hoe or ax when the soil was too tough to plow. The crop did not require a great deal of personal attention, but the first six to eight weeks after the plants appeared were crucial. Sprouting corn had to be guarded from birds and squirrels that enjoyed the buried kernels and young shoots. Nicholas Hesse reported that gray squirrels and blackbirds were a constant threat to newly planted fields of corn; deterring these creatures required two or three weeks of constant vigilance. Daniel Drake recalled the threat that these animals posed. One of his chores as a boy was to "repel these aggressors." With the help of his dog and an old shotgun, he chased off birds and squirrels. His trophies, he wrote, were "neither numerous nor brilliant; but the enemy felt my power."[41]

Fields also had to be cleared enough to keep weeds from entangling and choking the small plants. Farmers had to carefully hoe around their plants until they were knee high, as they could survive competition from weeds after a couple of months. Nicholas Hesse suggested that farmers plow between their rows of corn to keep weeds under control. The yield of corn in proportion to labor expended was better than most crops. It produced four times as much food as wheat and used one-tenth the seed. "Well-prepared" Missouri bottomland, along streams and rivers, could produce more than fifty bushels per acre, wrote Nicolas Hesse. Once the corn was able to survive without close care, families could then turn their attention to other farm chores, such as sowing a garden for fresh vegetables, clearing more land, or improving their primitive housing.[42]

Vegetable gardens were another important food source for farm families. John Mason Peck recorded that many of the settlers that he found scattered on the Missouri frontier about 1820 survived by cultivating corn and garden vegetables. Peck noted that these people raised cabbages, turnips, cucumbers, and melons. However, these were not the only crops grown by these farmers, who also cultivated lettuce, carrots, tomatoes, onions, pumpkins, and kitchen and medicinal herbs, such as sage, peppers, thyme, mint, and mustard. Frederick Steines noted in his diary that he grew potatoes, beans, peas, cabbage, and cauliflower in his garden. John Woods wrote that pumpkins, which could grow to sixty pounds, made good sauces and excellent pies. They could be easily sliced and dried for winter storage.[43]

Hogs, the most important livestock for Southerners on the frontier, supplemented hunting, corn, and garden vegetables. Southerners brought the combination of maize and hog agriculture west with them, but pigs were important livestock for farmers in the North as well. Hogs thrived in just about any area that had something to eat, so they were easy to raise. Farmers simply had to turn them loose on prairies or in woods, and they would feast on roots, acorns, nuts, and grasses. Pigs could take care of themselves and did not require herders to protect them from predators. They were gregarious animals that reproduced rapidly, usually with two litters a year. Hogs, whose semidomesticated state allowed them to run untended, were the "ideal frontier animals," wrote geographer John C. Hudson. James Bumgardner recalled that the woodland along the streams on his father's farm "fed, and even fattened, droves of hogs." William Shelton reported that after his family moved to central Missouri from Kentucky, they borrowed pork and lard from several neighbors until they could raise their own, "which did not take long," as their hogs reproduced quickly.[44]

Hogs could be transformed into many products, including bacon, ham, and lard. Almost all of the meat could be used, and there was little waste. They could be fed corn for fattening before sale, which improved meat quality and increased their size. Surplus hogs could be walked to a town for sale or slaughtered and packed in barrels. William Nash, for example, salted nearly 1,300 pounds of pork in December 1829, after winter had ended any threat of spoilage from heat. Freshly slaughtered hogs, packed in salt or pickled, could be preserved and sold in an era before refrigeration. Pork production made economic sense, as hogs provided more food pound-for-pound than beef and took care of themselves. Inexpensive river transportation helped keep costs low and provided access to markets for those who wanted to sell extra hogs.[45]

Missouri families also exploited the abundant natural resources around them. They collected strawberries, raspberries, and blackberries, as well as nuts when the opportunity presented itself. David Holmes Conrad recalled that wild strawberries covered the prairies "for leagues square. Nuts in every thicket, and at the head of them, the pecan nut growing wild in many places." W. L. Irwin noted that he found "blackberries by the bushel," as well as persimmons and grapes by the "wagon load," in Miller County, south of Jefferson City. Americans often cut down huge pecan trees to gain access to their nuts. Oak trees also provided plentiful acorns, he noted. Floodplains could produce more than 2,000 bushels of hickory nuts and 3,000 bushels of pecans per square mile. Residents also eagerly sought out beehives for honey and maple trees for sugar; both of these provided important sweeteners for families. Beehives were so widespread in Missouri, as well as across the eastern half of the continent, that a Saline County historian joked that all hollow trees had raccoons or honey in them. One man reportedly found seven "bee trees" in one afternoon along a creek in Chariton County. In an autobiographical recollection of the 1830s, Herbert Jones wrote that some farmers "hived several swarms of wild bees and domesticated them." Jones noted that farmers sold extra honey, as well as surplus vegetables, butter, eggs, and meat, to travelers or stores when possible.[46]

Daniel Drake recalled that "to get the honey was often a kind of frolic, made up of a few friends or neighbors." People worked together to find it, tracking bees and searching for appropriate locations for their hives. He wrote that this search often began near a flower patch or other blossoms. If this failed, they burned honeycomb to attract bees. Insects then returned to their homes, followed by humans who went to great difficulty to retrieve honey. People climbed trees, cut off limbs, or even felled large trees to capture a few quarts of honey. "The pleasure is in the finding and not the taking," Drake wrote.[47]

The production of maple syrup, from Missouri's abundant maple trees, provided another important sweetener (fig. 5). Like honey, it could be used to sweeten foods. Walter Lenoir wrote to his family in North Carolina, "the sugar tree is common here and most of the citizens make their own sugar." Maple syrup was harvested at the end of winter, just as warmer days in February and March caused the sap to run. Native Americans, the French, and Anglo-Americans all took advantage of the slack time before spring planting to gather sugar. Daniel Drake recalled that collecting syrup from trees was "work of great fatigue and exposure, but I recollect it with unmingled pleasure; for it was something out of the ordinary course of labor." People made horizontal cuts in maple tree trunks three to four feet above the ground and inserted spikes into the trees so the sap could run into buckets. Once they collected the syrup, it was boiled in large kettles until it granulated. The cold work included

5. Missouri's abundant maple trees provided a useful sweetener that was harvested at the end of winter. State Historical Society of Missouri, Columbia.

tending fires and chopping wood, as well as checking trees. Maple molasses sweetened fish, meat, and vegetables. Sugar was vital at the end of winter when foodstuffs might be almost depleted. It was often added to long-stored corn to help make it more palatable. Sugar production and honey gathering were important, for they helped diversify diets and preserve foods.[48]

"Farming was a hard occupation," noted historian Robert Leslie Jones. Families worked from dawn to dusk and often later. Some chores early in the day, or late at night, were completed by lantern or candlelight. Livestock always required care and feeding, pigs needed their swill, and milk cows might need to be taken to and from pasture. If a farm had sheep, lambing season could result in many sleepless nights, as people assisted with the delivery and care of new lambs. Plowing required miles of tedious trudging behind oxen, perhaps in broiling heat or cold rain. Fields and crops needed attention, and corn or vegetables might have to be weeded. Wood had to be cut for fencing, cooking, heating, or construction. Harvest time could be a race against time and weather. Work took far longer than can be imagined today—each ton of hay required eleven hours to cut, spread, and dry.[49]

Farm life was usually rewarding for a family, though. People relished their ability to make a living from the countryside and find independence. They prided themselves on their ability to plow a straight furrow or build a barn, and found fulfillment in their work and in their ability to cut hay or chop wood. Families were attached to their animals, from their horses and pets to newborn lambs and piglets. They took pleasure in the growth of their crops and a successful harvest. They noted the progress of their farms and the evolution of their buildings from log huts to frame houses, finding reward and happiness in their accomplishments. As parents aged, they helped their children start their lives as adults. Generations found usefulness in working the land and assisting each other.[50]

Farm families exploited the natural resources around them to produce the meat, vegetables, fruits, sweeteners, and other products needed for survival. After a year or two passed, the family could work to improve their farm, their diet, and their standard of living. Until that point, and often after, their fare would be dull and very repetitive. Jacob Lanius explained that a dinner in southwest Missouri consisted of corn, hog, chicken, coffee, butter, and "honey comb." Another missionary, Timothy Flint, found meals on the frontier to be the same: "good coffee, corn bread and butter, venison, pork, wild and tame fowls are set before you." Both men commented on how plentiful the food was, but neither praised its variety.[51]

People came to Missouri to secure their economic independence and gain a competency through the purchase of inexpensive and fertile land. Many, unable to buy their own land, had to rent property in hopes of earning income for later purchase. However, economic circumstances often stood in their way, as poverty, low prices, or bad luck reduced their opportunities. Those who did not own the land they lived on worked more than 20 percent of Missouri farms. Some never owned land, living as squatters. Most families spent their first few years practicing mostly subsistence agriculture and living in rudimentary conditions. Families had to create a farm out of the woods and prairies of central Missouri and worked to clear a few acres a year for crops. Many took part in the nascent market economy, even if only a few times each year. Jacob Lanius noted a clear division between the more commercial and developed areas along the Missouri River and its major tributaries and the more remote, less market-oriented areas isolated by limited transportation or geography. All endured the diseases that plagued nineteenth-century Americans, and widespread suffering and death were a normal part of everyday life. Cholera could wipe out a family in just a few days, while malaria left many in misery. Insects, from mosquitoes to bedbugs, added to the difficulties of life. Settlement had negative environmental consequences, leading to the spread of mosquitoes and the extinction of animals. Hogs and other livestock replaced bear, elk, and buffalo in Missouri within a few decades of their arrival.[52]

Hunting and corn, along with pork and garden vegetables, formed the pillars of American diets. Hunting helped feed people while they focused on the difficult work of building their farms. Corn was a staple crop for nineteenth-century Americans, for it was easy to grow and provided plenty of food. Thus, it allowed families to focus on important farm-building tasks, such as clearing land, planting gardens, and building homes. Vegetable gardens diversified diets and provided such nutrient-rich foods such as tomatoes, carrots, melons, and pumpkins. Hogs, which usually ran free and foraged in nearby woods, provided another important food source that required relatively little care. People also sought out berries, nuts, maple sugar, and honey to add sweeteners and diversity to their diets.

Pioneer families living in undeveloped regions with limited market access had to depend on themselves or their neighbors to feed themselves. Once families had assured themselves of a basic subsistence, they tried to improve the land they lived on or began to consider how to sell any surplus farm goods that they had been able to produce. Some families made butter or cheese and sold it or exchanged it with neighbors. Others did the same with extra sugar, honey, pork, or corn. Families on the frontier were often able to meet most of their food requirements from the fertile prairies, woods, and waters of Missouri. However, farm families needed each other for assistance in construction, plowing, harvesting, or other agricultural tasks. The next chapter explains the importance of such networks of mutual assistance for Missouri families.

5

THE COMMON DEPENDENCE OF MAN

In April 1824, Clarinda Tate notified her mother in Kentucky of the death of her infant son. The boy, born February 13, had lived but an hour. She wrote that the child had "breathed its last without a groan[.] I felt much resigned to the will of God." Clarinda had suffered from ill health during her pregnancy, having a "bad cold and cough," shortness of breath, and a pain in her left side. Her husband, James, had been troubled by back pain and confined to the house. "He lays himself up with hard work," she noted sadly. Their daughter Mary had also been sick, "taken with vomiting and purging of worms." Clarinda wrote that she had suffered much, but neighboring women and a skilled midwife had helped greatly. "Mrs. Henderson staid with me 3 weeks almost constent[.] She attended me night and day as tenderly as she could have don her own child." Clarinda recorded that she had company almost continuously for the past seven weeks. Clearly moved by the generosity of her neighbors, who had also helped build the family a cabin the previous October, she reported that they had done everything for her that they could. "Some come to see me that had not been acquainted with us before. I feel much attached to our acquaintences here they appear more like relations than strangers." She wrote that a neighbor had been so helpful, "she appears more like a sister than a neighbor. She is often sending me things we stand in need of." Though she missed her mother and had endured a terrible winter, Clarinda ended her letter by saying, "I feel better satisfied now than I ever did" with her friends in Kentucky.[1]

Few rural households could survive completely alone, and few ever tried. Farm families did not exist in a social or economic vacuum, and they depended upon on one another for mutual assistance and survival. Neighborhoods and communities were an essential and necessary part of life for nineteenth-century farmers. They provided security, comfort, and companionship. No family could produce everything that it needed by itself, and individual households depended upon each other. Women assisted in giving birth or took part in quilting parties, while men might help a family with communal physical labor such as a barn raising. Male slaves often completed work for neighbors who needed help, being loaned or hired out by their owners. Missouri residents also provided hospitality to travelers, giving assistance to people they would probably never see again. Farm families exchanged labor, tools, animals, agricultural products, and other help with each other, but they did not see such cooperation in solely practical terms. Neighbors shared work and recreation, including fishing, hunting, and going to church. People received emotional and psychological support from friends and neighbors, as well as enjoying crucial economic assistance.[2]

This cooperative and supportive behavior—variously called "reciprocity," "neighborhood exchange," or "borrowing"—included almost all aspects of rural and agricultural life, from assistance with clearing land to construction projects. Most farm families lacked the labor to complete many of these tasks or did not own enough livestock or tools to complete harvesting or plowing. Many farms also lacked dairy cows or large plots of grazing land, or farm families did not produce enough of all foodstuffs to feed themselves. Farm families did not possess the vaunted self-sufficiency claimed by many historians in the twentieth century. Thus, these families had to obtain part of their food requirements or labor needs from others. Such farm families had to enter into exchange relationships, not solely for profit or to increase their standard of living, but simply to feed themselves, have a place to live, or harvest their crops. Frederick Steines noted, "many farmers have neither carts nor wagons because their price is extravagant." He also wrote that his brother often borrowed his oxen for plowing or transport. This borrowing system provided crucial assistance to families during the initial years of agriculture in Missouri, as well as during the transition to some commercial production. In fact, such cooperation continued throughout the antebellum period, and the involvement of families in markets did not lead to any reduction in neighborhood reciprocity.[3]

Studies have demonstrated the inability of farm households to practice self-sufficiency. Bettye Hobbs Pruitt argued that the independence of American farmers was a "mythic vision." Pruitt found that a majority of farms in Massachusetts lacked one or more of the requirements necessary for a family to feed itself. These included land for crops; livestock for milk, meat, and work; pasture and hay fields for feed; and tools and equipment to complete a myriad of chores. As many as half of all inventoried farms lacked plows or oxen. One-third of farm families could not meet their own dairy needs, and most did not have enough pigs to meet their food needs. The poorest households, as can be expected, were the worst off. Two-thirds of the poorest farmers, those who owned less than twenty acres, did not own pasture for their animals to graze on or any swine at all. Almost half of this group did not own enough land to even grow all their food supplies.[4]

Since many families could not have been self-sufficient in food, these households could not have operated independently. They had to enter into exchange relationships to simply feed themselves. To meet the minimum food requirements, families had to turn to other farms for agricultural products, tools, animals, or grazing land. For Massachusetts farmers, and for those across the nation, agriculture was built on a foundation of interdependence, not self-sufficiency. Farm households could not operate as isolated units because they depended upon each other for survival. To meet their needs, farm households traded surplus production in one area with other families to compensate for insufficiency in another. Such neighborhood exchanges allowed farm families with surplus production to raise their standard of living through barter or sale. This borrowing system also helped poorer households feed themselves, because a family without pastureland could exchange grazing rights for a wagonload of hay, or barter the use of oxen for several bushels of crops. Most farms were not self-sufficient, but neighborhoods usually were. The interdependence of farms made them viable.[5]

In 1832, Charles Joseph Latrobe stumbled across a newly arrived farm family near Independence, in far western Missouri. The family, with a few slaves, had recently settled on 300 acres they had purchased the previous year. Neighboring women had come by to take part in a quilting frolic and were busily stitching together segments of wool and cotton. Latrobe observed, "a life in the woods teaches many lessons, and this among the rest, that you must both give assistance to your neighbor, and receive it in return, without either grudging or pouting." To lend a helping hand was laudable and natural, he noted. Neighbors helped each other in construction and harvest, as well as with smaller labors. The family fed Latrobe a "plentiful and homely" meal, cooked by a family slave, and treated him graciously, even while they lived a rudimentary life.[6]

This system of communal obligations and assistance existed throughout the United States. Tasks that were "too large for the individual"—such as clearing land or harvesting—were done in common. In *Sugar Creek*, historian John Mack Faragher explained how these community values operated in Sangamon County, Illinois. He discovered a "remarkable degree of gregariousness" among farm families, who spent time with their neighbors in work, play, and prayer. Faragher found that these families shared resources and provided crucial support to their neighbors through a "borrowing system" that allowed scarce tools, labor, and products to be distributed for the benefit of all. This network of assistance responded to neighborhood needs by sharing resources that were held in common, such as forests for livestock forage or wood for fuel. Farm households used the network of neighborhood borrowing for most transactions required for actual farming. The borrowing system was crucial to the everyday survival of the family farm, for it provided access to the material and labor that allowed farmers to survive and prosper. Families in Sugar Creek existed in a network of reciprocal obligations that demonstrated a "mixture of private and communal that characterized the backcountry economy." This system of neighborhood exchange also occurred in upstate New York, where historian Nancy Grey Osterud found that a similar system persisted throughout most of the nineteenth century. She noted that while many such exchanges were small, no more than help with milking a cow or borrowing a cup of sugar, they occurred frequently and made up what she termed a strategy of "getting by."[7]

John Bradbury, who traveled in Missouri just before the War of 1812, commented on the aid provided to new settlers in building a home. Money could not purchase the required assistance, but "that kind and generous feeling which men have for each other, who are not rendered callous by the possession of wealth, or the dread of poverty, comes to his relief." Neighbors arrived, even without being asked, on an appointed day when a "frolic" took place to help new arrivals build a house. "On the morning of the appointed day they assemble, and divide themselves into parties, to each which is assigned its respective duty. One party cuts down the trees, another lops and cuts them to proper length, a third is furnished with horses and oxen and drags them to the spot designed for the scite of the house." Another group made shingles, while another cut the wood for the roof. By the end of the night, all materials for construction were ready. The next day the family slept in their completed home. Bradbury wrote, "no remuneration is expected, nor would it be received. It is considered the performance of a duty, and only lays him under the obligation to discharge the debt by doing the same to subsequent settlers." Such assistance was not intended to only help the newcomer but occurred frequently throughout the year. Archibald Little Hager mentioned nine house, barn, shop, or stable "raisings" between August and November 1844 that occurred near his Missouri home.[8]

Historian Everett Dick fully agreed with Bradbury when he wrote, "the outstanding feature of frontier social occasions was the fact that with the exception of a wedding almost all of the earliest were connected with work." The whole community gathered to help neighbors with labor. In turn, they were expected to help all of their guests when needed. One of the first of these social occasions was "logrolling," where groups of neighbors went from farm to farm helping to clear fields of newly cut trees. Such work was the most difficult on the frontier, but it became a time of mirth, fun, and good neighborliness as families worked together to help each other. Trees were burned into pieces about ten feet long for transport; some could weigh hundreds of pounds. Men used handspikes, which were stout sticks about five feet long, to move them. Workers pushed handspikes under a log and arranged themselves on opposite sides to carry it off the field. Dick wrote that such hard work could be enlivened by humor, competition, and, of course, whiskey. Wrestling, lots of food, and dancing helped to make the occasion more enjoyable. One practical joke included putting one end of the stick in animal manure and then pushing it over to the man on the opposite side.[9]

Alcohol was part of everyday life in the early Republic, and people of all ages consumed it at all varieties of social occasions. Rural areas often lacked good water, and many Americans had difficulty finding access to clear, free-flowing springs or could not afford costly deep wells. Some feared cloudy water or swamp fevers; many disliked carrying water long distances or even thought that drinking it on hot days was harmful to one's health. Residents of St. Louis and New Orleans had to wait for muddy Mississippi River water to separate from sediment. Thus, most Americans did not see water as necessary for health, and alcohol seemed to have many advantages. The average American consumed more alcohol in the early nineteenth century than at any other time in U.S. history. Americans drank all sorts of such beverages, but especially enjoyed distilled liquor, including rum, gin, brandy, and, most often, whiskey. In fact, the word "whiskey" originated from Gaelic; it means "water of life," and many treated it as such. (Wealthier folk often enjoyed wine as well.) Adult men drank most of the alcohol, with about half of the male population consuming half a pint a day or more. On average, these drinks were about 45 percent alcohol, or ninety proof. Rural people drank whiskey at house-raisings, cornhuskings, and logrollings. Parents exposed their children to alcohol early, and boys drank liquor regularly. Families, workers, and the wealthy drank at all times and at all occasions, from elections to barbeques to harvests. Women who took part in communal sewing or quilting also drank whiskey. It was passed around at funerals and at militia musters as well.[10]

No event could be considered complete without a plentiful supply of liquor, and its availability was a sign of hospitality. Daniel Drake's father became a popular neighborhood figure when he received 100 gallons of whiskey in trade for a horse and provided small amounts of the liquor to friends without charge. Families made their own drinks from grain or fruit and shared them among themselves and neighbors. If they could afford it, farmers built their own small stills to produce alcohol. Access to whiskey and other such beverages helped Americans cope with tough or tedious labor, and men believed that whiskey invigorated them. Men, women, and children drank alcohol because it was, according to a history of early families in Missouri, considered "healthy and pleasant to the taste." It was an insult, and a reason to discontinue friendships, if a neighbor was not provided the opportunity for a drink. When visitors arrived in Missouri, Ovid Bell recalled, a high mark of hospitality included providing whiskey, sugar, spoons, and glasses for all. Visitors drank from gourds when life was too primitive to provide glasses. Alcohol had its negative effects, of course, inspiring fights, feuds, and murder. It wrecked homes, led to the abuse of wives and children, and drove many to early deaths. Sam L. Wilson wrote that his brother William had "given up entirely to drink" and appeared determined to bring "an end to his existence." He doubted his brother would live more than three or four more months. Joel Palmer reported, while on the Oregon Trail, that strangers provided a jug of whiskey one night. "Before bed-time all the men were completely intoxicated," he wrote.[11]

Daniel Drake provided an example of the intersection of alcohol and social gatherings. He recalled how the visit of justices of the peace to isolated towns gave rural families an excuse to assemble. Anyone with a grudge or litigation arrived at the selected location, sometimes a store in a small town. Business, legal and retail, could be conducted; many refilled their jugs of whiskey, and men prepared for a break from their normal agricultural labor. The presence of state-sanctioned justice did not deter vice, however. "Each day provided a bill of fare for the next," Drake wrote. Horse races, cockfights, wrestling, or fistfights enlivened the day. A fight often included choking, eye-gouging, or biting off opponents' noses, while onlookers cheered their favorite pugilist. Many, too intoxicated to ride their horses home, had to stay the evening in town. Fortescue Cuming, traveling on the upper Ohio River about 100 miles east of Cincinnati, related the story of a "stout young man" going to attend a "gathering" at a justice's court. This individual thought that sixty or seventy others would be there as well. Some were plaintiffs, and others were defendants. They went to wrestle, fight, shoot, gamble, and drink whiskey. This young man had his rifle and was ready for any "frolick." He chose to go to the court day because he had heard another man boast that he could whip him.[12]

The system of neighborhood exchange consisted of many different tasks that were shared in common or resources that were loaned from family to family. Neighbors helped each other with house-raising, harvesting, logrolling, land clearing, cornhusking, hunting, quilting, and sewing. They exchanged the use of their labor, their land (for pasturing or growing grain), and their livestock (for plowing). Archibald Hager noted in his diary that William Walker shared horses with Charles Ellis in late March 1851. People also borrowed tools and equipment, such as cider mills, wheelbarrows, plows, wagons, shovels, and soap- and candle-making materials, from each other. Charles Gilliam wrote that a neighbor brought a wagon over that needed its wheels repaired. Gilliam went to another neighbor to have his plow sharpened and also borrowed a handsaw in late January. When necessary, neighbors also gave food, loaned money, or provided credit. This trade was crucial for Missouri households, as they worked to build and nurture family farms. Such exchange networks served as a community economic safety net that provided assistance, social interaction, and support on both the rough edge of western settlement and in more developed areas.[13]

Another example of this system of mutual assistance included corn shucking (fig. 6). A family that needed help in removing the husk surrounding the ear of corn requested the aid of those in their neighborhood on a certain evening. The host family usually divided their large pile of corn in half, and competing leaders from visiting farms, often boys, chose teams. Once the signal was

6. Removing the husk surrounding an ear of corn was time-consuming. Families assisted each other with this labor, often working in competing teams. If a young man found a red ear of corn, he was entitled to a kiss from the woman of his choice. *Scribner's Monthly: An Illustrated Magazine for the People* (1874), 584.

given, each side furiously worked to shuck its portion of the corn before its opponent. Each side attempted to reduce its share of the corn by moving it over to its opponent's side. "Every now and then someone would throw an ear of corn and hit another on the head just for mischief," recalled David William Graves. Rival teams pushed corn across a dividing rail or stealthily pulled the rail toward one side. Accusations and denials flew back and forth. A brief fight between rivals often resolved disputes. Teams also passed a bottle of whiskey around. Any young man who found a red ear of corn was entitled to a kiss by the woman of his choice. The winning team found great entertainment in defeating the other party. A large meal followed, with the hungry and tired crowd enjoying meat, pork, pies, hot coffee, and other foods. A dance usually followed, enlivened, of course, by whiskey. Visitors often did not return until the next day, with the sober assisting their drunken neighbors home.[14]

Settlers who came to Missouri brought this system of assistance with them. Frederick Steines provided a fine summary of how this exchange system operated. Steines wrote in his letters that there were "various chores which are

7. This illustration shows the primitive and crowded living conditions of early settlers. A family might live in a cabin of fifteen by twenty feet. Nathan H. Parker, *Missouri As It Is In 1867: An Illustrated Historical Gazetteer of Missouri* (Philadelphia: J. B. Lippincott, 1867), 370.

performed by the neighbors in common." Most frequent among these were house-raisings, logrollings, and corn harvesting. He wrote, "neighbors are helpful in cleaning the land; then usually there is a party in the evening and through the night. There is eating and dancing." Steines cautioned his family in Germany that "here is the right place to speak of the necessity of remaining on good terms with everybody." He told the story of one of his neighbors, an American, who had put on a logrolling four months earlier. Only a few people showed up to help, and none of them were Americans. "Through some noncommendable deeds this neighbor had incurred the hate of the rest."[15]

Philander Draper explained in his reminiscences how the system of neighborhood exchange worked. Draper lived in central Missouri for almost all of his life and worked as a farmer, a merchant, and a businessman until his death in 1883. In his recollection, he described how pioneer farmers helped each other survive. "Distinctions of wealth or other such accidental circumstances had little influence" for families, he noted. "The common dependence of man upon his fellow man rendered all such mere accidents worthless. Physical helpfulness in time of need was superior to everything else." Draper described how neighbors from miles around would show up to help a family build a home (fig. 7). "Even if there were only eight or ten men in as many miles, each had to turn out and help his neighbor and they did it with a will." If corn had to be husked, the "usual practice" was to choose a day, set aside everything necessary for the task, and invite everyone within a "convenient radius." If wheat had to be harvested, "all in a like matter were expected to attend." People came with their sickles and helped harvest the grain. "Woe to the nabob who threw himself back on his dignity and proposed to hire his help because he had the means. His house would never raise nor his grain be harvested. He was severely 'let alone' and he found it good for his general welfare to remove to some more congenial locality."[16]

Other sources help to explain this system of mutual cooperation. William G. Bek translated diaries from German in the 1920s that recount how this system of neighborhood exchange operated for immigrants who settled along the Missouri River. One of these German immigrants was Gert Goebel, who came to the state in 1834 at the age of eighteen. He wrote that settlers were dependent on the cooperation of their neighbors, and a "request for assistance was hardly ever declined." Neighbors came from twenty miles away to help in raising the heavy logs needed for a new home. Goebel wrote that he "dare not decline such an invitation, because every year I was dependent upon the help of my neighbors myself." Similarly, Ethel Grant Inman recorded how the early social life of early pioneers was closely tied to neighborhood assistance in wood chopping, house warming, and logrolling. "While the men were busy at these labors the women picked wool, peeled apples or quilted. Here the tasks of pioneer life were shared and work that was ordinarily tiresome became a pleasant contest." When they took a break at noon, they all had the "best dinner that could be provided" on a table full of all the "good things of the community." In the autumn, there were husking bees for corn, apple ruts during harvests, and sleighing parties after it snowed. Though farm life was difficult and challenging, it was not "sordid and dull" for most families because "the social companionship of other people who too were striving with the soil" was "mingled with the hard work."[17]

Neighbors in Missouri helped to support each other throughout the year in a variety of ways. Mary Ann Kitzmillen noted a series of such exchanges from 1855 to 1858. Her family regularly went to the local mill to grind wheat into flour, but she did not record a payment for this, as she often did for items that might cost money. Thus, it is very likely that her family paid for milling with a portion of their crop. In October 1855, a neighbor built fences on the Kitzmillen farm and "took the last hog home," probably in exchange for his work. Kitzmillen's family also used a neighbor's cider press regularly, but she did not record any reciprocal exchange. It was very likely that this "debt" was paid with labor, farm products, or other assistance. Another neighbor, a Mr. Lightman, often helped with farm chores. She noted that he had helped them by mowing hay and cutting grain in the summers of 1856 and 1857. Her husband, Zebulon Kitzmillen, also appeared to have borrowed a wagon at least once. The family had to get salt for preserving pork, but she did not mention going to a nearby town as she did on other occasions. Therefore, she probably borrowed salt from a nearby family.[18]

William Nash, a farmer in central Missouri who owned land adjacent to the Missouri River, also recorded such exchanges in his diary. Nash took his grain to the local mill for grinding into flour, as did almost every farmer, paying for milling with a portion of his crop. He also helped his neighbors raise buildings, including a schoolhouse; he loaned horses or wagons when necessary and went hunting with nearby men. His fellow farmers borrowed tools and helped search for lost children as well. One neighbor, William B. Scott, brought him almost 200 pounds of apples and pears in November 1823. This was possibly to repay some prior assistance on Nash's part. Nash cared for two ill farmers, George Bartlett and John B. Moore, in October 1837. They may have repaid this assistance with their labor on Nash's farm, though he did not directly state this.[19]

Another example is that of Thomas Keyes Humphreys, who sold his farm and moved to Missouri in the autumn of 1835. Humphreys had lived near Charleston, Virginia (now West Virginia), and moved to live near Bellefontaine, in St. Louis County. He had grown corn, wheat, hay, potatoes, and rye on his farm in Virginia, where his slaves would have provided crucial farm labor. In September 1835, before selling his farm and heading west, he sold about half of his total crop of wheat—250 bushels—and had made $275. He also sold oats, wheat, potatoes, turkeys, geese, and chickens in nearby Harper's Ferry, but did not record how much he earned from these sales. Thus, Humphreys was obviously involved in some commercial production, which he continued when he arrived in Missouri. He withdrew $1,315 from his bank and settled his final bills in October. "Fixing and settling up my business for the West," he wrote in his diary on October 12. He found a farm that he liked in January 1836 and began to set up his new home with his family and slaves.[20]

Humphrey's diary demonstrated how the neighborhood exchange system worked to assist new settlers in Missouri. Even before he had purchased his farm, he had helped a neighbor "kill his hogs" on January 14. He then borrowed a wagon to haul corn in mid-February. Humphreys also helped out a traveler, "a stranger [who] came here from St. Louis, took sick with a chill and remained the night." In early March, he again borrowed a wagon and a horse. In mid-April, he went "after oats for seed" at a Mr. Garret's farm, from whom he borrowed $20 on April 30. Humphreys also helped a nearby farmer with sawing and took his slave Jim with him to assist a Mr. Lanham with planting his corn. In return, four days later Lanham brought one of his slaves, Jackson, over to help with plowing, as well as bringing a "load of hay." Once Humphreys had finished planting his own corn on May 18, he took his whole family to help another farmer finish his planting that afternoon. Three days later, he sent his slave Jim back to the same farm. At the end of May, another farmer, Aron Moses, came to help him "make rails to build the cross fence in the field." In June, he borrowed horses from Richard Cordell, went to a cornhusking, and loaned tools to Cordell, as well as "commenced making a cupboard for him." In return, Cordell and his slave, Israel, helped him in building a "spring house." Humphreys borrowed a cradle from another neighbor, a Mr. Gruell, to cut his oats, borrowed a wagon from another farmer, and received the assistance of Cordell's slave, Israel, for farm chores.[21]

This neighborhood exchange system continued in 1836 and 1837. Farm chores transitioned from work that could be completed during the colder months to the labor of plowing, planting, and caring for crops. On December 8, Humphreys noted that his neighbors helped him "raise the logs to our smoke house and workshop. Mr. Lanham was chief architect." Mr. Gruell came to help him "kill a beef" and two hogs, and a slave named Andrew assisted with unspecified work. In late January, Humphreys went to help a Mr. Conway "raise his stables," and in early February he "was all day helping to raise a smoke house for Mrs. Worthington." His wife, Helen, and four other farmwives worked together to sew a quilt. In early February, he was "making and nailing on shingles," possibly completing some carpentry work for a neighbor, since he reported "Mr. Cordell with us," possibly helping with the work. Humphreys also assisted Cordell "fix up an old house." In March, he completed carpentry work for another neighbor, as well as building him a kitchen door and helping to lay a floor for his house. Later that month, he asked a neighbor to return his harrow to help with planting. He also borrowed some potatoes, flour, and oats from several neighbors in late March and April. Once the warm weather began to return, the rhythms of agricultural life changed. On May 15, John Kearsley came to help with plowing; four days later Richard Cordell "came and assisted us in finishing to plant our corn." Over the summer, the neighbors exchanged tools, labor, foodstuffs, and wagons. They also loaned each other money, built fences and storage sheds, cared for the sick, gathered fruit, and pressed cider. Humphreys built a cider press that summer, and he reported on September 26, "Mr. Story brought load of apples to make cider." This cycle of work and assistance is recorded throughout the diary.[22]

Farmwife Pauline Stratton also recorded how this neighborhood borrowing network helped her family in the mid and late 1850s. She reported in May 1855 that her husband had "commenced plowing the Prairie with 3 yoke of oxen," using the animals and labor provided by a nearby neighbor, a Mr. Cook. A week later Stratton wrote that she had borrowed about forty cabbage plants from two other women. In August, she ran out of cornmeal, and a neighbor gave her some. In October, she received 106 pounds of beef from another farmer, Bob Stoneman, but she did not report why. (This could have been an exchange of foods or a form of payment for some assistance.) Stratton also gathered apples at a neighbor's orchard and then made cider at another family's house. In November, she "got another quarter of beef" from a neighbor named Gilbert when the family was "nearly out of meat again." Later that month, she also went to help a woman who was in labor, but the baby was born before her arrival. In January 1856, Stratton gave eight pounds of butter to another neighbor who had "visitors for 2 weeks & I believe they are nearly eat out." Later, in the spring of that year, she recorded that she ran out of cornmeal and "have borrowed from 4 of our neighbors." In August 1858, she used a loom from another farmwife for some weaving.[23]

There were drawbacks to such close interaction with neighbors, of course. Some people could be overly interested in the affairs of others, prying into the lives and activities of nearby families. It could be difficult to maintain much privacy in the countryside, too. People were expected to conform to set standards of behavior in a community. Those who refused to live by such ideas could suffer from ostracism as a penalty. Individualism was not an asset when strict moral and social standards limited individual expression. Residents of a community could also be judgmental, and they often gossiped about the intimate lives of those they lived near. Some imposed on their neighbors, demanding more than they deserved or taking more than they needed. Others gave less than they should have. Rivalries and mistrust could undermine relationships. Communities were crucial to family success, but they could often be oppressive.[24]

Despite potential drawbacks, men, women, and children truly enjoyed the social interaction with their neighbors, who were usually also their friends. Examples of unnecessary social activities abound in the sources. People visited their neighbors for companionship, hosted dinners, or went to them. They also participated in games, contests, and dances on a regular basis. Visitors often stayed for a few hours or even overnight. People exchanged not only labor but also foods, ideas, and opinions, providing emotional and psychological support to their friends and neighbors. Missouri residents also provided help to strangers and travelers, knowing that they in turn might someday need such assistance.[25]

Daniel Drake recalled that immigrants to the wilderness became "social and hospitable," since their isolation made them happy to see each other. People enjoyed having visitors and took part in an "abundance of small talk about the countries they had left, about their pursuits, their children, and their neighbors." He reported that rural families had many gatherings, often segregated by gender. Male-dominated gatherings, such as cornhusking, could be impolite affairs. "Profanity, vulgarity, and drinking were their most eminent characteristics." Gatherings of men often ended up with "the beastly intoxication" of at least a few. "Coarse jocularities were scarcely frowned upon by any." Female gatherings were usually more sober and well behaved. Mildred Arrington Huckstep Gillum wrote of a quilting and sewing match that she attended, with nearly thirty women and babies in attendance. Two big meals interrupted the day, with plenty of pies, cakes, coffee, and tea. Two quilts, six pants, six shirts, and three waistcoats were finished that day. She did not mention any violence, drinking, fighting, or misbehavior by either gender in her letter.[26]

Two examples from the late 1850s illustrate this constant social activity. Franklin Burt went to see friends and neighbors in January and February 1859, even as he cut and hauled logs for construction to a nearby sawmill. In one week at the end of January, he hosted neighbors for part of the day or overnight for five of seven days. They came after church or to help with work. In fact, Burt had so much regular company that he listed them in daily entries in his diary. He also visited neighbors who were ill and went to help a family shuck corn. In the last half of February, he stayed overnight with friends, or they stayed with him, one-third of the time. More than two dozen people visited his family or stayed overnight that month. Charles Wesley Gilliam provided another example of this. He had meals with neighbors, hosted overnight guests, and enjoyed the companionship of friends often. In mid-June 1858, he and his family spent most of the week with company at their home or staying overnight at another family's house.[27]

Families gladly hosted travelers in Missouri. Gustave Koerner and his friend Charles Friedrich, both of whom were recent German immigrants, took a journey by foot to Jefferson City from near St. Louis in October 1833. The farther west they walked, the fewer settlements they found. Koerner noted that women alone at home turned away guests, due to their husband's absence. Usually they were sent to another nearby place to spend the night. As soon as a man returned home, though, hospitality replaced any caution. "It was a self-understood matter that no decent looking person should be denied a night's lodging." Families fed visitors well. Koerner wrote that biscuits, corn bread, ham, or venison made up a typical meal. The two wandering Germans also shared any game they had shot during the day and often ate turkey or partridge for breakfast. One family shared a meal, coffee, and tobacco. They provided their visitors with a buffalo robe near the fireplace to sleep on as well as several pillows. "They were not refined, but behaved as well as any lord or lady could have done; of course, payment was refused." The two men often walked twenty or thirty miles a day. Koerner found the population of southern Missouri to be "very frank, open-hearted, hospitable and kind. There was very little refinement about them but also no rudeness." He judged these people to have limited mental horizons, but natural good judgment. Southerners were independent and confident folk, but the freedom from all restraints and the absence of police or the military led to excesses. Koerner thought they were "addicted to drinking" and capable of "almost any outrage."[28]

Martha Woods, moving with her family to Missouri from Virginia in 1857, recounted in her diary how strangers had provided company and assistance on the long trip westward. While in Tennessee, a man gave them squirrels for supper and helped them find corn for their horses. He "was very kind and obliging indeed." A week later, having crossed the Mississippi River into Missouri, they encountered a man from Pennsylvania. "He seemed to be a pleasant kind hearted person. Came to our camp and chatted for an hour or 2." On April 29, three men from nearby farms came to visit with the travelers, which helped the weary family enjoy the evening. The men told "many anecdotes and thrilling adventures." Ten days after this, in Saline County, Missouri, the family stopped for the night without a place to stay. A nearby farmer, originally from Virginia, sent them corn and meal without charge. "He says he would not give a cent for a Virginian that would not give an old Virginian a few bushels of corn." When they arrived at their destination, relatives offered them a place to stay, with one cousin convincing a friend to move in and loan his house to the Woods family. "Our neighbors are so very liberal that we feel almost ashamed of ourselves as we have been here so short a time we have no means of returning it."[29]

Other travelers found Missouri residents equally hospitable. William Graham Johnston, heading west across Missouri to join the gold rush in March 1849, found himself in unknown territory. An attempt at fishing left Johnston and a companion "lost in the woods, and wandering about promiscuously." They stumbled across a log cabin and were greeted by a couple, who asked them to join a noontime meal. "We needed no urging to accept the invitation," he wrote. The two men, their search for fish forgotten, enjoyed ham and eggs, corn bread, onions, and coffee. Their hosts then pointed them in the correct direction, and they quickly found their way to their camp. A Maryland surveyor, Joseph Shriver, sent to examine routes for a road to Jefferson City, also recorded the hospitality of people in the area. Shriver spent time with an old man who claimed to be a Revolutionary War veteran. Shriver and his party discovered that their host wanted to provide them with "everything he had good to eat." After weeks of living on corn bread and butter, they found his generosity "a treat to us."[30]

Pauline Stratton, Thomas Humphreys, Philander Draper, and others provide excellent examples of how the neighborhood exchange system operated in central Missouri. Farm families, as demonstrated here, depended upon each other throughout the year in a myriad of ways, from assistance with seasonal and labor-intensive farmwork to the use of tools that not all families owned, to the exchange of foodstuffs when someone ran short. In these ways, such mutual aid helped both newcomers and more established farm households to meet their needs.

The legendary stereotype of a completely self-sufficient farm family is a myth that conceals the true interdependence of Americans. Families depended on each other for assistance with a wide variety of tasks. No family could produce everything it needed, and people exchanged tools, animals, food, and labor when needed. Such aid helped families to clear land, harvest crops, and construct buildings. People assisted their neighbors with harvesting, cornhusking, and land clearing, as well as in smaller, everyday exchanges. Neighbors also helped each other by building fences and loaning equipment, livestock, and tools. Families cared for each other's sick and wounded. They also exchanged foods and helped in childbirth, as well as enjoying the companionship of their friends and neighbors. These tasks allowed families to feed and house themselves and successfully survive the first few hard years of farm making. The network of neighborhood exchange supplied some farm families with the foods that they needed but could not purchase in nearby stores because of distance or transportation difficulties. It allowed them to feed themselves and improve their farms so they could more easily and more quickly begin to transition to producing agricultural goods for market. Neighborhood exchange also temporarily replaced the more formal commercial structures of stores, credit, and market participation that settlers had left behind when they migrated to Missouri. This exchange system continued throughout the antebellum era, and the increase in commercial activity did not erode the bonds among communities.

Migrants to Missouri came in search of the economic independence that they might not be able to achieve elsewhere and had to survive a difficult transition period of primitive living, often isolated from local and regional markets. For most, initial settlement required a temporary period of largely subsistence agriculture, where families had to build a new farm. The immigration of thousands of families after 1815 transformed the region from a generally uninhabited region into a changed landscape of farms, villages, and small towns. The state of Missouri contained 140,000 people in 1830, with most of this number living in a fifty-mile-wide corridor along the Missouri River. Increasing settlement steadily pushed the borders of settled areas farther away from the Missouri River in the 1830s. By 1840, when the state had a population of 383,000, almost all of the current state counties had been organized. The northeast region in the Chariton River valley and northwest areas near Independence and St. Joseph had been settled, as well as the banks of the Osage River in the south-central section of the state. The plains north of the Missouri River filled in rapidly after 1840, but most immigrants avoided the Ozark Mountains south of the Missouri River, probably because of the region's rough terrain and isolation.[31]

After several years of tough living, farm families normally had cleared enough land and planted enough crops to begin to improve their basic conditions. Once families were able to feed themselves, they looked to the production of surplus crops that they could sell or barter for goods they could not produce themselves. Such items included sugar, coffee, spices, and gunpowder. They also began to use income from surplus production to buy things they chose not to produce themselves, including clothing, utensils, or shoes. Sometimes they were able to meet these needs within the context of neighborhood borrowing, but the presence of towns or improved transportation links allowed them to sell or exchange surplus production. Often the first farm goods sent to a local store involved those produced by farmwomen, such as eggs, butter, poultry, or cloth. The next chapter details the many contributions of women to the family economy. It shows how female labor aided in earning much-needed income for their families and helped with the transition from a mostly subsistence and local existence to a more market-oriented one.

6

COOK, NURSEMAID, AND HOUSEWIFE

White farmwomen in the antebellum United States operated as economic producers in their households. They often took part in the growing formal market economy and earned income for their work, as well as completing a wide range of traditional household duties. Women provided crucial domestic labor that helped to support their families in both subsistence and market production. Not only did they cook, clean, and provide child care, they also produced, preserved, and gathered foodstuffs, including vegetables, poultry, and milk products. Women processed raw materials from outside the home and produced foods and other items for household or market use. In fact, female labor usually provided from one-third to one-half of a family's food consumption. Some women also helped to earn money or barter credit through the sale of the goods they produced, which included poultry, eggs, cloth, butter, and cheese. An example of this was Eliza Wallace, who wrote to her sister, "I pay for nearly all mine and Catherines Clothes by marketing[.] I have my butter engaged the year round at ten cents." Such income helped obtain goods that families could not, or chose not to, produce on their own and allowed them to begin to purchase useful items such as shoes, utensils, or manufactured clothing that improved their families' standard of living.[1]

The contribution of women to antebellum farm life has been little explored in the history of Missouri.[2] This is mostly due to the lack of available sources. Women in antebellum Missouri played substantial roles in the family economy, completing important tasks through paid and unpaid labor. Some contributed to their households with involvement in the market economy that existed outside their homes. Those most likely to be involved in such transactions lived near towns or close to the Missouri or Mississippi River, the areas with the most demand for items that were produced. The opportunity to make money through the sale of female-produced goods increased greatly after the 1820s as steamboats allowed the greater distribution of goods throughout Missouri and as an expanding population supported general stores in growing towns across the state. Many women chose to take part in such activity and took advantage of the opportunity to earn additional income for their families. They also completed a complex variety of work to support their households at home. In the past several decades, historians have detailed greater female involvement in the formal cash economy, finding that women have often helped to support their families through unexpected paid work.[3]

Farming, according to historian Susan Sessions Rugh, would be unprofitable and unsustainable if families did not have the unpaid work of farmwives and mothers. Households could not have afforded to pay an outsider to complete all the tasks that farmwives did. Families cobbled together their livelihoods by using the domestic labor of women, children, and slaves; the subsistence and commercial farm work of men; as well as neighborhood exchange and barter. Very few antebellum farmwives escaped a life of hard physical labor, wrote historian Jeanne Boydston, for "family life depended on the smooth performance of an extensive array of unpaid occupations in the household."[4]

Women suffered from the burden of a "double day" as they supervised and trained children, as well as completing all their expected household tasks (fig. 8). Melinda Napton, wife of a judge and lawyer in Saline County, bore eleven children and managed the family farm while her husband was frequently absent from home for two decades. Her husband, William, complimented her on her everyday labors, including her skilled and tireless sewing, knitting, cooking, and health care for their family. Women often operated as economic partners in their families, and their labor sometimes helped keep the family farm business from failing during tough times. While many sources are unable to demonstrate that women earned income for the family economy, their own labor usually allowed their husbands to earn money from their work.[5]

The diary of Mary Ann Kitzmillen, a farmwife who lived in Lewis County in northern Missouri, illustrates the laborious tasks of antebellum women. In one week in late May 1855, she worked in her garden planting corn, beans, beets, and cabbage, and spent at least one day making soap, which was a time-

8. Women completed a vast array of tasks to help support their families, often juggling several tasks at once. J. P. Newman, ed., *Golden Links in the Chain that Connects Mother, Home and Heaven*. (St. Louis: N. D. Thompson, 1890), 56.

consuming chore. Soap making required collecting grease, fat, and tallow from meat, in addition to lye from wood ash, and then boiling it all together. Ash left in a barrel produced lye when water was poured over it. Women, with the aid of children, measured appropriate amounts of lye and grease and boiled it in large kettles. After boiling, they poured the mixture into containers to harden before use. Kitzmillen also planted potatoes in rows in the family orchard and hosted her sister and her young niece. She did all of this while "very sick" for at least one day. In addition, Kitzmillen also completed all of the other usual chores of farmwomen, ranging from cooking to washing. Over the next two months (June and July) she recorded that she planted beans, cabbage, and potatoes in her garden; collected cherries and raspberries; and spent at least one day doing the "girls washing" and another day baking. At the same time she kept track of the work of her husband—noted as "Z," shorthand for Zebulon—in the fields, mowing hay, plowing corn, and cutting grain. He was aided by their sons and by the occasional neighbor.[6]

Mary Ann Kitzmillen also detailed her work during the summer and the fall harvest. She labored in her home and garden, washing, cleaning, gathering grapes and chestnuts, helping with cornhusking, and caring for the crops in her garden. She did "laundry all day," churned butter, and boiled maple syrup. Kitzmillen also "went to the shoemakers" several times, at least once to get the men shoes. On several occasions she mentions chores, such as "hauling corn" and "sowing wheat," but does not tell who was completing these actions, and it is quite possible that she assisted with them. Her contributions to the family economy also included profitable labor, such as when she sold a turkey and twenty-four little chickens on December 8, 1855. She did not report how much she made from this exchange, but simply that she had sold them.[7]

A large farm family consumed enormous quantities of food. Farmwives, along with their daughters, usually spent much of their day preparing meals. They dedicated their mornings to cooking. Meat, eggs, cheese, corn, and vegetables had to be harvested, collected, or obtained from storage. Gravies, jellies, milk, butter, and coffee and other drinks normally accompanied family meals and needed to be prepared as well. Women baked bread from corn or wheat daily, prepared three or four vegetables for meals, and roasted, smoked, or stewed meat. They also cooked chicken or pork, dried fruit or spices, and pickled vegetables. Helen LaTourette recalled that her mother cooked at the fireplace in their family's log-cabin home southeast of St. Joseph. She used frying pans and kettles that she swung over the fire, as well as an oven built next to the fireplace. LaTourette's mother, whose name was not identified, cooked biscuits by the fire and sweet potatoes in the coals. LaTourette fondly remembered apple, peach, and blackberry cobbler, as well as chicken pies and bread. A nearby spring kept butter and milk cool. Until stoves became widespread in the 1840s and 1850s, women cooked meals directly over coals in a fireplace, a back-breaking and dangerous responsibility that accompanied bringing water from wells or streams, cleaning dishes, and managing children. Daily chores, such as cleaning and sewing, along with the weekly cycle of housework and the seasonal rhythms of a family farm, kept farm-women constantly busy.[8]

Vegetables were an important part of people's diets. Each family usually set aside about an acre of land near the house for a kitchen garden. After fathers or sons plowed the land, the cultivation and care of the garden plot fell to the women and children of the household. They raised everything from cucumbers and potatoes to carrots, pumpkins, and kitchen and medicinal herbs. Women and children planted onions and potatoes in early spring, followed by lettuce, carrots, and turnips in April. Tomatoes could be started early indoors, and seedlings moved outside after the last chance of frost. Other vegetables, such as cucumbers, melons, and pumpkins, were planted in May. Farmwives and their daughters and sons hand-watered and weeded young plants. Once plants had survived their first weeks, vegetables could be harvested throughout late spring and summer.[9]

The labor of children was as valuable as that of their mother and father. They were the most versatile and adaptable laborers in a family and could easily be employed in a wide variety of chores. Children spent countless hours completing essential duties for their families for which their parents did not have time. Boys usually did men's work, but when needed they completed female labor, such as milking cows or cooking. Normally, girls labored with their mothers in the home and garden, but they often completed tasks that fell to boys, including herding animals and harvesting crops.[10]

Boys completed work that changed according to their age. Younger boys, not yet ten or eleven, did less physically demanding tasks. These included helping to plant corn, taking care of livestock, and gathering nuts and berries. As they grew older, boys took on more difficult chores. By the time they became teenagers, most had assumed the responsibilities of adult men. When he was a boy in Kentucky, Daniel Drake helped his father clear brush by cutting saplings and tree limbs. He also helped with planting and took corn to a mill; he fed cows and kept the fire lit, too. At the age of twelve, he began to assist in plowing. Within a couple of years he was using a sickle and scythe in the fields and cutting wood and splitting fence rails. As he was the oldest child and had only one sister, Daniel had to sometimes help his mother with churning butter, washing clothes, or milking cows. "She had urgent need, daily and nightly, of all the assistance I could give her," he noted.[11]

Children provided crucial labor for most farm families. Both boys and girls helped in clearing land and preparing it for planting. Older children assisted in plowing, while younger ones broke up clumps of soil or planted kernels of corn. Boys and girls helped plant the large family vegetable garden and cared for it. Children also gathered wild plants and wood and brought water back home from nearby springs or streams. They helped care for the many animals a farm family owned, including horses, cows, pigs, sheep, and chickens. Both sexes learned to drive and herd livestock at an early age, bringing cattle in from the fields for milking or taking them to pasture early in the day.[12]

Daughters, while sometimes working outdoors with their brothers, usually spent their time with their mothers inside the family home. Starting at an early age, they cooked, cleaned, washed, sewed, and completed the many demanding duties expected of farmwomen. Girls and young women learned to make soap and candles, knitted and weaved, processed and preserved food, and cared for their younger siblings. Daughters also helped their mothers make butter or raise poultry to be sent to markets. Farmwives relied on the labor of their female children in such pursuits. The work of younger women, like that of their mothers, had few limitations. It also provided them with domestic training for their adult lives.[13]

Women and girls were also usually responsible for caring for poultry and cows. They tended flocks of geese and chickens, fed and milked cows, and churned butter and made cheese. Careful planning could provide a steady supply of eggs and fresh-killed chicken for most of the year. Girls, occasionally aided by their brothers, assisted with the routine of milking cows twice a day and in tedious tasks like making butter. Henriette Bruns, a German farmwife living in the village of Westphalia, took care of her garden; stayed busy with washing, sewing, and making soap; and managed 100 chickens, sixty to seventy pigs, two cows, as well as geese. Female work provided important foodstuffs for their households, which helped to diversify farm families' diets and sometimes provided income from goods sold to merchants or necessities from exchanges with neighbors.[14]

In November 1836, Henriette Bruns arrived in Missouri with her husband, Dr. Bernhard Bruns, and their young son. She was twenty-three, fifteen years younger than her husband, and left almost her entire family behind. They had immigrated to the United States from southwest Germany to live about 100 miles west of St. Louis, near the town of Westphalia. Dr. Bruns had decided to leave his home for many of the same reasons that his compatriot Frederick Steines had—cheap land, fertile soil, low taxes, and greater opportunity. The family lived in a "simple log cabin" with "sparse furnishings," Henriette wrote in her letters home. These letters have been collected in the book *Hold Dear, As Always, Jette: A German Immigrant Life in Letters*, which details her life and experiences over nearly sixty years in Missouri. Her writings provide a detailed look at the life of a farmwife and German immigrant and help to show the varied, and exhausting, work of a rural farmwoman in antebellum Missouri.[15]

Henriette Bruns struggled for seventeen years in Westphalia to raise her children, manage her household, and complete all the tasks expected of a wife and mother. Like most frontier women, she dealt with many of the same crises and challenges that plagued antebellum Americans: sickness, drought, death, and isolation. Her husband and children; her oldest brother, Franz, and his family (who had emigrated with them); and several laborers and their families lived with them, or nearby, for the first few years. Despite this crowding, Bruns was often left alone for long periods when her husband left home to attend to his widely scattered patients. Her children kept her very busy. "We could plant only a very few vegetables because the little fellow took too much of my time. The few things on the stiff upper land did not succeed very well. Now we have many people and little to eat. A great worry for the housewife!" She wrote that she would need to dig up some fresh potatoes so that her family and their workers would have enough to eat. "What else should I complain about? That I am very often vexed? That it is no fun to represent cook, nursemaid, and housewife in one person?" She also gathered nuts for her family, harvesting a large bag in one hour. The Bruns family battled a recurring fever that attacked them over a period of years. In the summer of 1838, she wrote that the fever reappeared six times, afflicting both her and the children. She struggled with constant illness and weakness, writing, "my feet do not want to carry me up the hill again after I have gone down into the garden."[16]

Bruns balanced caring for her children with her other household duties. She had a new baby, Johanna, in the spring of 1839 and another boy, Rudolph, two years later. In between, in June 1840, she wrote that she was glad that they had moved to Missouri, but she also noted "how lonely I am; there is not another congenial female being with whom I could exchange now and then my feelings when I need some relief and would forget the daily worries and cares and set those aside for a short time." She added, writing to her distant brother, "I rarely get to go out of the house." She stayed busy with milking, washing, sewing, making soap, and constant child care. In the summer of 1841, dysentery sickened all of her children. Three of her children—Johanna, Max, and Rudolph—died in September. Grief-stricken, she wrote in despair to her brother in Germany, "with all of them the last words and dying glance was 'Mother!' And so it is not surprising that I wished I could have gone with them."[17]

However, she persevered, held her family together, and continued to manage her household and bear children. Bruns had seven more children in the next eleven years, five of whom lived to be adults. They continued to live near Westphalia until 1853. Then her husband decided to move to Jefferson City, the state capital, and run his business in the city. She rented rooms out to boarders to help pay for the "terrifically high" rent in the town. They lost two sons in the Civil War. Dr. Bruns died in 1864, leaving his wife to care for their remaining four young children. She made a living by running a boardinghouse and renting rooms to state legislators. For part of her last years, she lived with a daughter and her family, maintaining orchards and gardens and raising chickens, some presumably for market sale. Henriette Bruns died in November 1899 at age eighty-six. Her life demonstrates the daily hard labor and grinding workload of a rural farmwife in central Missouri. She survived illness, loneliness, and the death of five children, while completing all the expected duties of a farmwife. Her life shows the struggles of antebellum women and their important unpaid work for the family economy. Though she did not produce farm goods for market sale, her life helps to illustrate the myriad ways in which female labor helped support these women's families.[18]

Women's work was never-ending, as shown in the examples of Henriette Bruns and Mary Ann Kitzmillen. In addition to a grueling routine of daily tasks, farmwives and their daughters often spent their evenings working at spinning wheels, weaving and making clothing for their families.[19] J. A. Ward, who lived near Troy, thirty-five miles northwest of St. Louis, reported that "my mother made all the cloth that clothed her family" and headed the family as a single parent for forty years. Helen LaTourette recalled that she and her sisters "all learned to knit when we were quite small." All sewing was done by hand. The children wore homespun clothing, and her mother made clothes, linen, towels, and sheets for the family. Girls helped produce stockings and mittens. LaTourette fondly recalled how her mother, her sisters, and she had knitted and made quilts by candle- and firelight; a brother often read to the family in the evenings. In addition to sewing, women also preserved and pickled foods, and made candles as well as blankets and quilts. Beatrice Fink described her daily work in Missouri to her relatives in Germany in a letter mentioned in the book *German Settlement in Missouri*: "Besides attending to the things my dear mother taught me, such as cooking, baking, washing, ironing, sewing, knitting, mending, etc . . . I can milk a cow, which gives me great pleasure; also I can make trousers and vests and coats. There is no work I dodge and I am not ashamed to perform the humblest tasks." In Missouri, farmwomen did all of these tasks—and more, as a shortage of labor on frontier farms often led to women and children being drafted into completing tasks normally performed by men. When necessary, they assisted men with labor in the fields, barns, and forests—picking apples, plowing, harvesting crops, and slaughtering larger animals.[20]

Martha Tyler Overall was born in 1840 near Fulton, Missouri, on a plantation owned by her father. Both of her parents died when she was four years old, and her oldest sister and brother took charge of the estate. Her siblings took in boarders in the 1840s to help meet their expenses, as did her sister and her husband who lived in Jefferson City. Since the town was small in the 1840s and usually crowded with visitors, "every family took in boarders." Women, being responsible for housekeeping, completed all of the cooking, cleaning, and other work that maintained the household and provided services to boarders. Thus, in this way they helped their families through cash earnings.[21]

Overall grew up quickly, marrying young and taking on the responsibilities of a wife and mother. After her sister died in 1851, she wrote that her "heart almost stood still at the calamity." She was then sent to school in Louisville, Kentucky, for three years before she married at age eighteen. After marriage, she lived with her husband and a slave couple on a small farm west of the town of St. Charles. Though she provided relatively little information on this phase of her life, she did have two daughters and boarded in St. Charles or St. Louis during much of the Civil War. When they did live on their small farm, she helped in harvesting apples from their five-acre orchard. She noted in her memoirs, "the fruit was gathered and piled under each tree, and then carefully packed in barrels and shipped to St. Louis. We bought a hand 'Cider Mill,' and the refuse apples were made into cider." Her husband was a merchant who was often absent from home on business, which would have left her to run the family farm alone. Though she does not explicitly acknowledge harvesting, packing, or shipping apples, it is possible that she took part in this work. In this way, she helped earn money for her family.[22]

Margaret Blauff Hillenkamp was a German immigrant who came to live near St. Charles in 1835. She brought vital income to her family through sales of eggs and wool clothing and also helped her husband, Friedrich Hillenkamp, with hard physical labor. While no documents written by Margaret Hillenkamp survive, we do know about her life from one of her husband's surviving letters, penned in May 1843. He wrote that his wife had assisted him in clearing, and then cultivating, about twenty acres of their farm. They had planted an orchard, and he took the fruit to sell in nearby St. Louis. He also wrote that they had taken several hundred eggs from her chickens to sell as well. The cash they earned from these sales allowed them to purchase "all their necessary household goods." In a January 1846 letter, Hillenkamp noted that his wife had "helped him in every kind of work where her circumstances allowed"—in other words, when she was not pregnant. The family also kept sheep, probably using their wool for weaving. Historian Linda Pickle argues that Margaret's weaving was possibly sold at market and that her contributions to the household were "vital to the economic success that she and her family attained in Missouri."[23]

Another woman whose work proved crucial to her family was Sally Dodge Morris. She spent decades living in Missouri, helping to support her family—and substituting for an ill husband on a regular basis—by sewing coats for market sale, gathering bushels of nuts, and hunting for meat. Sally, the daughter of a missionary from Vermont, moved with her family to Bates City in western Missouri in 1821 to work among the Osage. She was ten years old at the time and would spend most of her life in the state. In 1893, she wrote a thirteen-page autobiography for a writing contest that told of her life in Missouri as a young woman. After she married Milton Morris in 1831, she often found herself alone on their farm with their two children when he had to go to a mill forty or fifty miles away. In his absence, she managed the farm and household. If a traveler needed to cross the river nearby, she took them across in a canoe and helped "swim the horses and ferry the men. Mr. Morris sick half the time, we would take the two children in the canoe and hunt, and cut bee trees and gather nuts." She also earned income for the family. "I made forty coats by hand, besides pants and vests, and took the pay in corn, pork, potatoes, beans, home made cotton cloth &c." In the 1840s, Morris continued to make money for her family. She wrote that sometimes neither she nor her husband saw but one silver dollar "an entire year, and I got that for making a coat." One year—"having no money"—they camped out on the Big Osage River and cut down pecan trees to gather the nuts. After collecting sixty bushels, they sent all of it to St. Louis and earned $1 per bushel. She wrote that this was the "entire amount we had for our store bill for one year when there was nine in the family." Even at the age of eighty-two she was "doing the housework for four in the family," washing, mending, and cooking for everyone.[24]

Elise Dubach Isley, another young woman in western Missouri, was the daughter of Swiss immigrants who came to live near St. Joseph after they landed in the United States in 1855. Shortly after reaching northwestern Missouri, Elise's mother died, and she had to take over her duties. She recalled that it was good that she had given her doll to a friend, "for in the same grave with my mother I buried my childhood. Although I lacked a month of being thirteen years old, I had no more time for dolls. I had to be mother to my two younger brothers and soon was to be housekeeper for my father." She told her son that her father knew that "after I assumed the duties of a home, I would be so busy with my housework that I could no longer attend school." The family settled in a log cabin north of St. Joseph, near Amazonia. Her father wanted to settle near the town "because of the market it afforded" and also because his brother lived nearby. She completed all of the housework, although she was not yet fourteen when they moved in. "I not only cooked, swept and washed, but made butter and cheese, cut out and fashioned clothing, and at certain seasons manufactured soap and candles."[25]

Elise and her family began to take part in the expanding commerce of the region as soon as they arrived at their new home near St. Joseph. Her father purchased a wagon, a plow, furniture, a stove, utensils, and livestock once they had bought their land. She wrote that her family had never heard of "diversified farming," but that they practiced it nonetheless. They earned income in a number of ways—from field crops, livestock, and the sale of butter, eggs, timber, and oxen. The family regularly took its farm produce across the river for sale. She referred to these trips as her "trading excursions." Elise rode horseback to take her butter and eggs to market, returning with dry goods and groceries. She sometimes crossed the frozen Missouri River on the way south to St. Joseph. Elise was responsible for making the butter and cheese and taking care of chickens and their eggs. So here, she was accountable both for the production of these market items and for their sale. Thus, she helped her family not only through her domestic labor and subsistence production but also through cash income or credit earned by the sales of market goods.[26]

Similarly, James Williams also recalled how he took his mother's chickens and eggs to market in the 1850s to earn money for his family. Williams was born in May 1834 at his parents' farm in Cass County. Later the family moved north to reside in the Clay County area. His father died when he was fourteen, "leaving us in the wilderness in a double log cabin, two brothers, two sisters, and a weakly mother, with little to live on after the doctor bills and burial expenses were paid." James and his brothers helped their mother run the farm, but he provides little information on her. In 1855, after his "mother had raised a fine lot of nice chickens," he took them to sell to the soldiers at Fort Leavenworth. Two towns to the east, Plattsburg and Haynesville, were too small to absorb the sale of the 150 or so chickens that he had. A neighbor told him that a "good spring chicken" could be sold at Fort Leavenworth for twenty-five cents each. "So we decided to market our chickens," Williams noted. He built a chicken coop eight feet long, divided it into three compartments, attached it to a wagon, and headed for the fort. It took two days for him to reach the fort, and he sold all of the chickens to the hungry soldiers. He earned $3 a dozen and recalled that he had twelve to fifteen dozen chickens. Thus, he earned from $36 to $45 this one trip from his mother's work at home. Williams then reported that he had "some goods to buy," including a sack of salt (which almost was ruined by a thunderstorm), and returned home.[27]

The diary of Pauline Stratton, a farmwife who lived near Syracuse, Missouri, details her household management and domestic duties, as well as how her work helped to bring in much-needed income and store credit. Her family lived about twenty-five miles south of Boonville and had moved to central Missouri from Virginia in 1855. Pauline and her husband, Thomas, had five children. They owned 11 slaves, more than double the Missouri average of 4.8 slaves per owner, as well as more than double that of the average of Cooper County of 5.2. Their slaves included one ninety-five-year-old woman and five others of prime working age who were between sixteen and thirty-eight years old. The other five were children who were fifteen or younger, including one infant who was one year old. The Strattons' human property provided them with a significant labor force and made them one of the largest slave-owning families in their township. For the whole county, they were in the top 15 percent of slave owners. Eighteen people lived on the Stratton farm, with eight slaves and three children thirteen years old or older. Their slaves and children helped with work in the fields and also assisted Stratton with gardening, cooking, washing, and butter production. The large labor force available helps to explain the productivity of her household. Even with all this help, she stayed almost constantly busy, helping to manage her household and its production of farm goods. Stratton completed all of the usual jobs of an antebellum rural farmwife, including cutting out a pair of brown pants for her husband, making soap, planting and caring for her garden, and constantly mending or fixing clothing.[28]

Like other farmwomen, she often had to step outside the gender boundaries of her time and do work that normally fell only to men. In early July 1856, she recorded in her diary that she had been hauling wheat and harvesting oats. Here the flexibility of female labor allowed her to complete both domestic, gender-appropriate tasks as well as more masculine and physical labor. On occasion, males sometimes completed the work of women. She wrote that her son John, age thirteen, was "making a little butter now" during the spring of 1859.[29]

A large rural household, such as Stratton's, required tremendous amounts of labor. Pauline Stratton did not escape the daily burdens of farmwomen, but the work of her children and slaves reduced it. She assigned the care of chickens to her daughters, for example. Two of her slave women, Aga and Dilsy, kept the kitchen fire lit and helped with cooking. They also completed the family washing and helped with sewing and weaving. Stratton still worked in the garden, preserved foods, processed meat, and made butter, soap, and cider. She also spent countless hours making clothing for the members of her household, both slave and free. Her slaves undoubtedly made her life easier, though. They also helped produce foodstuffs for family consumption and market sale.[30]

Pauline Stratton's diary, which covers the years 1856 to 1862, detailed her regular sales of eggs, butter, and other products to merchants in nearby towns, as well as the occasional traveler or party heading west. Income from these sales was used for a variety of goods to benefit her family. She purchased both luxuries and necessities, including sugar, linen, plates, cups, hats, coats, shoes, and clothing. Her notes are not always complete, and the disorganized nature of her diary makes estimating the exact economic contribution to her family difficult to determine. However, the actual cash and credit earned by female-produced goods in the Stratton household was significant. It was also often earned year-round, as opposed to the seasonal income that male-dominated work during fall harvests and animal slaughtering brought in.[31]

In 1856, Stratton sent a steady stream of products that her household made to nearby towns. On February 16, she sent thirty-nine pounds of butter to a merchant named Bell. In return, she bought a set of plates, six tumblers, a set of cups, a pitcher, and a saucer. Two months later, in April, she sent twenty-seven and one-half pounds of butter to the same store. She was very busy during the summer and autumn, recording work in the fields, sewing, planting and harvesting her garden, making soap, patching clothing, and caring for her children. Pauline Stratton, her family, and her slaves produced 138½ pounds of butter in 1856. However, due to a very low price of three cents per pound in April, she earned less than usual, only $16.52.[32]

In the first four months of 1857, she sent ninety-one pounds of butter to market, receiving in return a coat for her son John and twenty-one yards of calico. As in the previous year, the butter production of the Stratton farm came to a halt in the late spring and summer. This was due to the inability to keep butter from spoiling in the midyear heat and also possibly due to the heightened demand for labor during the summer. In the fall, once temperatures fell, the family renewed their production of butter. In late December, Stratton sold "60-odd lbs" of it in town. In 1857, she was able to sell about 150 pounds of butter and earn an estimated $22 for her family. Three years later, between May 1860 and April 1861, she sold 290 pounds of butter to nearby towns.[33]

During these years, Pauline Stratton helped to earn a substantial portion of her family's income, selling more than 600 pounds of butter. If we assume that the Stratton household produced 200 pounds of butter each year in the late 1850s, this can be compared to an estimated average household butter production in Cooper County of 77 pounds per year. This number is calculated by figuring an average household size of five, based on the census returns from Lebanon Township and a sample of other sections of the county. The county produced 208,100 pounds of butter in 1860; dividing this sum by the number of households—2,705—provides an estimated average of 77 pounds of butter produced per household. Thus, the Stratton household seems to have produced at least two-and-a-half times as much butter as average households in the county.[34]

But she did not confine her commercial activity solely to one item. Whenever possible, it seems, she took the opportunity to try and sell the products of her poultry and livestock. In November 1858, a peddler and an Irishman bought thirty-six pounds of butter; she used $5.40 in credit to buy cloth. In April 1859, Stratton sold three pounds of butter and four dozen eggs to cattle drovers heading for California. Her other sales that year helped earn $27.37 in cash and merchant credit. In 1860, a very active year for the family farm, Stratton reported that she sold cloth, chickens, eggs, butter, and bacon. This would have earned an estimated $69.35 for her family. In November 1860, the family also sold eight barrels of corn at $2 each, for $16. They also killed three hogs and sold their meat for at least $39, as well as selling one calf for $18.[35]

The total income from the various farm operations managed by Pauline Stratton in 1860 was substantial and almost equal to the amount of money earned from the sale of corn and livestock—$73. So, it is possible that the monthly income earned by Pauline Stratton may have exceeded the cash income of her husband on occasion. Despite its imperfect information, Pauline Stratton's diary is an important record of the role women played in the family economy. Her work helped buy clothing, plates, food, and shoes for her family, improving their quality of life and making her children's lives easier. In fact, depending on market prices and her husband's work, she may have earned a majority of family income in some seasons.

By the 1840s and 1850s, farmwomen in central Missouri pursued more market participation than they had previously, producing butter, cheese, poultry, and other farm goods for sale or exchange. Earlier, in the 1820s and 1830s, farmwomen had engaged in more subsistence production, focusing their labor mostly on the family economy or their neighborhood. Here their production of clothing and foods, ranging from vegetables to butter, supported their families with unpaid domestic labor. But with continued migration and the new towns and transportation links that grew throughout the region, the possibility of market participation opened up new opportunities for women such as Pauline Stratton. Such farmwomen took advantage of the chance to sell their farm goods in local markets to earn income for their families. Their children and slaves, if any, helped them in these pursuits. By the start of the Civil War, such market activity by rural farmwomen was an expected and unexceptional aspect of the family economy.

Women in antebellum America played substantial roles in the family economy, completing important tasks through paid and unpaid labor. Female labor did not just produce vegetables, milk, butter, eggs, and cheese, and gather fruits and nuts for the family's table. It also often helped to produce a variety of farm goods, which could be sold for cash or mercantile credit to purchase necessities or to improve the household's standard of living. Market involvement helped farm families better their lives by providing access to desired items that they could not manufacture themselves or by allowing them to buy relatively inexpensive, mass-produced items that they chose not to make. A woman's earnings also helped to diversify her family's income and made surviving lean times easier. While historians have often ignored the crucial economic role of paid female work, recent research has shown how important this income was for many farm families. Missouri farmwomen who took part in the expanding market economy played an overlooked and underappreciated role in antebellum agriculture.[36]

The next two chapters explain the continuing expansion of the market economy in the region. Continued immigration and increasing settlement, combined with the integration of central Missouri into the national economy because of the transportation revolution, laid the foundation for the increased participation of residents in commercial activity. Migrants had moved west with a long-standing interest in profiting from market participation. In the final stage of market expansion, economic development enabled ambitious immigrants and settlers to make money. This transformation changed the social and economic life of the region as consumerism spread throughout central Missouri and as families embraced opportunities to produce more goods for sale or barter.

7

A GREAT BUSINESS IS DONE

Once American and European migrants surged over the Appalachian Mountains in the late eighteenth century, they pursued commercial opportunities. But "markets cannot affect the behavior of people if people lack access to them," noted historian David Danbom. Rivers provided this access. Peddlers and flatboat stores met rural consumer needs until the development of towns and transport integrated western areas into an expanding national market. Steamboats allowed the cheap movement of goods and people up rivers and linked Missouri to other regions. These vessels utterly changed the economic life of the antebellum West, reducing travel time and slashing the cost of goods, providing access to a cornucopia of consumer items. Missourians took full advantage of the new opportunities provided by improved access to markets, collecting cattle for sale to overland migrants or selling surplus farm goods downriver. The Santa Fe trade, beginning in the 1820s, as well as migration to Oregon in the 1840s and 1850s, spurred the growth of towns and market demand in central Missouri. The California gold rush also encouraged the economic development of the state, rewarding many who produced for the market economy in central Missouri.[1]

In the 1820s, minister Timothy Flint wrote that the Ohio and Mississippi Rivers contained scores of boats full of Americans selling products from Kentucky, Illinois, and Missouri. "The products and ingenuity and agriculture of the whole upper country of the west" were for sale. Boats had arrived from regions thousands of miles apart, he noted with some exaggeration; sometimes a collection of these vessels covered a few acres. Flint wrote that boats loaded with planks from southwest New York mixed with "Yankee notions from Ohio." Pork, flour, whiskey, hemp, and tobacco could be found in Kentucky boats. Illinois farmers sent cattle and horses, while Missourians exported furs and lead. Some boats, he recalled, were loaded with ears of corn or turkeys "that gobble most furiously," while others had barrels of apples and potatoes or cider or dried fruits. "Every kind of spirit manufactured in these regions" was sold onboard as well. Henry Vest Bingham also noted the extensive commerce on rivers. He wrote of seventy or eighty keelboats and barges at St. Louis in June 1818. Bingham estimated that each boat could carry 30 to 100 tons of goods. Only one steamboat was docked in the city.[2]

The American drive to make money was shown by the great variety of goods and services for sale on these waterborne craft. Some boats operated as floating mercantile shops, while others were the equivalent of a floating tavern. While traveling on the Mississippi River, Flint found that more than 100 boats had landed in New Madrid, a small river town in southeast Missouri. He watched a "tinner's establishment" float by, which made and sold various metal articles. Another vessel, a blacksmith's shop, manufactured axes, scythes, and other iron tools. The aquatic blacksmith even shod horses. There was also a dry goods dealer on a boat. Indeed, Flint declared, every spring brought forth "new contrivances of this sort, the result of the farmer's meditations over his winter's fire." Christian Schultz, traveling along the Ohio and Mississippi Rivers in 1807 and 1808, found a floating grain mill. The boat moved up and downstream "wherever [a] customer calls" and proved "valuable in a country so destitute of mill-seats such as this." Missourian Thomas Beckwith also noted the commercial interests of western farmers. He recalled that farmers in western Kentucky had loaded boats with corn, hogs, cattle, lumber, or "whatever they had for sale." Other flatboats sold "every thing you could buy in a store," including wagons, plows, ropes, bells, silk, sugar, coffee, and molasses. These floating merchants tied up their boats near a town or village and remained for a few days, until the residents were supplied with the goods they wanted. Then the small ship headed downriver to another community.[3]

Another form of waterborne opportunity existed before the Civil War. Steamboats burned wood for fuel, and wood yards were stocked next to rivers. On the southern Mississippi River, slaves often prepared them. When the supply of fuel ran short, a steamboat pilot steered to the nearest wood lot. The boat tied up to a tree, with planks put down to serve as a gangway. Crew and deck passengers helped carry wood onboard. Deck passengers, often flatboat crewmen returning home upriver, received a 20 percent discount if they assisted with fuel loading. Money, or the promise of future payment, was left in exchange. Sometimes vessels left behind corn or pork. Such employment could be very profitable, as steamers might need to replenish their fuel every thirty to forty miles. Steamboats did not have the space to store more than about ten cords of wood and had to stop several times a day for fuel. Basil Hall, traveling on the Mississippi River in April 1818, recorded that a steamboat could burn thirty cords of wood a day. A vessel could burn more than 500 cords on a round trip from New Orleans to Louisville. Thousands of these woodlots existed along riverbanks in the Mississippi River valley. Abundant forests, as well as an American drive to make money, encouraged their operation.[4]

Thomas Beckwith wrote of how his father and other Missourians took advantage of the moneymaking opportunities provided by steamboats. When the vessels required wood, their bells were rung when within 200 or 300 yards of a landing. Farmers then set out with a boat full of stacked wood and tied up to the stern of the steamboat. Then the crew, and sometimes passengers, helped move it to the deck. According to Beckwith, the vessel would run at half speed for about an hour, load the fuel, and then cast off. The farmer, presumably with cash in hand, would then float back downriver to his home. Beckwith wrote that his father sold about 1,200 cords of wood each year and earned $2.50 a cord.[5]

Antebellum Americans exploited their natural surroundings in the search for profit. They rafted tens of millions of board feet of lumber downriver every year, shipped hundreds of tons of Minnesota ice to southern markets, and loaded thousands of bushels of coal on huge flatboats for industrial use. Some massive log rafts were 100 feet wide and 600 feet long and floated to New Orleans, sometimes from northern Wisconsin or Minnesota. Each could contain hundreds of thousands of board feet of lumber. Other boats might carry hundreds of barrels of potatoes or flour. Americans also sold pork, hay, apples, and wood, usually at several stops along the Ohio or Mississippi as they headed downriver. One unique cargo was made up of beehives. The boat owner worked his way south to avoid the cold, presumably selling his honey along the riverbanks. Plantations along the lower Mississippi often concentrated upon producing a limited number of crops and purchased fruit, meat, or other foodstuffs from the floating shippers and merchants to help feed their slaves.[6]

9. Peddlers helped to spread consumerism by transporting goods to rural customers. *Harper's Weekly* (June 20, 1868), 393.

When Americans settled in the Mississippi River valley in the late eighteenth and early nineteenth centuries, a variety of retailers followed. Itinerant peddlers and roving merchants helped meet the demand for material goods in isolated regions (fig. 9). They served an important purpose in antebellum America. These businesses were often the only source of merchandise for settlers until populations became large enough to justify permanent stores. Such retailers helped to spread consumerism by expanding the geographical reach of mass-produced goods to areas with limited transportation and low population densities. Limited numbers of customers in rural areas reduced the ability of merchants to make a profit and establish stores. Long distances also reduced the ability of customers to travel to towns or stores. Thus, peddlers took the products to their customers. By taking a variety of items into the countryside, they helped spread market values into rural areas and hastened the involvement of households in the commercial economy.[7]

Many Missouri families lived away from stores or easy transportation links in the early nineteenth century. William S. Bryant and Robert Rose argued this in a history of early settlement in the state, noting that only a limited number of "necessary" items were available in the few stores. Wagons sometimes came to these frontier regions from St. Louis, loaded with goods that settlers desired. Families traded meat, honey, and butter for what they wanted. "The arrival of one of these wagons always created a sensation, and everybody turned out to buy and sell." Surplus farm production was sent to New Orleans by flatboats, keelboats, and even canoes, they wrote.[8]

"Yankee traders" served the less populated western areas, such as Illinois or Missouri, in the early nineteenth century. They moved by boat or by wagon, taking merchandise that they sold to residents from their transient stores. These peddlers sold corn, pork, bacon, and whiskey, as well as coffee pots, clocks, tools, and even furniture, to a dispersed population with few towns. Like river traders, they stayed in a neighborhood until they disposed of their goods or moved on to better markets. Often, they visited county courthouses on court days in search of customers; a number of peddlers would then provide a wider variety of goods to local residents who came into town. (Traveling tree peddlers had a bad reputation for selling low-quality goods, and the *Michigan Farmer* cautioned readers about such "wandering speculators.") Some permanent merchants started as peddlers, but accumulated enough capital through hard work and thrift to open up their own businesses in towns. One such entrepreneur, Jared Warner, who later established his own store in Wisconsin, traveled more than 1,000 miles in the summer of 1834 in Ohio, Indiana, and Illinois. Collis P. Huntington, Jim Fisk, and Levi Strauss all began their business careers as peddlers. Westward migration and the increase in population provided new opportunities for merchants and traders, who flocked west after the end of the War of 1812.[9]

Well-known examples of these roving merchants were the famous Yankee clock peddlers. These men made their way across the United States into every corner of the country in search of customers. They were often the subjects of wicked humor. Such peddlers, with their wagon of timepieces, made it into impassable and trackless areas where wheeled vehicles supposedly could not reach. They pursued the chance for gain across rivers and through dense forests, only asking if anyone lived nearby, looking to sell them a clock. Efficient peddlers packed their goods for presentation, looking to awe backwoods folk into a purchase. One scheming salesman, according to John Ludlum McConnel, managed to convince a family to adorn each wall of their home with a clock. These traveling merchants could estimate their possible customer's wealth and interest based on their clothing. A farmwife with an apron or a calico dress, for example, may have acquired a "taste for buying," claimed McConnel. If a house had glass windows, the family might have need for a clock, too. Some counties in Missouri, such as Audrain and Warren, had laws restricting the activities of peddlers. Such limitations excluded them from selling goods in entire counties and punished them with fines up to $50 for violating the law.[10]

The naturalist John James Audubon was a partner in stores in Kentucky until financial problems pushed him west. Audubon and his partner loaded their merchandise onto a boat and set off down the Ohio River. They had 300 barrels of whiskey, powder, and other goods on a keelboat. Audubon and his crew had to pull their boat upriver against the Mississippi's current, having rafted down the Ohio River. Winter and a frozen river forced them to camp on the side of the waterway for more than six weeks. Once they had arrived in the small southeast Missouri river town of Ste. Genevieve, they found "a favorable market. Our whiskey was especially welcome, and what we had paid twenty-five cents a gallon for, brought us Two Dollars." They sold most of their stock and made a good profit in Ste. Genevieve, a place with low supplies and a pent-up demand for merchandise. Audubon then quit the retail business and sold out to his partner, who began his own store in the town.[11]

Americans came to Missouri seeking fertile and affordable land that would allow them to earn a competency, a higher standard of living, or a better quality of life. Though settlers were forced to rely on subsistence farming for the first few years of settlement, they quickly produced surplus goods for market sale. They did not see subsistence farming as particularly noble or desirable for long periods. Families preferred to live near transportation and wanted access to markets. "Away from the river the want of communication made farming unprofitable," recalled Gustave Koerner. Property distant from the Missouri River could be "fine prairie lands, easy to cultivate; but as they were far from the markets they were considered by many then and for years to come, as almost valueless."[12]

Few farmers preferred the spartan and primitive life of the rude pioneer, where dirt floors, drafty cabins, backbreaking work, and a monotonous diet dominated their lives. "Most settlers craved permanency and certainty," wrote historian James E. Davis. They wanted transportation improvements and access to markets. Peter Hardeman Burnet remembered life in western Missouri before steamboats reduced prices and increased the supply of goods. He wrote that the cost of shipping things upriver by boat led to high prices, with items such as coffee, salt, and iron being especially expensive. "Everything farmers purchased was very high," he noted. But Lisbon Applegate recalled "certain luxuries," such as coffee, "must be had" even in the absence of stores. Fortunately for settlers, a ready-made highway existed that allowed them to take advantage of commercial opportunities. Without inexpensive and easy access to markets downriver, families in Missouri would have remained on the fringes of the American economy.[13]

The vast inland interior of the United States was particularly dependent upon river transportation. Good roads were rare, and railroads only became widespread late in the antebellum period. The Missouri River played a key role in the state named after it. Initially, it had opened the region to settlement and provided access to markets. Later it operated as a major highway for the state. Missouri rivers flowed through eight million acres of fertile land, about 20 percent of the entire state. Few families in the Mississippi River valley lived more than twenty miles from a river. This was fortunate, for roads in the antebellum United States were terrible. Most barely deserved the name, as mud holes, stumps, and stones made transport hazardous; when wet, they became rutted and swampy. Rural communities lacked the resources or the labor to build a decent transportation infrastructure and normally focused on building shelter, clearing land, and raising crops. Country roads usually led from a village to a nearby town, mill, or store and were built to serve local needs.[14]

Even late in the antebellum period, travel by road was challenging. Lisbon Basye, who traveled to the lead mines of southern Missouri in spring 1852, usually only made about ten miles a day by road. On March 18, he wrote that his wagon had "stalled several times at mud holes." The next day the road froze "hard enough to bear the wagon, which was a help to us; had it not been the case we could not have got along, for the ground would have been too soft." Traveling west of Boonville a week later, he was impressed by the road he was on and wrote, "from Boonville out some 10 miles it is nearly a solid lane." Returning north at the end of May he traveled thirty miles in one day on a good road, but such rapid movement was unusual.[15]

Flatboats, barges, and keelboats, which were simple vehicles for carrying heavy cargoes, provided early river transportation (fig. 10). These vessels helped make early settlement and commerce in the West possible. Flatboats were large, rectangular floating boxes that flowed with the current, up to five miles an hour in floodwater, and could carry thirty to forty tons of freight.

10. Flatboats could carry thirty to forty tons of freight. Farmers across the United States built such vessels to take their produce to market, even after steamboats populated western rivers. Samuel A. Drake, *The Making of the Great West, 1512–1883* (New York: Charles Scribner's Sons, 1897), 164.

These vessels were normally ten to twenty feet wide and thirty to sixty feet long, with a crew of four to six. A roof covered most of the deck, providing cover for people and cargo. The largest flatboats could be 100 feet long and carry hundreds of barrels of farm goods. They made their way downstream during high water in the spring or, less often because of low water, after autumn harvests. Farmers built flatboats to help them export livestock, grain, whiskey, and other products. They provided transportation in areas steamboats did not visit and could be easily and cheaply made using available tools.[16]

Flatboats were "convenient and necessary auxiliaries to trade and agriculture," wrote James Hall. He estimated that there might have been 4,000 flatboats descending western rivers in the 1840s, in addition to steamboat traffic. Charles Joseph Latrobe described these vessels as broad, flat arks with a deck several feet above the waterline. Usually they had a narrow ledge around them, to assist in using poles for navigation and movement. Animal skins, drying in the sun, were frequently nailed to the sides. Oars helped propel larger craft, and they often had sails as well. Some carried livestock and hay for the animals. Some boats, Timothy Flint observed, carried entire families downriver. They were "fitted up for the descent of families to the lower country, with a stove, comfortable apartments, beds and arrangements for commodious habitancy." Livestock, poultry, dogs, and people traveled together, with plows, looms, and other important equipment stored on the roof.[17]

Keelboats and barges—both long, narrow craft built to reduce resistance—provided the much more difficult upriver transportation. Barges carried heavier loads and operated in deeper waters on larger rivers, while keelboats worked in shallower waters. Both of these craft had to push upstream against the current, sometimes with the help of a strong southerly wind and a large sail. Normally though, such boats were forced upstream using human muscle power. They usually had seats in the bow for men to row. These craft stayed close to shore to avoid the strongest currents. The trip from New Orleans to Pittsburgh, nearly 2,000 miles, could take four months of backbreaking labor. Boats could move upstream at an average speed of about fifteen or twenty miles a day. Passengers, who might take a few weeks to float down to New Orleans from Missouri, had to then return home, which took several months until the advent of regular steamboat service along the Mississippi River in the 1820s and the Missouri River in the 1830s.[18]

Many noted the problems of travel on the Missouri River. The writer Washington Irving described an American Fur Company expedition up the river in 1810, providing an example of the difficulties of travel before steamboats. Men propelled the boats upriver using their muscles, employing oars, poles, or even grappling hooks to pull from tree to tree. Masses of driftwood and floating trees that had collapsed into the river were hazards. Sunken trees threatened to impale boats with jagged roots or limbs. Boats made their way upriver in a zigzag course, men often wading through cold water to pull the craft against the current. Sometimes the river was too swift to make any progress. To battle the tedium and exertion, men often sang songs, with an oarsman leading and the others responding in turn. John Wyeth, traveling up the Missouri River in 1832 on his way to Oregon, wrote that his steamboat had to proceed "very slowly and carefully" due to obstacles in the river known as snags and sawyers. Snags, loose trees caught in the riverbed whose branches pointed upstream, could not be seen above the water. Trees that floated in the river, dangerously bobbing up and down in the current, were known as sawyers. These threats were the "chief terrors of the Missouri and Mississippi rivers," he noted. Some boats moved so cautiously that their passengers disembarked and walked along the riverbanks for entertainment. By the 1840s, improved vessels appeared, which reduced problems such as these.[19]

Until the advent of the steamboat, commerce flowed almost entirely in one direction—south. The cost for upriver freight was five times the downstream cost in the 1810s, and it took four or five times as long to make the trip. Because of such difficulties, most of the country west of the Appalachian Mountains had limited access to the imported merchandise and manufactured goods available in those areas with easy transportation links. Movement of goods overland by wagon was simply too expensive and inefficient. The high cost prohibited the transport of agricultural products, limiting the economic development of western states and territories. The vast majority of all river commerce flowed downstream before 1820, and traffic upstream was very limited, with only a few keelboats and about twenty barges making the trip each year.[20]

This one-way market system began to change in 1817 when the first steamboats made their way up and down the river highways of the West (fig. 11). Steamboats were an ideal transport for the Mississippi River valley because they employed the existing river network. The vast region between the Great Plains and the Appalachian Mountains was often lightly populated in the antebellum period. Railroads would not tie the region together until after the Civil War. As transportation costs fell, previously isolated households were added to regional and national markets. Families could then choose to produce for the commercial economy. Over time, as settlement moved west and new areas were incorporated into the national economy, the time lag between settlement and commercial agriculture decreased. By the middle of the nineteenth century, this lag was as little as a decade, and farms closest to rivers produced the greatest surpluses.[21]

Between 1815 and 1860, the United States experienced a transportation revolution that made the transition to a market economy possible. Canals, steamboats, and railroads replaced primitive roads and one-way river shipping. These forms of transport solved the problems of moving goods and people quickly and cheaply across a country where distances were often measured in thousands of miles. Canals, such as the Erie Canal, connected waterways that had been previously isolated by geography. This eliminated barriers to movement by river. Steamboats allowed upriver transportation that had been

11. Steamboats changed economic life in Missouri by providing rapid and inexpensive transport on America's many rivers. This vessel, the *J. M. White*, completed the run from St. Louis to New Orleans in less than four days in 1844. Emerson W. Gould, *Fifty Years on the Mississippi* (St. Louis: Nixon-Jones, 1889), 627.

severely limited by downriver currents. Railroads proved even more useful in integrating the national economy, since they could be built virtually anywhere and were not limited by the need to employ waterborne trade. Railroads had much less importance for Missouri than states farther east, however, and rivers remained the dominant form of transport until after the Civil War. Improved transportation tied disparate regions together and allowed the easy exchange of products, helping the United States to develop a vast self-sustaining domestic economy. An example of this integration occurred in southern Wisconsin in 1837. Lumber harvested in New York State was used to build a new home. The wood was cut in Pittsburgh sawmills and then transported by steamboat to the Wisconsin Territory, astonishing settlers. Businesses in Massachusetts also exported hundreds of thousands of brooms to northeastern and national markets, with the aid of improved transportation.[22]

The rapid and inexpensive transportation provided by steam power in the West dramatically reduced travel time and changed economic life. The first steamboat was built at Pittsburgh in 1811, but the War of 1812 halted new construction. In 1815, the steamboat *Enterprise* made its way upriver from New Orleans to Pittsburgh. The first such ship docked in St. Louis on August 2, 1817. Within two years there were thirty-one steamboats on western waters, mainly running between Louisville and New Orleans. Steamboat operations began on the Missouri River in 1819 when the *Independence* reached the towns of Franklin and Chariton, 250 miles above St. Louis, and brought flour, whiskey, sugar, and iron. There was no regular steamboat service on the Missouri River until 1829, but ships made it upriver occasionally. In 1821, it took ten days to travel by land from St. Louis to Franklin; steamboats cut this time by up to 80 percent a decade later. By the mid-1830s, steam power had linked the towns and rural regions in central Missouri to the larger American economy. Port towns such as Jefferson City and Boonville became thriving commercial centers for their agricultural hinterlands. The fast and cheap transportation provided by steamboats brought about the "economic emancipation" of the West, according to historian Louis Hunter. Steam navigation began to tie the nation together after the War of 1812 and caused a revolution in the standard of living in the states in the Mississippi River valley.[23]

Steamboats helped transform this region from a primitive frontier society into a bustling commercial region. Robert Baird noted in 1834 that the introduction of steamboats "effected a complete revolution in the internal navigation" of the Mississippi River valley. Merchandise of all kinds was "now carried between the extremest points for a very small amount." Upriver freight prices fell, and the cost to move goods declined by up to 90 percent between the War of 1812 and the 1830s. Inexpensive and easy access to markets in other parts of the country allowed the Mississippi River valley to develop economically and escape a dependence on limited, local markets. The cost of manufactured items, as well as that of sugar, salt, coffee, tea, and other products, fell drastically. Prices dropped 50 to 75 percent for sugar, coffee, salt, and other goods. Lower costs and increased supplies of such items gave Missouri residents access to material goods that improved their lives. Steamboat transportation also reduced serious price differences between St. Louis and other cities. Large quantities of merchandise at competitive prices were chiefly available in St. Louis and upriver in Missouri because of the reduced transportation cost.[24]

Steamboats did not replace flatboats, which populated western rivers by the thousands until the 1850s, but they became increasingly important for trade. In 1826, at least one steamboat stopped in St. Louis every day from late spring to early fall. The next year 259 steamboats arrived in the city, most of them coming from New Orleans and bringing retail goods. In 1831, five boats traveled up and down the Missouri River, transporting people and goods. Eleven years later, twenty-six steamboats worked on the Missouri, accelerating the import and export of goods and people. "There are 150 or more steamboats up the river in the course of the year, and a great business is done and increasing," noted R. Rowland from Jefferson City in 1840. In the early 1840s, regular steamboat service occurred between Glasgow, located 100 miles east of Kansas City, and St. Louis. When the California gold rush brought tens of thousands of migrants to the transcontinental trailheads in western Missouri and Iowa, the number of vessels more than doubled.[25]

Steamboats initially made most of their money from transporting people, but this changed by the 1840s, when the transport of goods dominated. Many more passengers moved up the Mississippi River than down it, including immigrants heading west and boatmen heading north after delivering their cargoes to New Orleans. The busiest shipping seasons were the fall, after harvest, and the spring, when the river was highest. The decline in freight costs in the late antebellum period encouraged the export of surplus farm goods to New Orleans from western states. The efficiency of steamboat transportation increased dramatically in the 1820s and 1830s, as freight capacity grew and more lightly constructed vessels appeared. The weight of steamboats fell, allowing them to operate in shallower waters and over longer seasons. Travel time also fell, as speeds increased and rivers were cleared of obstacles. The increasing productivity of steam transport—combined with decreasing costs—helped tie areas on the edges of settlement into the national market. In the 1850s, the *Weekly Tribune*, in the western Missouri town of Liberty, announced prices for farm goods such as oats, corn, potatoes, and ham in St. Louis and New Orleans. Near the end of the decade the paper began to quote Cincinnati prices as well, showing the interest of the local population in outside markets and commercial participation.[26]

Melinda Houston Estes commented on the importance of steamboats and the difficulties of travel in a 1901 reminiscence. Her family had moved to Missouri in 1817, first settling near Franklin, then moving farther west to live near Liberty four years later. They carried with them only "things absolutely necessary," such as utensils, clothing, and bedding. She recalled that there was not a store in Clay County in 1821, which she called "wild-looking country" where the people "came with guns in their hands." For their first year in the area, her father crossed the Missouri River to go to an Osage trading post to buy items the family wanted, such as calico and blankets. Nearly eighty years later, she remembered when the first store opened in the town of Liberty in 1822. "It was followed by others soon afterwards." Steamboats did not begin to run regularly on the Missouri River until the late 1820s, she recalled. With no good roads, everything had to be hauled by wagons "hundreds and hundreds of miles" or moved upriver by keelboat. "Nothing heavy could be brought into the county," and coffee and sugar were expensive and scarce. Though Estes does not explicitly say it, steamboats brought a revolution in living standards by significantly lowering the costs of goods and increasing the opportunity to enjoy a variety of products.[27]

As the regional economy expanded, St. Louis became a major collection point for agricultural produce. Steamboats arrived regularly from places near and far, ranging from Louisville, Cincinnati, and New Orleans to Peoria, Galena, and Leavenworth. The city accepted pork, tobacco, whiskey, hemp, beef, and corn from Missouri, as well as farm goods and iron from Illinois and the upper Mississippi River valley, for downriver shipment. Steamboats gave Missouri farmers an advantage over their Ohio valley rivals because the Missouri River and its tributaries were navigable even at lower water stages. The river was also less likely to freeze than the Ohio River. The booming agricultural business pushed the fur trade into secondary status, as the transportation revolution brought the expanding national market to Missouri. Frederick Steines commented on this commercial growth on July 21, 1835, noting how "the state of Missouri is on the rise is shown by the future lively steamboat travel. Almost daily boats travel on the Missouri. They are favorable auspices for inhabitants there." Phillip Hone, a New York merchant who visited St. Louis in June 1847, noted his astonishment at the commerce of the city's waterfront. Fifty large steamboats took and discharged cargo, and vessels constantly arrived from throughout the Mississippi River valley, full of people and products. Hone wrote in his diary that the entire levee was covered with huge piles of lead and thousands of barrels of flour and bags of corn, as well as many hogsheads of tobacco.[28]

The commerce of St. Louis and the Mississippi River impressed many. George Huse visited St. Louis in 1846 and was surprised at the extent of commerce on the city's waterfront (fig. 12). "It was much larger than I had supposed, more pleasantly located—and also much more of a business place. I never saw

12. A view of St. Louis shows the city's bustling waterfront in 1840. Anna Paschall Hannum, ed., *A Quaker Forty-Niner: The Adventures of Charles Edward Pancoast on the American Frontier* (Philadelphia: University of Pennsylvania Press, 1930), 124.

business more brisk in Boston than it was there." He counted more than forty steamboats at the city's levee, which operated as its wharf. The ships were busy loading and unloading. He walked down to the levee to see what goods were being shipped. There Huse found hemp, flour, tobacco, corn, wheat, and a variety of other articles, as well as "groceries of every kind, and altogether too much of one kind—whiskey—shoes, brass clocks, and hard ware and stoves in quantity." William Switzler, traveling north on the Mississippi River with his father in 1836, wrote in his diary, "we daily passed numbers of large rafts and flat boats, in which the produce of the upper country is exported to New Orleans." More than a decade later, in 1847, James Cowan noted flatboats and rafts, "almost innumerable," on the rivers below St. Louis. German immigrant Eduard Zimmerman called St. Louis a "second New Orleans." The city, he wrote, collected "inestimable quantities of produce" from the Missouri and upper Mississippi valleys and sent them south.[29]

A number of small towns grew up along the banks of the Missouri River. It operated as a ready-made highway, and, like the interstates of today, settlements grew up along its route. Towns from St. Louis to St. Joseph—500 miles upstream—were located on the Missouri River because of the easy transportation it provided. St. Louis remained the state's largest city throughout the nineteenth century and served as a link between the smaller towns to the west and New Orleans downriver. The towns, and the services they provided, helped to develop their surrounding areas. They served as economic and social centers for settlers and migrants, and as outfitting or supply stations for the rural areas around them. While traveling on the Missouri River in August 1836, Frederick Gustorf watched as a steamboat captain searched for a new town about fifty miles west of St. Louis. Once he found it, the craft unloaded "a lot of merchandise" for a store that was one of two log cabins in the village. Gustorf reported that the town had existed for only a few weeks and that twenty "very excited" farmers awaited the arrival of the steamboat.[30]

Towns retained a rough and primitive character, despite the influx of business and settlement. The state capital, Jefferson City, had unpaved roads, alternately deep in dust or mud, depending on the weather. "Dust, dirt, and mud, and the effects of dust, dirt, and mud were everywhere," John Lewis Peyton observed in 1848. Dried mud covered houses, vehicles, and people. A tough caste of country folk, attracted by the fact that court was in session, shocked him with their dress, manners, and appearance. These stout, heavily armed men drank whiskey, chewed tobacco, and took part in jumping contests, wrestling, and boxing. Good humor ruled the day until evening, "when fiery liquor caused many to lose their heads."[31]

Towns initially arose because they served as a river port, a center of trade, or a county seat. Intersecting transportation routes aided in town development, as did the presence of institutions such as a land office or a bank. Towns grew because of these advantages, which allowed them to outstrip smaller villages in the surrounding countryside. One example of such growth is that of Franklin, the westernmost town in central Missouri in the 1810s and early 1820s. This location gave it a monopoly on the trade of the quickly populating area. It had a post office, a public land office, a newspaper, and a circuit court. It also served as the initial starting point for the Santa Fe trade in the 1820s and benefited from westward-bound rendezvous and outfitting traffic. Franklin's merchants offered a wide variety of services to area farmers and sold items including cotton cloth, construction materials, groceries, and household furnishings. Merchants brought their supplies by mule from St. Louis several times a year to meet the burgeoning demand of settlers. Customers exchanged salt pork, tallow, beeswax, and tobacco for store goods. Towns like Franklin collected and sent agricultural production downriver to St. Louis and New Orleans via mercantile intermediaries; farmers themselves also floated their farm goods to market. The Fayette *Missouri Intelligencer* wrote that the town presented to the observer "a busy, bustling, and commercial scene." In the late 1820s, river floods wiped it out. Boonville replaced Franklin as the local commercial center, while the Santa Fe trade moved farther west to Independence in 1827.[32]

Towns served the economic needs of nearby populations, and this included exporting surplus farm goods. Hemp was an important crop for slave owners along the Missouri River, who had brought the crop west from Kentucky and Virginia. Hemp fibers were used to make rope to tie together cotton bales, as well as to make slave clothing; when antebellum cotton production soared, so did the demand for hemp. Growing it took large amounts of year-round and intensive labor, usually completed by slaves, who could be compelled to complete the backbreaking labor the crop required. Slaves planted, cultivated, and harvested the plants from April to August. Hemp was then cut, dried on the ground, and collected. It was put out in the field to rot, which allowed it to be broken. Hemp breaking, or crushing, occurred in January, February, and March and separated the fibers of the plant. This allowed fibers to be used to produce rope, bags, or clothing. Hemp was often sold to nearby merchants or shipped downriver from port towns such as Liberty or St. Joseph. Steamboats carried so much hemp in some years that it was stacked as high as the smokestacks.[33]

Commercial growth in towns such as Franklin or Liberty contributed to the economic development of the region. Towns provided a link with the world beyond the rural household and close neighbors. They attracted a diverse mix of enterprising men, such as merchants, land speculators, and tavern keepers, who pursued business opportunities and profit. Settlements acted as gateways to the traffic of people and goods, allowing the local exchange of products and the chance to enjoy things imported from outside the region. Other towns grew along the river as well, serving the same functions for their small hinterlands as Franklin. Columbia was established in 1821 and quickly became a trading center for Boone County. Jefferson City became the state capital because of its central location and nearness to the river. It prospered as a market center for its area and gained a stage route by the 1830s. The town of Independence also became a major center for western trade and emigration. It became the jumping-off point for the Santa Fe trade in the 1830s, once steamboats were able to carry merchants and their outfits farther west. Like other towns, it had a variety of businesses that served disparate groups, from overland migrants to fur trappers. One emigrant, traveling west from Kentucky to California in 1849, noted the people had camped out for miles around the town and that the streets were so crowded it was almost impossible to move about.[34]

The Santa Fe trade contributed significantly to the growth of towns, such as Independence, and to the increasing commerce of Missouri. Missouri became the main supply base for this business, providing pork, flour, and other foodstuffs from local farms. The trade also encouraged settlement, as it gave farmers a market for their produce. Josiah Gregg wrote in his classic account of the southwestern trade, *The Commerce of the Prairies*, that Independence was "a place of much bustle and active business." Rocky Mountain traders, trappers, emigrants, and merchants bought supplies or outfitted themselves in the town. Gregg wrote that he purchased flour, bacon, coffee, sugar, beans, and crackers in the town before he headed for Santa Fe in 1830. Traders usually also bought other provisions, as well as mules, oxen, and wagons, before departing. Local stores provided a wide variety of goods for the traffic and its participants. In the 1840s, Independence became a starting point for the Oregon and California Trails.[35]

The Santa Fe trade began by accident in November 1821, when a Missouri trader named William Becknell reached the New Mexico capital with a small group of men. For the three decades before this first venture, Spain's commercial restrictions had impeded any such trade, but Mexican independence ended these limits. The severe depression that followed the Panic of 1819 left farmers unable to sell their surplus agricultural goods. Many could not earn the cash to pay their mortgages, and people went in search of markets and profits. Becknell was one of these debtors. He had already lost property to his creditors and hoped to find financial redemption in the Southwest. The Missourian had advertised for men to join him on a trading expedition across the plains. Becknell had headed west into Indian country hoping to sell the goods he carried, which included cloth, tools, kitchen utensils, and household goods. His party intended to trade their merchandise for horses and mules, as well as to hunt bison and other animals on the plains. The group had left Franklin not knowing Mexico had declared independence and that the Spanish colonial trade limitations would be lifted. They encountered a detachment of Mexican soldiers who informed them that they would be welcomed in Santa Fe. The company quickly crossed to the city, sold their goods in November at a high profit, and returned home with news of their great success. Becknell paid off his creditors upon return.[36]

The news of Becknell's good fortune spread and encouraged further such trading missions. Josiah Gregg, whose father was a member of Becknell's second expedition to Santa Fe, noted, "the favorable reports brought by the enterprising Captain stimulated others to embark in trade." In May 1822, Becknell's second caravan left for Santa Fe with twenty-one men and three wagons. Other parties left as well, and Gregg estimated that one caravan of fifteen men left Franklin with $4,000 to $5,000 in merchandise. Early merchants may have earned profits of 100 percent, and in 1824 the trade earned a caravan of about eighty Americans $180,000. In 1823, the Franklin *Missouri Intelligencer* wrote that it was "gratifying to learn that these enterprising adventurers have made a profitable trip." They returned with more than 400 mules, a "quantity of beaver," and a "considerable" amount of silver. The paper noted that the furs and livestock would "bear a profit" if taken for sale to the eastern states. However, the silver coin brought back to Missouri was probably most important, for the specie would help to "impart activity" to the depressed Missouri economy.[37]

In 1830, Richard Gentry, a Columbia tavern and stable keeper, wrote several letters home to his family describing his success in the trade. Gentry had made his first trip to Santa Fe in 1827, after borrowing $863 by mortgaging his property, livestock, furniture, and slaves. He purchased a wagon, eight oxen, food, and his goods and set out for the city. He was successful in the trade, for he left home twice more. On July 4, 1830, he wrote to his wife from Santa Fe after a long, but profitable, journey. "I am glad to be able to state that trading here is very good indeed, better than it has been. I am selling my goods, and may be able to start home soon." He informed her that he would buy some mules with his profits, as "I can make good money out of them" by returning to Missouri with the animals. Gentry told his wife to have his son set out for Santa Fe, to help him drive the mules back home. Seven months later, he sent his father in Kentucky a letter, writing that he had "disposed of my goods to advantage, in fact made good money and have been able to satisfy the mortgage on my furniture and stock." He had bought mules and herded them back home, sleeping at night with pistols nearby and a faithful dog to guard his livestock. "I will feed them [mules] during the coming winter and hope to bring them to Kentucky in time for the spring trade, where I hope to sell the thirty-nine to good advantage."[38]

The Santa Fe trade encouraged the economic development of Missouri. The trade brought between $100,000 and $200,000 in silver to the state each year in the 1830s, which helped fuel the frontier economy. The export of merchandise from the towns of western Missouri created new business opportunities or supported existing mercantile shops. James Josiah Webb wrote in *Adventures in the Santa Fe Trade, 1844–1847* that he had purchased most of his goods in St. Louis—spending $1,800 for one trip—but had "outfitted" in Independence. Here he had spent $100 for a wagon, $112 for oxen, and $100 on other goods. On a later trip, he bought fifteen yoke of oxen, three new wagons, and "sufficient goods to make two good loads to pay duties on." Webb took 12,500 pounds of goods to Santa Fe on this trip. He was just one of many independent traders heading west. No one firm dominated the trade, and small merchants—men like Richard Gentry and Webb—took part on a semiregular basis. In 1828, merchants transported $100,000 in goods to Santa Fe. By 1837, about $500,000 in merchandise was taken for sale. American merchants in Missouri were so intent upon making money from the Santa Fe trade, reported the Columbia *Missouri Intelligencer* in 1831, that medicines sent to New Mexico had directions written in Spanish and were packed in cases solely for export to the Southwest.[39]

This brisk and widespread business activity, argued historian Dorothy Dorsey, "transformed the region of central Missouri into a veritable hive of industry." Evidence from Alphonso Wetmore supports this contention. A veteran of the War of 1812, he had lost his right arm fighting the British. Wetmore had then settled in the Boonslick and became a lawyer and merchant. While living in Franklin, he began to take part in the trade with New Mexico. He wrote in an 1831 letter to Secretary of War Lewis Cass that the Santa Fe trade had steadily increased since it was first established and that Mexican dollars were the main currency in the state. Many Missourians made a profit off the trade, and farmers and artisans gained "advantage" from it. The whole community, he argued, benefited from this "interesting traffic." This trade influenced Missouri for decades. Septimus Scholl, a farmer near Independence, wrote to friends in Kentucky about the booming Missouri economy in 1848. "We have flush times here this winter and spring owing to the [Mexican] war and Santa Fe trade[.] Our mules and wagons very much in demand at fair prices."[40]

Missouri also benefited from the migration to Oregon, which began in 1841. A small stream of initial emigrants soon grew, with more than 1,000 people heading northwest by 1843. Two years later, more than 3,000 people left for Oregon, drawn by free land and pushed out by economic problems in the United States. Francis Parkman described the bustling town of Independence in his book *The Oregon Trail*. He wrote that the hotels were crowded and that the gunsmiths and saddlers were "constantly at work providing equipment" for departing migrants. Almost every day, he noted, "steamboats were leaving the levee and passing up the Missouri, crowded with passengers on their way to the frontier." More than 1,000 emigrants camped out near Independence in the spring of 1846. "A multitude of shops had sprung up to furnish the emigrants and Santa Fe traders with necessaries for their journey; and there was an incessant hammering and banging from a dozen blacksmith's sheds, where heavy wagons were being repaired and horses and oxen shod," Parkman recorded. This migration made "good business for Missouri," historian Daniel Walker Howe noted. Emigrant parties left from western Missouri towns for the Oregon Trail, which led across the plains and over the Rocky Mountains to the fertile valleys of the Pacific Northwest.[41]

The discovery of gold in California turned this limited movement into one of the greatest mass migrations in the history of the nation. Gold fever spread across the country in late 1848. Newspapers repeated stories of incredible opportunities for wealth. Books, pamphlets, and guides, as well as businessmen and politicians, also promoted California. Tales of unparalleled riches spread across the country. One letter, published in the Missouri *Republican* in May 1849, claimed that "men are here nearly crazy with the riches forced suddenly into their pockets." Thousands who caught the gold fever decided to leave for California immediately. So many young men considered leaving Missouri that their families feared they could not effectively run their farms. In 1849, more than 80,000 Americans left for the gold fields. Many took ships to Panama, crossed the Isthmus, and then found transport to California. A smaller number risked the long voyage around South America. Most people, however, decided to cross the continent by land.[42]

The overland migrants provided a huge economic boost to Missouri, especially in the spring when most people came west to the towns at the beginning of the California and Oregon Trails. Twenty-five thousand people left for California from Missouri River towns in 1849, and 50,000 departed on the overland trails the next year. Parties often purchased livestock, foodstuffs, or other items in St. Louis before heading upriver on steamboats. They also picked up supplies in western Missouri towns, such as Independence or St. Joseph. John Hawkins Clark, in St. Joseph in 1852, wrote, "oxen, horses and mules are brought in from the surrounding country to sell; the merchant has anticipated all the wants of the emigrant and has everything needed for an 'outfit.'" Clark noted that St. Louis was "very lively" and "full to overflowing with California bound immigrants." He made a very modest estimate that emigrants spent thousands of dollars in the town every year. Others, such as Edwin Bryant and his party, bought in Independence "a long list of small articles" required for his journey.[43]

William Kelly described St. Louis when he reached the city in 1849. The farther west he proceeded, "the more intense became the California fever. California met you at every turn, every corner, every dead wall; every post and pillar was labeled with Californian placards. The ships seemed to contain nothing but articles for California." The excitement of gold fever influenced everyone. Advertisements about California and excerpts of letters from miners filled newspapers. Everyone also talked about California. Kelly and his party purchased weapons in the city, but waited to buy wagons and livestock in Independence. A "mob" of people joined him for the steamboat trip upriver. The passengers ate the vessel empty of food, and it had to stop in Boonville for more provisions. Men looked for mules in the town. In Independence, Kelly's group bought sixty mules and horses, as well as five wagons. Sam Wilson wrote to his mother in April 1849, "You would not credit your sences to see the vast number that are crowding the streets of every city town and village making preparation[.] You see men of every age from the gray headed to the boy in his teens, the rich and poore though not many of the latter, men from every state in the union."[44]

Emigrants spent money all along the Missouri River. They usually passed through one of the jumping-off points—Independence, St. Joseph, or Council Bluffs—on their way west. Often they spent some time and money in these towns, packing the stores, saloons, hotels, and boardinghouses. They also paid for transportation, lodging, livestock, food, drink, and other required items from St. Louis to Iowa. Emigrants took steamboats upriver, stopping in places such as Jefferson City, and paid for ferrying across the Missouri River in Glasgow, 100 miles east of Kansas City, where the ferry and boats there could not keep up with the wagon traffic. Unfortunately, the crowded and unsanitary conditions on these vessels helped spread cholera, killing many before they crossed the plains. Steamboats often stopped to load wood from stations along the river, as William Swain recorded in his diary. "The passengers all helped and had a good exercise," he explained. People ate and drank in saloons in Boonville and fixed wagons in Georgetown. Parties hired local men to work as guides, drivers, and teamsters for the trip west. This was helpful, as William Graham Johnston noted that such men "understood mules as though they were blood relations."[45]

Merchants offered everything travelers could need, gathered from the surplus production of the countryside, or brought upriver from St. Louis. Farm families provided enough food and livestock to meet most of the demands of emigrants, according to historian Walker D. Wyman. Septimus Scholl wrote to his family, "we farmers are securing a portion of the spoils as our surplus Bacon corn Beef and pork are in brisk demand." He noted that the price of beef cattle was good and the land productive. "If trade would keep as good as it now is we would make money for every kind of produce," Scholl observed. He estimated 300 wagons of merchandise would also leave for Santa Fe in the spring of 1848. Emigration to Oregon and California kept the price of livestock and wagons high, since neither "ever returns." Departing parties may have bought most of the surplus bacon, bread, flour, and meat of the region, wrote Wyman. One party crossing northern Missouri purchased corn and hay throughout the month of April as they headed west. Colonel James B. Tate, with a different group, noted in his diary in April 1849, "corn is very scarce." Even if the produce was available, the price could be steep. Charles D. Ferguson reported as his party left St. Joseph for Council Bluffs, "we could obtain hay and corn of the farmers much cheaper." They needed the feed for their animals, as the late spring of 1849 had delayed the growth of grass for their livestock.[46]

Overland migration also led to a great demand for livestock. "The California trade has produced quite a revolution in the cattle trade in Missouri," noted an 1853 report. The price of cattle had more than doubled since the gold rush had begun, and raising cattle had become "about the most profitable business our farmers can enter into." Livestock could be fed cheaply over the winter on cornhusks and sold to spring migrants. An agricultural journal reported that overland emigrants had purchased most of the extra mules and oxen in the state of Missouri in 1849. Some of these groups drove cattle to California to sell for higher prices than they could receive in Missouri. For example, Charles

Kleinsorge, a young German immigrant, left St. Joseph in 1854 with a group of ninety people heading for California. He reported that they had purchased 940 horses and cattle to take with them. More than 100,000 cattle may have been driven to California the year Kleinsorge left.[47]

A gold strike in Colorado in 1858 brought a new rush of emigrants just before the start of the Civil War. The discovery brought a wave of people, mostly men, to western Missouri, which served as a departure point. River towns, such as Kansas City and St. Joseph, benefited from the heavy traffic in people and goods in 1859. William Yates and three other men, for example, bought corn from farmers as they headed west across Missouri in the spring. They also paid for their animals to be ferried. The Colorado gold rush greatly increased demand for beef in Missouri. Enterprising livestock owners traversed the state searching for cattle to sell for food and for oxen to pull wagons across the plains. Cattle were also driven north from Texas to meet the demand for beef from overland emigrants and gold seekers in the 1850s. Local businessmen took advantage of those heading west, promising an "assortment of Pike's Peak Outfitting Goods," such as blankets, boots, and shoes.[48]

The great engine of growth in the United States was the creation of a self-sustaining domestic market. It was based, in large part, on population growth and migration that spurred economic development. The migration of thousands of people not only expanded the national market but also created a local market that extended into new territory and brought new farmland and resources into use. Larger populations helped overcome the problem of undeveloped markets weakened by a lack of customers or producers. Town growth encouraged economic activity, and steamboats linked people and markets together. Roads, ferries, and boat landings helped people export farm products, while mills, stores, and warehouses encouraged trade and settlement. Missouri grew quickly and contributed to the creation of a self-sustaining market in the region. The state's population steadily increased at a rate about seven times the national average, from about 66,000 in 1820 to nearly 1,200,000 inhabitants by the time of the Civil War. All of this immigration continuously added a growing demand for food for migrants during their first several years of farming. After a few years, families demanded greater access to nonessential goods to improve their standard of living in their new homes, driving the region's economy through their production and consumption.[49]

Americans migrated westward seeking land, independence, and opportunity. They settled near rivers, as waterways provided transportation and gave them access to downriver markets. Rivers served as conduits of commerce in the antebellum period and helped Americans take part in the expanding market economy. Farmers and traders who sought to make money sold everything from foodstuffs, livestock, and tools from boats on rivers. Those who did not live near a town or store were able to purchase goods that they wanted. Roving peddlers and mobile merchants helped meet the demand for material goods, moving from neighborhood to neighborhood selling their stock. Families satisfied their economic desires through such brief market interactions.

In the two decades after the end of the War of 1812, the transportation revolution tied Missouri to the rest of the country. Steamboats provided a rapid and inexpensive way to import and export goods into central Missouri and greatly reduced transportation costs upriver. Steamboats integrated Missouri into the national economy and accelerated the growth of markets in the region by allowing residents to purchase the inexpensive material goods that had been previously denied to them because of high transport costs. The Santa Fe trade also contributed to economic development by increasing demand for mercantile goods and by increasing the supply of currency in the state. Overland migration to California and Oregon provided further stimulus to the riverine economy. The presence of steamboats and a growing population also pushed economic growth. All of this human movement and commercial activity encouraged the growth of the market economy. Permanent stores and the merchants who operated them replaced temporary or migratory retailers and aided in the spread of market participation among rural families. The crucial role that merchants played in fostering consumerism is the focus of the next chapter.

8

A STORE ALMOST IN SIGHT

Gottfried Duden lived in central Missouri in the 1820s and encouraged the immigration of his fellow German citizens in his book *Report on a Journey to the Western States of North America and A Stay of Several Years Along the Missouri.* After three years of living on a farm located on the Missouri River west of St. Louis, he wrote of the possibilities available for European immigrants. He glorified pioneer life and emphasized the plentiful natural resources and the availability of cheap land in Missouri. It was "extremely alluring to settle down in regions where one has such complete freedom of choice," he explained. Americans benefited from the fertility of the land and the plentiful game and fish. River connections were "splendid," and the Missouri River was "navigable without interruption for over two thousand five hundred miles," he exaggerated. Communication via steamboat was "exceedingly easy," and the region's rivers tied Missouri settlers to the rest of the nation. Briefly stated, Missouri was ideally suited for commerce and farming. It provided outstanding opportunities for European immigrants, he boasted.[1]

Market participation was one of the opportunities for immigrants. Duden noted, "wherever population had grown to a certain level, there also a market will soon develop for the products of the soil, and no one would be more pleased than the farmer who can leave it to the merchant and to speculators to send goods long distances." No immigrant or settler could "get along without the intermediary service of a merchant," he added. Anyone who had something to sell turned to storekeepers, who then sold the goods on commission or bought them from the farmer. In the 1820s, rural residents brought in wax, tallow, furs, skins, and minerals and received brandies, flour, and other goods in return. According to Duden, Missouri farmers tried to produce as many of their necessities as possible themselves—this was the "ambition of every farmer"—so no money had to be spent on basic foodstuffs. (This changed in the following decades, however.) He wrote that American farmers "spend their cash with a much easier mind for luxury articles, for things of one's fancy." He also noted the interest in commercial activity of local farmers, writing, "some farmers, for instance, use the hours of bad weather for making shoes, for building barrels, and for making other implements. All of this is then transmitted to a storekeeper for sale." A St. Louis newspaper advertisement provides an example of this. It noted that brooms, whiskey barrels, and hides could be sold to merchants in the city.[2]

Rural families needed to be able to sell their surplus agricultural produce. General stores, providing a wide variety of items, fulfilled the key role of middlemen for Missouri residents. Farmers preferred local merchants to the more risky and time-consuming use of flatboats to transfer their produce to markets. Fluctuating river levels, possible low prices, transportation difficulties, and distance pushed rural families to use nearby stores. Storekeepers took locally produced agricultural goods for credit, barter exchange, or sometimes cash payments and provided Missourians with access to goods from outside the region. "Commercial markets for agricultural surpluses drew the backcountry into regional trading systems," wrote geographers Warren R. Hofstra and Robert D. Mitchell. Rural areas were pulled into markets tied to exports and imports, as local consumer demand rose. Population increases, urban growth, and demand for export surpluses stimulated commercial development. Agricultural income allowed farm families to increase the consumption of items they did not produce. For example, families in the Shenandoah valley in the late 1700s owned clocks, teapots, and coffee mills.[3]

Consumerism linked the countryside to towns, which then tied rural areas to river transportation and larger markets downriver. Town stores, a key part of this commercial system, exported farm products outside the region (fig. 13). Such stores allowed rural residents to take part in the expanding national market and promoted their consumerism. Few farm families ignored the chance to improve their standard of living by selling a portion of their agricultural production. They sold or exchanged their surplus farm goods for things that they chose not to make themselves, or for goods they could not make, such as coffee or tools. The Boonville merchant firm of Walter and Ballantine, for

13. This image of a store in Fort Dodge, Kansas, shows what trade in rural Missouri may have looked like. *Harper's Weekly* (May 25, 1867), 329.

example, promised to pay the "highest market rates" for corn, wheat, bacon, butter, and eggs that their customers brought in. (Other merchants in Boonville advertised china, wine, nuts, and "nicknacks to suit the epicure.") Over time, rural Missourians decided to purchase more goods at local stores and produce fewer farm goods for household consumption. They bought more whiskey or clothing at stores and made less for themselves. Families also eventually purchased more items of all sorts from stores. In this way, farmers were able to improve their lives by taking part in the growing market economy.[4]

Missouri farmers did not hesitate to participate in commercial activity when the opportunity presented itself. In fact, they often went out of their way to pursue opportunities to make money. The Franklin *Missouri Intelligencer* reported in 1819 that local farm goods had been taken to stores to exchange for manufactured goods. In March 1824, the same paper reported that six boats full of bacon, tobacco, furs, beeswax, and ham took advantage of the high spring water to take their cargoes to New Orleans. Dewitt Clinton Basey, who lived in the small town of Brunswick, located just north of the Missouri River, observed such activity. He recalled that the town was a center of trade for rural families as far away as the Iowa border. Basey reported that he had seen forty to fifty wagons in town with heavy loads from the countryside. Visitors brought pork, bacon, beeswax, honey, fur, and tobacco to town. In return, they received items they could not produce themselves, such as sugar, dry goods, salt, and hardware. Stephen Hempstead lived on a farm five miles from St. Louis and sent wagonloads of produce to the city in the 1810s and 1820s. Hempstead's slaves and workers raised a variety of crops, including corn, wheat, and vegetables, and took the surplus to market.[5]

Carr Pritchett and his family left behind "poor, worn fields" in Virginia and came to Missouri in 1835. They settled in Warren County about thirty miles northwest of St. Louis. The family purchased property and "managed to clear a few acres of land and raised a small crop of tobacco, digging up the ground with our hoes." After they sold their eagerly-awaited first crop of tobacco for $32, Pritchett recalled how happy he was that he could buy his mother, who had made all of the family's clothing for years, a calico dress and a "few necessaries for the family." Over time, through hard work, thrift, and self-denial, his family built a successful farm "and came to enjoy not only the necessities but also many of comforts of life" that they acquired through market participation.[6]

Rural families began to search for ways to sell surplus produce and purchase nonnecessary items soon after settlement. In the Ohio River valley, farmers began to market surplus crops by the third year after establishing a farm. Those who lived near rivers found it easier to find a market for their produce. Initial commerce often involved selling farm products to new immigrants who arrived with some cash to buy food, seeds, or tools to help start their own farm. Midwestern farmers, by the 1820s, looked to take part in commercial markets and escape the primitive life of subsistence agriculture. The same was true for Missouri. Farmers in central Missouri moved "as quickly as possible" from subsistence to commercial farming, argued R. Douglas Hurt. Surveyor Joseph Shriver, traveling west of Jefferson City in September 1829, wrote that livestock, corn, hemp, and tobacco were the main crops. A "good market is had at any point on the Missouri River—wherever a good steamboat landing is found." Vessels carried away the produce of the countryside and left necessary articles and some luxuries, he added. "This state presents facilities for making a fortune in various ways."[7]

Families in central Missouri sold their agricultural products to market towns when possible, especially after steam transport tied market centers to downriver commerce. Often, though, they lived in an area that was not close to a town or that did not enjoy easy transportation. Distance from stores or towns usually precluded significant market participation. In these situations, farmers usually sent their surplus produce to the closest town on an irregular basis, after harvests or after a significant amount of locally produced goods such as chickens, honey, or corn built up. Towns like Franklin, Liberty, and Independence served as trade centers for commercially minded rural farmers, as well as merchants and Santa Fe traders. Such places served as the centers for exchange, encouraged farmers to produce a surplus, and allowed them to benefit materially from their market activity.[8]

One of the crops Missouri farmers produced for market was tobacco. Slave labor was important for its production, as tobacco cultivation and preparation for sale took almost all year. It was a demanding crop that kept farmhands busy. Workers prepared fields and sowed beds of seeds in early spring. Plants that sprouted were then transferred to fields. Constant care was needed to control pests, such as worms and beetles, to keep weeds at bay, and to ensure quality leaf production. Lower leaves had to be pruned to encourage growth higher on the stem; worms had to be removed by hand. Harvesting was also a tedious process, with slaves or workers cutting, drying, and stripping leaves to cure them and prepare them for market. By the time the tobacco was ready for sale, fields were readied for a new crop. Boone County, the largest producer in the state, grew 1,700,000 pounds of the crop in 1840.[9]

Gert Goebel, a German immigrant who settled in the town of Newport about forty miles west of St. Louis, wrote of the lack of involvement by his compatriots in trade when they first settled in Missouri. He noted that German immigrants, through their hard work, proved that they could farm land south of the Missouri River that earlier American migrants had bypassed and considered unfit for cultivation. However, roads were poor, and settlers were unable to transport surplus produce because they lived too far from the river. Livestock could be driven to market or sold to travelers on occasion, but there was a lack of cash in the area and no local demand for extra wheat, barley, or corn. Families fed surplus corn to farm animals, because it was "too inconvenient to take grain to St. Louis by wagon and it was quite a while before people began to buy wagons." Since it was impossible to make any profit from farming, families sent children to St. Louis to work and make money. The boys worked in brick plants and the girls in kitchens and as nursemaids; they sent back their earnings to help their families buy more land. Here Goebel illustrated the problem of economic geography, writing that market participation was limited by a lack of transportation. Distance from markets also kept Lucy Bradford's family from regular involvement in commerce, as they lived about 100 miles southwest of St. Louis, near Rolla. The family hauled items such as sugar, coffee, salt, and rice from St. Louis twice a year. Bradford recalled that there "was no market for butter, eggs or any farm surplus. Livestock ate extra grain before being driven to market."[10]

For those who lived near rivers and towns, merchants served an important purpose for frontier society. They functioned as middlemen between farmers and wholesalers. They helped rural families market their extra farm production and allowed farmers, in return, to purchase goods that improved their quality of life. Markets created opportunity for farmers, who produced cider and shoes, picked cherries, or hauled firewood in the quest for profit. Midwestern merchants were midwives to capitalism, helping to bring the market economy to the rural population. They helped "liberate" western residents from the primitive living conditions of early settlements, argued historian Lewis Atherton. Once a store opened up in their community, farmers and their neighbors no longer had to produce their own food and clothing as well as other items they needed to survive. Dewitt Clinton Basey wrote that he could pay off his store debts with bearskins, honey, or beeswax. These items operated as "legal tender," and "you could pay debts with them if you had no money." In the town of Liberty, the firm of Wilson and Sedwick advertised sheet iron stoves, kettles, and scales for sale, and promised to pay eighty cents a bushel for flax seed. Another firm in the same town accepted hemp, wheat, and honey in exchange for store goods.[11]

By offering credit in exchange for farm goods, merchants encouraged the development of a commercial economy in regions where banks or currency were absent or rare. Storekeepers helped the western nineteenth-century economy operate because they had access to capital and credit. They transferred farm goods to outside markets and provided raw materials to artisans and manufactured goods to families. Furthermore, they promoted rural consumerism by providing the residents of central Missouri with the chance to barter or sell farm goods.[12]

Merchants gave settlers access to the material goods required for a reasonable level of comfort. Families desired not only necessities such as tools, spices, and cloth but also items they decided to buy from a store instead of making at home, such as brooms, utensils, candles, and plates. They also purchased nonessential and luxury goods, such as china, gloves, clocks, chocolate, window glass, and inkstands. Sarah Randelman Barnes recalled that her parents sold chickens and surplus crops to stores in St. Louis, crossing the Missouri River in a boat to reach the city. She proudly noted that her parents quickly improved their economic position by participating in local markets. They earned money to purchase food and clothing and were able to buy a sizable farm and build "a good house and a large barn."[13]

The town of Liberty functioned as a center for trade for Clay County, in far western Missouri. It was the only town of any size in the county until the growth of Kansas City. Transportation difficulties in the 1820s had limited the participation of rural families in the spreading market economy downriver. By 1826, steamboat visits had increased, and local merchants began to sell groceries and cotton goods, such as bonnets and dresses. A spring bonnet show at the Big Shoal Meeting House, a Baptist church, provided an example of enthusiastic market involvement. The second Sunday in May was a major social event for the area, where local women could show off their newly acquired and colorful bonnets.[14]

Luke Shortfield provided another example of rural consumerism. Shortfield moved to Missouri in 1831 to help his older brother Joseph manage a business near Franklin. They established a new store in the village of Pike Bluff. Even before it was completely finished, "the people for miles round came in every day and inquire[d] when the goods would arrive." There was another merchant in the county, but he was too distant for nearby residents, who eagerly awaited the new store's opening. The local population showed up to see $6,000 worth of goods landed—six or seven boxes of dry goods and thirty or forty other packages, Shortfield noted. The brothers offered such popular items as hardware, shoes, coffee, salt, and hats for sale. "The beauty of the business was, no flaming advertisements or red-letter hand bills were required to make known the establishment of a new store in a new place." Everyone nearby, he wrote proudly, took an interest in their business. People spread news of the new merchants far and wide. Shortfield reported that they did "a good business." He was less happy when a half-sober doctor accidentally removed the wrong tooth the next year.[15]

In Harrison County in northwestern Missouri, rural families took advantage of the opportunity to improve their standard of living by selling farm produce in the nearest market center. In the late 1830s and 1840s, early settlers supplied themselves with most of the farm goods they needed, since families away from the river were far removed from markets farther downstream. The closest town was Liberty, eighty miles away to the southeast. Families gathered their surplus crops, loaded up a wagon, and chose someone to make the weeklong round trip. This individual then bartered all of the produce for the best possible price. These frontier residents most wanted tea, coffee, salt, cloth, and dye; they sent honey, beeswax, and raccoon and mink skins in exchange. The beeswax, made into yellow cakes, functioned as currency and was worth twenty-five cents a pound. Mink skins were worth twenty-five cents each, while coonskins earned fifty cents each. When the driver returned, the farmers divided their goods and any money left over.[16]

Once the town of St. Joseph was established in 1843, about fifty miles away, it became much more attractive as a market center. Families took their surplus produce there until merchants set up shop in the nearby town of Betheny. Farmers were then able to market their crops directly to a local merchant. Other stores were also established in smaller towns in the county. The barter trade in honey and animal skins rapidly faded, and residents began to sell the products of their own labors, rather than those gained from the land around them, to local merchants. Families sold butter, eggs, chickens, bacon, and cattle to merchants and purchased coffee, sugar, molasses, flour, salt, and candles. In 1859, residents received ten cents a pound for butter, $1.25 for a dozen chickens, ten cents a pound for ham and bacon, and $3 for every 100 pounds of cattle. They paid $1 a pound for tea, seventy-five cents for a gallon of molasses, and twenty-five cents a pound for coffee. Residents suffered from low prices for their goods, but paid dearly for those they wanted to buy.[17]

Another example of the frontier demand for mercantile goods can be found in Ruth Ralls Fisher's reminiscence of her family, which had moved to Missouri in 1841 from Indiana. She recalled that her grandfather, Silas Haley, worked as a cattle buyer and that he was often away from his family. They lived in north-central Missouri, near the towns of Brunswick and Laclede, where

Haley went to obtain "supplies" for his family. Whenever Silas Haley returned home, his wife and children celebrated because his arrival brought such treats as brown sugar, raisins, and other sweets. He also carried home shoes, boots, calico, and even silk from town stores. Fisher wrote that the store cloth was a luxury and only "enjoyed by the more fortunate." An old store receipt found in his papers from 1860 listed some of the items he purchased: indigo, saltpeter, calico, a bottle of wine, and one watermelon. Another receipt four years later showed that he spent $110.30 on calico, satin, shoes, boots, cloth, whiskey, and a dress pattern.[18]

Markets created opportunity for farmers, who produced or collected goods such as eggs, butter, beeswax, animal furs, or tobacco to sell or barter in market towns. Once a store opened up in their community, farmers could access store goods and begin to buy things they wanted, such as coffee, candy, shoes, or clothing. W. L. Irwin was clearly relieved when he wrote to family back in Pennsylvania, "we have a store almost in sight." But farm families were not solely profit-seeking and produced much of their needs throughout the antebellum period. Outside markets complemented household strategies, usually combining some market participation with some household production of food and goods. Neighborhood exchange continued, as families assisted each other with labor and foodstuffs. Rural Missourians did not embrace household autonomy at the expense of their communities; they combined household, neighborhood, and market production to meet changing needs.[19]

A wide variety of goods would have been available to rural Missourians. Most of these items could be classified into seven different categories: fabrics, food and drink, hardware, clothes and accessories, household goods, personal items, or miscellaneous. (An extraordinary advertisement by Jesse Brown, a dealer in "staple and fancy groceries" in Westport, near Kansas City, offered lobster, in addition to brandies, spices, and coffee.) Sugar, spices, alcoholic drinks, meat, and butter were usually in demand. Families frequently made clothing at home, sometimes using fabric acquired from stores. However, people often bought items such as shoes, boots, gloves, and hats, which were more difficult to make. Customers normally purchased manufactured items such as pots, pans, utensils, and dishes from merchants, since it was difficult to make such durable metal things. Another category, hardware, included merchandise used in construction, agriculture, and hunting, or with livestock. It encompassed everything from nails, shot, and iron to hoes, saws, and spurs.

A last group, personal items, contained all sorts of small comforts that modern Americans take for granted, such as razors, combs, paper, and glasses. All of these things were available in Missouri stores. A study of a general store in the Ozark Mountains, southwest of St. Louis, identified fabric, clothing, food, and sewing items as making up 51 percent of all purchases. Whiskey was the single best-selling product. Sugar and salt were the most common food purchases, both often used for food preservation. Nonessential items bought at the store included coffee, tobacco, and alcohol.[20]

Two examples of mercantile businesses illustrate the importance of storekeepers in the spread of consumerism in the region. The first of these were stores run by the Payne family. In 1828, twenty-one-year-old Moses Payne opened up a general store in Columbia in partnership with his older brother Jacob. Moses had lived in Boone County, Missouri, for five years, after most of his family had moved west from Kentucky following the death of his father. Jacob had managed another store in Harrodsburg, Kentucky, from 1826 to 1828 and had served as a deputy sheriff in the state to help support his family. A third brother, Andrew Payne, also went into business with them. The three brothers opened up the firm J. U. Payne & Brothers in Columbia, just as regular steamboat travel began to tie central Missouri to eastern states.[21]

The brothers expanded their business in the following years, paying close attention to their customers. Their firm opened in June 1828, with goods brought west from Kentucky and purchased from a merchant in Versailles, Missouri. The store prospered, and at the end of their first year they had sales of $17,202.47. Only about 30 percent of this was in cash, with the remainder on credit or via barter. In their second year, ending June 1, 1830, they had $46,361.80 in sales. Only about a quarter of this amount was paid in cash, though. In 1831, Jacob opened up a second store in Fulton with his brother-in-law. He wrote to Moses on December 20, 1831, that store sales were "tolerable," ranging from $50 to $75 a day. The brothers also opened up a store in Rocheport farther west, as the state's population grew and expanded upriver. Moses seems to have been especially attentive to customers, as O. Williams wrote to him in July 1832 and requested that he pick up a bill of goods. Williams asked him to fill it while on his annual trip east to purchase items for the store. Another customer, George W. Ferguson, wrote to Moses to inform him that their store was out of sole leather. Ferguson noted, "the neighbors request you to keep leather in the neighborhood." But Payne did not just work to make his customers happy. He also had to ensure that store goods purchased from wholesalers in New York or Philadelphia made it to Missouri. When shortages arose, he had to buy goods from fellow retailers in St. Louis at higher prices than he would have preferred.[22]

Like all western merchants' stores, the Payne family stores carried a wide variety of items and accepted payment in a number of ways. They stocked a surprising variety of drugs, including Epsom salts, quinine, sedatives, and even opium. They accepted both cash and bartered goods in payment. Customers sometimes used locally made artisan goods to pay their accounts. For example, a local tinner received $8.50 in credit for six tin buckets and eight coffeepots he made. Often these artisans paid their accounts with finished goods like shoes, gloves, or hats made from raw materials purchased from the Paynes. (The records of another merchant, in Franklin, show that customers paid their bills with wood, eggs, chickens, apples, and hay.) The stores also accepted bacon, pork, skins, hemp, and whiskey in barter for store goods. Whiskey sold better than any other liquor and was usually in demand in western stores. It earned thirty cents credit per gallon and was sold back to customers for fifty cents a gallon. Cotton was credited at eight cents a pound and homemade soap at six cents a pound.[23]

Records from 1842 and 1843 from another merchant family, the Aulls, show that they took a number of items in payment for debts. Wheat was the most popular item accepted in these two years ($3,180.59), followed by hemp ($1,245.62), bacon ($994.12), flaxseed ($650.86), and lard ($202.69). They received most of the wheat—60 percent—during harvest season, from mid-September to November. The Aulls collected such surplus agricultural production and sent it to St. Louis and New Orleans for sale.[24]

Like the Paynes, James and Robert Aull migrated west to central Missouri to seek their fortunes. They moved to Lexington in 1825 and opened a retail store. In the next five years, they opened up more stores—one each in Independence, Liberty, and Richmond, Missouri. The Aulls stocked their store, in part, with local goods bartered by customers and then resold these same goods, such as whiskey, salt, beans, tobacco, and vinegar. They also imported hundreds of varied items from eastern wholesalers each year. One store's 1833 inventory showed six different kinds of blankets for sale, including blue, green, and broad-striped varieties. They also had mugs, teapots, cups, and seven different types of plates. Robes, ostrich feathers, silk gloves, trunks, cotton candy, wine, and a bewildering number of different medicines were also available. They exported tobacco, beeswax, furs, honey, hemp rope, and pork to New Orleans, though they only sent four hogsheads of tobacco south in 1828. The Aulls exported 60,000 to 70,000 hemp and bale ropes each year, manufacturing them in a small rope-making factory they owned. They also sold foodstuffs to the government for supplying American Indians or to troops at Fort Leavenworth. Their customers, like those of the Paynes, rarely paid in cash. Customers often settled their debts with barrels of whiskey, beeswax, tallow, sugar, or homespun linen. The Aulls also allowed customers to pay their bills through labor, which included cutting brush for the business.[25]

In the autumn of 1839, customers in their Lexington store purchased necessities far more than other items. Salt, sugar, and coffee were popular, as were shoes, hats, and suspenders. People also bought nails, gunpowder, knives, buttons, and fabrics such as calico and linen on a regular basis. (In Concord, Massachusetts, for example, households quickly abandoned producing their own cloth when they were able to purchase inexpensive textiles from local stores.) Items that were rare, only appearing once or twice out of nearly 1,000 items, were a quill and ink set, nutmeg, a spade, a pitcher, and lace. A typical entry, from June 27, listed the sale of twenty-six pounds of flour, a pound of powder, and four combs. Cash payments for store goods were rare, and most transactions were through barter or credit. Customers rarely bought any items that could be made or grown at home—such as soap, whiskey, candles, butter, clothing, or food products—until later in the antebellum period. Farm families, who used surplus farm goods to gain income for necessities or the occasional luxury item, produced these things at home.[26]

However, entries fifteen years later in the 1854 Lexington store accounts show that customers purchased a greater variety and number of items. They bought more goods of all types from the store and seemed to be making fewer products at home. The store's patrons obtained whiskey, candles, potatoes, butter, tobacco, maple syrup, combs, and ham regularly. Necessities such as coffee, sugar, boots, nails, shoes, and gunpowder continued to appear throughout the sample. Newer and less essential items like table covers, flannel, silk, cups, tea, and paper appeared repeatedly. An average transaction could be for six pounds of Havana coffee (September 14), a pair of shoes (September 30), or ten pounds of tobacco, two pounds of soda, a flask, and whiskey (September 16). There were more cash payments for goods than fifteen years earlier, but just barely. Cash payments accounted for about 15 percent of their business during this time. Noncash transactions continued to make up a large majority of all transactions throughout the antebellum period. Customers continued to pay by barter or through credit, as they had earlier. Though the region lacked a banking system, or much cash at all, rural residents actively took part in their local market economy because of credit offered through merchants.[27]

Other mercantile records portray a similar evolution in consumption. The records of Jacob Wyan, a merchant in Boonville from 1819 to 1822, show that his customers purchased necessities far more often than any other goods. Items that sold the most included some obvious things that farm families might need on a relatively isolated frontier region, such as cotton, gunpowder, sugar, tobacco, and calico. Shoes and gloves also sold well, as did thread, buttons, and ribbons. Customers bought some of these items to help them make things, such as clothing, at home. Other items that showed up regularly included other manufactured items such as combs, knives, and nails; people bought utensils, cups, and plates much less often. Items rarely purchased included inkstands and books. Food and drink were also in low demand, with little cheese, butter, whiskey, or brandy purchased. Thus, most customers obtained items that they could not make themselves—sugar or gunpowder, for instance—from stores, while producing most of their own food, clothing, and beverage needs.[28]

Customers at another store in Fulton, fifty miles to the east of Boonville, demonstrated an increased interest in purchasing a greater variety and greater number of goods nearly two decades later. Irwin Hockaday's records in 1838 and 1839 show that customers most often purchased the same items as they did nearly two decades earlier in Boonville. Almost every day Hockaday sold sugar, tobacco, cloth, and leather. Less often, but still very regularly, customers bought shoes, tea, buttons, coffee, nails, plates, cups, and tools, which included shovels, files, knives, and axes. Patrons also spent money on items that were rarely bought in 1819 and 1820, such as teapots, razors, needles, or soap. Approximately once a week clients purchased a book or paper. No one purchased whiskey for eight months, from late September 1838 to June 1839. Patrons also bought very little food, other than the rare bit of butter or some apples, and only a few pairs of shoes. They purchased a lot more cloth than finished goods, such as shawls or gloves, leading to the conclusion that residents of the area continued to make most of their own clothing (other than shoes or the rare glove or pair of socks). Customers in the late 1830s acquired more nonessential items than did the patrons of Jacob Wyan's store in 1819 and 1820, but their consumption of these items was less than in later decades. However, the consumption of all goods accelerated toward the end of the antebellum period, as shown in the Lexington store records of James and Robert Aull.[29]

Market participation tied rural families into a world of debt and rising and falling prices that could have negative consequences for household autonomy. While markets provided the opportunity to improve a family's material status and comfort, they brought additional risk and uncertainty. As people became dependent on stores for goods, they incurred and increased debts to storekeepers. Debts might tie a household to a store that offered lower prices than competitors. Falling prices for farm-produced goods could leave families in ever-increasing debt, as they attempted to maintain their standard of living. Customers could also be tempted to continually produce more for market sale—more chicken, more butter, or more pork—limiting their independence and economic options.[30]

They also ran the risk of being hounded by merchants for debts. This usually occurred when stores ran into economic difficulties, often as unpaid accounts swelled. In January 1833, James Aull wrote, "as we have been engaged in business for a number of years we have a large amt. credited out." He added that they were determined to be out of debt by the end of the year. To "attain so desirable an object" required limited purchases of new goods, as well as turning their "attention principally to collecting" debts. This plan did not work out as hoped, though. Three years later, James Aull estimated that his customers owed him $150,000. Tough times for merchants could produce equally challenging circumstances for their rural customers, who might have to pay debts when prices were low or their own debts high. Households might be pushed to pay debts when they could least afford to. James and Robert Aull pursued those who owed them money, sending notes, often bearing 10 percent interest, after those they could locate. If debts went unpaid, they brought suit against individuals. They also requested that postmasters find officers of the law who would present bills. These people received 10 percent of the amount collected.[31]

Aull dedicated a lot of time to tracking down those who owed his business money. On January 26, 1833, he pursued a customer who owed money from August 1829, requesting that a business contact collect a debt for $27.21. He charged $5.06 in interest and gave him six months to pay, "with some good man for security." One day previous he had sent a collection notice to another man in Illinois. "If not promptly paid to be put in suit forthwith," he instructed. Aull charged 10 percent interest, an amount allowed by the state of Missouri. A letter to another former customer on January 29 threatened to charge interest if the debt was not paid within three months. He pursued an old debt from 1825 as well. Aull threatened others who had debts two years old with a lawsuit if payment did not come. Sometimes people had a month to pay. But if payment looked unlikely, he instructed constables or other officers to begin suit immediately. The firm also sent notices to men in Louisiana and Arkansas. However, Aull considered it "doubtful" these would be paid.[32]

When not tracking down rogue clients, storekeepers had to travel to New York or Philadelphia to obtain goods for their stores. They often made these long trips, which could take several months, once a year in the winter. The Paynes purchased thousands of dollars of goods while in Philadelphia in March 1831, including luxury items such as black silk lace, white satin, scarves, men's gloves, and cigars. They also picked up more practical materials, such as saws, anvils, kegs of nails, and bags of coffee and pepper. When they had finished their purchases, they had these items shipped to them over the Appalachian Mountains and down the Ohio River or by boat to New Orleans and then up the Mississippi River. They also purchased coffee, brown sugar, and rum in New Orleans and picked up manufactured items in the Ohio valley to reduce transportation costs. Merchants usually enjoyed six months of credit with no interest and then were charged 6 to 10 percent interest for the next six months. They had to make final payment within one year of purchase. In Missouri, almost all goods sold at two to three times eastern prices. After returning, many merchants publicized the arrival of new goods. Richard D. Law, from Fayette, advertised a variety of merchandise, including dry goods, hardware, groceries, boots, and shoes. Law also announced he had shawls and silk for sale, asking for wheat and flax seed from customers.[33]

General stores benefited from the credit system, as their customers were able to buy goods without cash. Merchants provided generous, long-term credit, most likely for business necessity but also possibly for neighborliness. Without this credit system, rural families would have been unable to buy the goods they wanted. Credit and barter allowed the development of rural consumerism and, by tying new consumers into the expanding market, pushed commerce into the rural hinterlands of towns. Merchants, of course, preferred customers to pay in cash, but this was unlikely due to a shortage of currency.

There were serious risks to storekeepers whose customers ran up large debts. Merchants often carried massive customer credits on their books that could run into the tens of thousands of dollars and could go unpaid for years. One accounts receivable ledger from the Aulls listed 2,797 unpaid debts, ranging up to $10,000, which was probably a large loan to a fellow businessman or family member. Most of these debts were less than $20. The total outstanding debt of the Aull businesses exceeded $150,000 in 1836. That year James Aull dissolved his partnership and sold off his stores in Liberty and Richmond; only his Lexington store remained open. Moses Payne, however, was much more successful and ended his life a wealthy man.[34]

Customers' buying habits changed over time, as the transportation revolution lowered the costs of goods beginning in the late 1820s. Steamboats brought in large quantities of inexpensive things and allowed the export of the agricultural production of the state. The opportunity to buy store items cheaply and export surplus farm goods led rural residents to make the logical choice to make fewer things at home and take more corn, pork, or eggs to the local merchant. The family production of whiskey, candles, butter, and tobacco for home use fell. Instead, families focused on taking more of these things to local stores to buy items they could not make at home or that they no longer chose to produce for home consumption. The list of goods that rural families could buy was long, and the usefulness for them was obvious. Items such as nails and tools had clear benefits for farmers. Powder was crucial for hunting, and cotton, cloth, and calico for making clothing. Pots, pans, and utensils were useful in the kitchen. Cheap transportation changed everything by eliminating barriers to market participation, lowering prices, and pushing farmers to change their production and consumption habits. This market behavior, which emerged in the three decades before the Civil War, is a contrast to the more subsistence economy practiced earlier in the nineteenth century. While Missourians may have wanted greater market participation, barriers limited their involvement until improved transportation encouraged greater commercial activity.[35]

Frederick Steines noted in a letter to a friend in 1836 that he could buy hundreds of items from local stores and that there was a constant demand for artisan labor and store goods in his area. Steines chose to take part in the commercial economy of central Missouri because market involvement provided him with the opportunity to make money and improve his life. He purchased land, sold farm produce, and bought goods that he chose not to make himself.

Steines arrived in Missouri just as the commercial economy was taking off, as steamboats tied the region to the larger capitalist market. Migration, settlement, the Santa Fe trade, and the California gold rush fueled the economic boom in the region. Steamboats opened western regions to widespread market involvement, exchanging agricultural production for eastern goods. Growing populations supported larger markets for store goods and provided greater surpluses for trade with merchants. Families in Missouri embraced commercial activity, and they benefited from access to staple foods, manufactured tools, mass-produced clothing, and luxury goods.[36]

Americans had moved to Missouri with an interest and acceptance of commerce. They expected to take advantage of the market opportunities available in the region to help them gain a competency. In the early part of the nineteenth century, flatboat stores, roving merchants, and itinerant peddlers had met the consumption needs of farmers in the West. Once permanent stores were established and merchants began to export and import goods in large amounts with the assistance of steam power, Missouri became increasingly tied to the larger economy. Farm families along the Missouri River were then able to express their pent-up desires for the opportunities that a market economy presented. Men like Richard Gentry profited from the Santa Fe trade, while others such as Thomas Beckwith or Basey Dewitt sold or bartered surplus farm goods at stores. Women such as Mary Ann Kitzmillen and Pauline Stratton also demonstrated how farm families embraced commercial activity through their production of farm goods for market sale and their purchase of store merchandise. Merchant families such as the Paynes and Aulls migrated west and set up businesses to meet the commercial needs of rural families. All of these people, pursuing their own individual or family goals, helped spread a market society in central Missouri.[37]

Merchants operated as vital middlemen in the agricultural economy of the West. They provided families with the opportunity to exchange surplus farm products for goods that improved their lives. Storekeepers helped settlers to transition from mostly subsistence farming to increased commercial activity, giving customers the chance to market agricultural goods. They also promoted rural consumption by providing residents with long-term credit, permitting them to purchase desired items even when they did not have an immediate way to pay for them. The production and consumption of Missourians changed before the Civil War. Farm families purchased a greater number and diversity of items at local stores by the 1850s than they had in earlier decades. They also began to produce more goods for exchange at stores. However, market participation came with inherent risks. Falling prices or debts could threaten a family's independence. Merchants pursued deadbeat clients for hundreds of miles, threatening lawsuits or high interest to recover debts. Despite risks, rural Missouri families embraced market production and enjoyed higher standards of living because of their participation in the commercial economy.

CONCLUSION

The Louisiana Purchase did not simply add land to the United States—it thrust aside European rivals and opened the center of the continent to a flood of ambitious, avaricious, and land-hungry migrants. Americans surged into Upper Louisiana in the early nineteenth century, building on the mix of agriculture and commerce established by the French and continued under the Spanish. The region had strong economic ties to outside markets, sending grains, furs, and skins down the Mississippi River in the eighteenth century. But American settlers brought an intense commercial spirit and exported far larger quantities of crops, as well as a greater variety of farm products. The "industry" of the Americans in Upper Louisiana, as noted by Nicolas de Finiels, John Bradbury, and others, led to increasing economic development, as they built more farms, started new businesses, and pursued economic opportunities wherever they could. With American migration came an expanding market society, full of an eager and entrepreneurial people, which eventually transformed Missouri.

Missouri provided opportunity for Americans and Europeans, such as the German immigrant Frederick Steines, who criticized the acquisitive nature of his neighbors. These newcomers brought an acceptance of the market economy west with them, whether they came from Virginia, Kentucky, or New York. Alexis de Tocqueville commented on Americans' love of money and their interest in farming and trade, as did other European observers in Missouri. Most antebellum migrants came from the upper South and settled near rivers, as soils were more fertile and waterways provided easy transportation and market access. They also brought slavery west with them, but the peculiar institution did not impede involvement in the growing market economy, since Southerners had long demonstrated an interest in commerce. Few Missouri residents resisted the lure of markets or the chance to better their lives with coffee, sugar, shoes, or clothing that they did not have to make. Some chose to live away from settlement. Many took advantage of the chance to enjoy the material opportunities provided by trade, as Henry Schoolcraft observed in a remote area of the Ozarks.

Families came to the state in search of a competency, or comfortable independence. They sought productive and affordable farmland to provide for themselves and their children. Good land allowed them to produce a surplus for market use, to accumulate money for more land, or to buy things to ease their lives. Missouri provided a chance for a competency to many, but not all. Starting a farm was expensive, and those who lacked capital often had to struggle to build it; many never could and were forced to keep moving west or south in search of the dream of land ownership. Thousands of families found success and improved their lives, though. Newcomers spoke highly of the region in their letters. Some came in search of opportunities that were disappearing east of the Mississippi, starting new businesses or farms. Others bragged of cheaper land or market opportunities. The rush to accumulate property often led to heartbreak, and many lost their hard-earned gains. Increased opportunity did not always result in equal opportunity.[1]

The land provided almost everything a farm family could need, and it was a fine place to grow grains, vegetables, or other crops. But life was tough and could be short. Building a farm required many years of hard work, and disease was a constant threat. Corn and pork served as a foundation for diets, and hunting was crucial for early settlers. Foodstuffs gathered from the countryside—honey, berries, and nuts—helped families in the first years of farm building. Good fortune and many years of labor often provided a family with the security they desired. Successful harvests, improved farms, and frame homes demonstrated their accomplishments.

Rural households depended on each other for assistance and survival. No family could produce everything that it needed by itself; some families did not have livestock, land, or other necessities. Women helped deliver babies or shared food, while men might help a family with construction or with clearing land. People pursued honey and hunted animals together, cared for those who were sick, and loaned tools to those who did not have them. Community labor helped bind people together, as work mixed with dancing or drinking. Families shared labor, animals, equipment, and other help with each other, and the growing commercial economy did not undermine this system of mutual assistance. People may have looked to make money from the market economy, but they did not seek advantage at the detriment of their neighbors.[2]

Farmwomen, their children, and slaves produced many of the first items a family made for market use. They made money or earned barter credit through the sale of poultry, eggs, and butter. Such income helped obtain things that families could not produce on their own, or chose not to, and allowed them to begin to buy useful items such as shoes, utensils, or manufactured clothing. Female labor was crucial to the success of a family farm, as their unpaid labor, ranging from cooking and child care to washing and soap making, allowed a farm to survive and prosper.[3]

Americans enthusiastically pursued market participation in the nineteenth century. Peddlers and flatboat stores met rural consumer needs until the transportation revolution connected Missouri to the rest of the country. Steamboats changed life by providing an inexpensive way to import and export goods. They tied Missouri into the national economy and accelerated the growth of the region by bringing affordable material goods that had been blocked by high transport costs. Overland travel and commerce, such as the Santa Fe trade and Oregon migration, spurred the growth of towns and market demand in central Missouri. The California gold rush also encouraged the economic development of Missouri, providing further stimulus as tens of thousands of people headed west through the state.[4]

Merchants provided families with the chance to exchange surplus farm products for goods that improved their lives. Storekeepers helped settlers to transition from mostly subsistence farming to increased commercial activity. They also promoted rural consumption by providing credit for store purchases. The production and consumption of rural families changed during the antebellum period. Farm families purchased a greater number and greater diversity of items at local stores in the 1850s than they had in earlier decades. Customers bought things that they had previously made at home, including whiskey, soap, and clothing. They also began to produce more goods for exchange at stores, such as corn or pork. But market involvement came with risks. Low prices or debts could threaten family autonomy. Merchants also pursued their debtors, threatening lawsuits and charging high interest rates. Despite these threats, rural Missouri families enjoyed improved lives because of their participation in the commercial economy.[5]

The end of the antebellum period brought more challenges for rural families than opportunities. The Civil War tore Missouri apart, as vicious guerrilla warfare brought chaos and widespread destruction. Refugees fled across the state, assassination became common, and both sides committed atrocities. Guerrillas controlled much of the countryside, and business ground to a halt. The collapse of slavery and military demands for labor made farming difficult. The state lost up to one-third of its population during the conflict. However, Missouri recovered rapidly after the war ended in 1865, as people moved into unsettled rural areas. Unfortunately, the good times came to a quick end in the mid-1870s when an economic depression hit the nation.[6]

Life continued to be difficult in the following decades. Violence and lawlessness returned, as gangs like the James boys undermined postwar stability. Drought and locusts added to people's troubles. In the late nineteenth century, farm families became "increasingly vulnerable to forces beyond their control," according to historian David Danbom. While rural families enjoyed lives of greater abundance than previous generations, falling crop prices and high interest rates made debts a greater threat than ever before. Competition and economic growth began to undermine the communal bonds of the antebellum era. Increasing market involvement brought increasing insecurity.[7]

The postwar capitalist economy held less opportunity and increasing risk for Missourians. Growing market dependence left rural families vulnerable to price fluctuations, competitive pressures, or crop failures. Farmers went deeper into debt to purchase new machinery to increase output. In the late nineteenth century, they had to sell more of their production to pay the costs of implements, mortgages, and shipping by railroads. New machines replaced farm workers, usually the children of farmers. Younger family members often had to leave rural areas for cities, eroding family and community bonds. A growing class of wageworkers suffered from competitive pressures to produce cheap goods for distant markets. They had little control over their lives. Wage reductions, harsh economic depressions, and a lack of regular work took their toll. In the depression of the 1870s, thousands of hungry and jobless men roamed St. Louis.[8]

In the countryside, a family's chance to gain a competency fell. It became harder to buy land and establish an independent farm after the Civil War.

The number of tenants increased, as families rented land because they could not afford to buy. In 1880, owners cultivated 72.7 percent of Missouri farms, while the remainder paid rent in cash or a share of their production. After Illinois, Missouri had the highest percentage of nonowners in the north-central region, an area of eleven states and territories. The invisible hand of the market economy provided decreasing chances to find opportunity, security, or autonomy. Many did eventually purchase land, though. Barriers to success were not insurmountable, but simply higher.[9]

A far larger international market also reflected global food supplies and prices, rather than regional or local ones. Thus, locally poor crops did not always lead to higher prices because of shortages. Reduced production only left farmers in greater difficulty. Transportation improvements also led to vast new regions being settled. These new farmlands and their increased supplies helped to keep agricultural prices from rising, which would have helped indebted families. As insecurity grew, so did resistance to the new economic order that industrialization created. Strikes, outlaw violence, vigilantism, and even the Populist movement demonstrated the clash between tradition and economic growth in Missouri. Widespread resistance to the market had finally arrived.[10]

Missouri was never a bucolic agricultural paradise before the Civil War. Life was tough, and the chance to get ahead was never fairly distributed. But the opportunity for average white families (and, of course, their wealthier kin) to gain a competency was more widespread than after the war. Antebellum rural people had the choice to participate in commerce and the flexibility to produce more or less for market use. Transportation improvements had not yet tied together international agricultural markets, and global production had not begun to keep prices down. Rural adversities multiplied in the late 1800s, making it harder to start and keep a family farm. Expensive storage and transport, as well as increasing American output, increased farm costs and reduced income. Commercial farmers had little control over their own destinies. The opportunities for improving life that the market presented before the Civil War decreased in Missouri in the decades after the war.[11]

ACKNOWLEDGMENTS

A long project such as this incurs many debts, both professional and personal. This book began as a dissertation at the University of Kansas (KU) and has since evolved into a much more readable book. Jonathan Earle was an exceptional adviser (translation: humane and fair) and remains an academic role model. Others at KU, including Peter Mancall, Joshua Rosenbloom, Ted Wilson, Rita Napier, Jennifer Weber, Kim Warren, and Don Worster, provided insight, assistance, and high standards. The Humanities and Western Civilization Program served as home for most of my time in Kansas. The interdisciplinary mix of scholars and students, as well as its extraordinary director, James Woelfel, provided friendship and support for five years. Jim, David Dewar, Greg Douros, Brian Drake, Matt Waldschlagel, and Jane Pierce helped make working in Bailey Hall not only tolerable but also occasionally fun. Ten years before I started at KU, I took a history class from Oliver Rink, at California State University, Bakersfield, that convinced me to abandon a business major and pursue history. Now retired, Oliver was a great teacher and mentor. I can thank him (or maybe blame him) for my career as a historian.

The State Historical Society of Missouri helped with research through a Richard S. Brownlee grant, and Stephen F. Austin State University provided a summer faculty research grant. Iowa State University (ISU) generously provided summer research funds, course releases, and faculty grants during revision. ISU is wonderful place to teach and write; the state is also a great place to call home. The chair of the history department, Pamela Riney-Kehrberg, read the entire manuscript and saved me from embarrassing errors of fact and clarity. My colleague Kevin Hill also read every chapter and gave many useful suggestions, reminding me that paragraphs should be less than an entire page in length. Others have commented on various stages of this book, including Susan Sessions Rugh, Jeannie Whayne, David Blanke, Steven Sodergren, Maddalena Marinari, and several anonymous reviewers. Their feedback has improved my work greatly. The staffs at the Missouri Historical Museum in St. Louis and at the State Historical Society of Missouri (SHSM) have been extremely helpful as well. The people at the University of Iowa Press have been superb, with special thanks for Catherine Cocks. Her interest in this project, and support and patience, is greatly appreciated. James Harlan at the University of Missouri helped with a map, while Anne Cox at SHSM assisted with images for this book. Robert Burchfield completed outstanding copyediting work, and his dedication is greatly appreciated. Parts of chapter 6 first appeared in "Mothers of Commerce: Antebellum Missouri Women and the Family Farm," *Missouri Historical Review* 104 (July 2010): 187–197. Sections of chapters 7 and 8 were first published in "Frontier Capitalism: Market Migration to Rural Central Missouri, 1815–1860," a chapter in *Southern Society and Its Transformations, 1790–1860*, edited by Susanna Delfino, Michele Gillespie, and Louis M. Kyriakoudes (Columbia: University of Missouri Press, 2011).

Friends from outside academia, or "normal people," as a student once commented, have provided essential distraction and friendship for many years. Greg Olson was my scoutmaster and has been an inspiration and a model of human compassion and decency for most of my life. I cannot thank him enough for all that he has done for me. Patrick Witcher has been a good friend and ally for more than fifteen years. He helped make teaching in inner-city California bearable and sometimes humorous. Eugenia Morain and Angela Capobianco have served as surrogate family for many, many years, and their love and grace is a gift. This book is, in part, dedicated to my grandfather Henry George Welcome, who did not live to see his grandson finish his education. Hank never enjoyed the privilege of a college education, but nonetheless he inspired me to pursue my dreams inside academia with his own intellectual pursuits. My greatest debt is to Yana Reid, who has lived with the book almost as long as I have. She endured writing and editing on our honeymoon in New Mexico, in addition to the varied insults and abuses that academia inflicts on spouses and partners. I cannot adequately express how much I appreciate her selflessness, humor, patience, and love.

NOTES

CHAPTER 1

1. William L. Barney, *The Passage of the Republic: An Interdisciplinary History of Nineteenth-Century America* (Lexington, Mass.: D. C. Heath, 1987), 9, 14; Jacqueline Barbara Carr, *After the Siege: A Social History of Boston, 1775–1800* (Boston: Northeastern University Press, 2005), 87; David B. Danbom, *Born in the Country: A History of Rural America* (Baltimore: Johns Hopkins University Press, 1995), 86, 95; D. W. Meinig, *The Shaping of America*, vol. 1, *Atlantic America, 1492–1800* (New Haven, Conn.: Yale University Press, 1986), 358; James A. Henretta and Gregory H. Nobles, *Evolution and Revolution: American Society, 1600–1820* (Lexington, Mass.: D. C. Heath, 1987), 226; Joseph J. Ellis, *His Excellency: George Washington* (New York: Vintage Books, 2004), 269.

2. George Rogers Taylor, *The Transportation Revolution, 1815–1860* (New York: Harper and Row, 1951), 35, 63–64, 89, 396–398; Stuart Bruchey, *Enterprise: The Dynamic Economy of a Free People* (Cambridge, Mass.: Harvard University Press, 1990), 225–227, 233; Douglass C. North, *The Economic Growth of the United States, 1790–1860* (New York: W. W. Norton, 1966), v; Jeremy Atack and Peter Passell, *A New Economic View of American History: From Colonial Times to 1940* (New York: W. W. Norton, 1994), 161; Louis C. Hunter, *Steamboats on Western Rivers: An Economic and Technological History* (New York: Octagon Books, 1969), 22–23. New York City population includes Brooklyn.

3. Hal S. Barron, "Rediscovering the Majority: The New Rural History of the Nineteenth-Century North," *Historical Methods* 19, no. 4 (Fall 1986): 141;

Charles Sellers, *The Market Revolution: America, 1815–1846* (New York: Oxford University Press, 1991), 123, 138, 153, 161, 208, 346, 374.

4. Daniel Walker Howe, *What Hath God Wrought: The Transformation of America, 1815–1848* (New York: Oxford University Press, 2007), 5–6, 44–47, 217–221, 563–569; Gordon Wood, *Empire of Liberty: A History of the Early Republic, 1789–1815* (New York: Oxford University Press, 2009), 2–4, 317–325, 702–708; John Majewski, *A House Dividing: Economic Development in Pennsylvania and Virginia before the Civil War* (New York: Cambridge University Press, 2000), 7–8.

5. Beatrice Craig, *Backwoods Consumers and Homespun Capitalists: The Rise of a Market Culture in Eastern Canada* (Toronto: University of Toronto Press, 2009), 13, 19; Naomi Lamoreaux, "Rethinking the Transition to Capitalism in the Early American Northeast," *Journal of American History* 90, no. 2 (September 2003): 438–439, 461; Joyce Oldham Appleby, "The Vexed Story of Capitalism Told by American Historians," *Journal of the Early Republic* 21, no. 1 (Spring 2001): 14; Richard Lyman Bushman, "Markets and Composite Farms in Early America," *William and Mary Quarterly*, 3rd Series, 55, no. 3 (July 1998): 361–366.

6. Wood, *Empire of Liberty*, 317, 322–323, 706–707; Stephen Aron, *American Confluence: The Missouri Frontier from Borderland to Border State* (Bloomington: Indiana University Press, 2006), 22–23, 50–51; Simpson Kensinger to Lewis Kensinger, November 7, December 20, 1858, Kensinger Family Papers, State Historical Society of Missouri, University of Missouri, Columbia (SHSM); William Davis Jr. to William Van Lear, November 30, 1838, Missouri History Papers, Missouri History Museum Archives, St. Louis (MHM); June 13, 22, 1846, Charles Peabody Diary, Journals and Diaries Collection, MHM. (When quoting from these and other letters and documents used throughout this book, I have retained the spelling, punctuation, and capitalization of the originals.)

7. Diana Mutti Burke, *On Slavery's Border: Missouri's Small Slaveholding Households, 1815–1865* (Athens: University of Georgia Press, 2010), 9, 13, 29, 34, 48–51, 57; R. Douglas Hurt, *Agriculture and Slavery in Missouri's Little Dixie* (Columbia: University of Missouri Press, 1992), xi–xiv, 6–7.

8. Kathleen DuVal, *The Native Ground: Indians and Colonists in the Heart of the Continent* (Philadelphia: University of Pennsylvania Press, 2006), 103–104; Colin G. Calloway, *One Vast Winter Count: The Native American West before Lewis and Clark* (Lincoln: University of Nebraska Press, 2003), 362–365, 380–

382; Willard H. Rollings, *The Osage: An Ethnohistorical Survey of Hegemony on the Prairie-Plains* (Columbia: University of Missouri Press, 1992), 6–8, 235–237; Anne F. Hyde, *Empires, Nations, and Families: A History of the North American West, 1800–1860* (Lincoln: University of Nebraska Press, 2011), 239, 314–317.

9. William E. Foley, *The Genesis of Missouri: From Wilderness Outpost to Statehood* (Columbia: University of Missouri Press, 1989), 1, 6–7, 24–25; James Neal Primm, *Lion of the Valley: St. Louis, Missouri, 1764–1980* (St. Louis: Missouri Historical Society Press and University of Missouri Press, 1998), 3–6, 39.

10. Carl J. Ekberg, *French Roots in the Illinois Country: The Mississippi Frontier in Colonial Times* (Chicago and Urbana: University of Illinois Press, 1998), 239–246; Aron, *American Confluence*, 29–35, 42–43, 58–59, 67–68.

11. Primm, *Lion of the Valley*, 8–21; Tanis C. Thorne, *The Many Hands of My Relations: French and Indians on the Lower Missouri* (Columbia: University of Missouri Press, 1996), 66–70; Aron, *American Confluence*, 50–54; Jay Gitlin, *The Bourgeois Frontier: French Towns, French Traders and American Expansion* (New Haven, Conn.: Yale University Press, 2010), 26–28.

12. Hiram Martin Chittenden, *The American Fur Trade of the Far West: A History of the Pioneer Trading Posts and Early Fur Companies of the Missouri Valley and the Rocky Mountains and of the Overland Commerce with Santa Fe* (New York: Francis P. Harper, 1902), 1:3–11, 40–43; William E. Foley and C. David Rice, *The First Chouteaus: River Barons of Early St. Louis* (Chicago: University of Illinois Press, 1983), 18–21, 38–41, 72; Andrew R. L. Cayton, *Frontier Indiana* (Bloomington: Indiana University Press, 1998), 276, 279.

13. Foley, *Genesis of Missouri*, 30–32, 40–42; John Francis Bannon, "The Spaniards in the Mississippi Valley: An Introduction," in *The Spanish in the Mississippi Valley, 1762–1804*, ed. John Francis McDermott (Urbana and Chicago: University of Illinois Press, 1974), 11–13.

14. Wood, *Empire of Liberty*, 15, 112–113, 358; Richard B. Morris, *Forging of the Union, 1781–1789* (New York: Harper and Row, 1987), 233–234; John G. Clark, *New Orleans, 1718–1812: An Economic History* (Baton Rouge: Louisiana State University Press, 1970), 206–207.

15. Wood, *Empire of Liberty*, 113–114; Clark, *New Orleans*, 209–210; Louis Houck, ed., *The Spanish Regime in Missouri: A Collection Of Papers And Documents Relating To Upper Louisiana Principally Within The Present Limits of Missouri During The Dominion of Spain From The Archives Of the Indies At Seville, Etc., Translated From The Original Spanish Into English, And Includ-*

ing Also Some Papers Concerning The Supposed Grant To Colonel Morgan At The Mouth Of The Ohio, Found In The Congressional Library (Chicago: R. R. Donnelley and Sons, 1909), 2:256–257, 261.

16. Wood, *Empire of Liberty*, 316; Houck, *Spanish Regime in Missouri*, 2–3, 11–13.

17. Wood, *Empire of Liberty*, 316–317; Thomas D. Clark and John D. W. Guice, *Frontiers in Conflict: The Old Southwest, 1795–1830* (Albuquerque: University of New Mexico Press, 1989), 84; Clark, *New Orleans*, 211–214; Percy W. Bidwell and John I. Falconer, *History of Agriculture in the Northern United States, 1620–1860* (New York: Peter Smith, 1941), 164, 168, 171–172, 182.

18. C. Richard Arena, "Land Settlement Policies and Practices in Spanish Louisiana," in McDermott, *Spanish in the Mississippi Valley*, 57–60; Clark, *New Orleans*, 207–208; Gilbert Din, "Spain's Immigration Policy in Louisiana and the American Penetration, 1792–1803," *Southwestern Historical Quarterly* 76, no. 3 (January 1973): 255–257, 266–267.

19. Neal O. Hammon, ed., *My Father, Daniel Boone: The Draper Interviews with Nathan Boone* (Lexington: University Press of Kentucky, 1999), 107–110; John Mack Faragher, *Daniel Boone: The Life and Legend of an American Pioneer* (New York: Henry Holt, 1993), 228–230, 237–238, 242, 246–247.

20. Hammon, *My Father, Daniel Boone*, 110, 112; Faragher, *Daniel Boone*, 248–249, 260.

21. Lawrence Kinnaird, "American Penetration into Spanish Louisiana," in *New Spain and the Anglo-American West: Historical Contributions Presented to Herbert Eugene Bolton*, ed. George P. Hammond (New York: Kraus Reprint, 1969), 1:222–226; Gitlin, *Bourgeois Frontier*, 48–49, 65.

22. Nicolas de Finiels, *An Account of Upper Louisiana*, ed. Carl J. Ekberg and William E. Foley (1803; repr., Columbia: University of Missouri Press, 1989), 1, 10, 69–70, 76–77.

23. Finiels, *Account of Upper Louisiana*, 63–65.

24. Carl J. Ekberg, ed., *A French Aristocrat in the American West: The Shattered Dreams of De Lassus de Luzieres* (Columbia: University of Missouri Press, 2010), 202–203, 217.

25. Amos Stoddard, *Sketches, Historical and Descriptive, of Louisiana* (Philadelphia: Matthew Carey, 1812), 214, 221, 224, 230, 293–296; John Bradbury, *Travels in the Interior of America in the Years 1809, 1810 and 1811; Including A Description of Upper Louisiana, Together With the States of Ohio, Kentucky,*

Indiana, And Tennessee With the Illinois and Western Territories, Containing Remarks And Observations Useful to Persons Emigrating To These Countries, in *Early Western Travels, 1748–1846*, ed. Reuben Gold Thwaites (Cleveland: Arthur H. Clark, 1904), 5:9, 259–260.

26. Louis Houck, *A History of Missouri: From the Earliest Explorations and Settlements until the Admission of the State into the Union* (Chicago: R. R. Donnelley and Sons, 1908), 2:238, 255–258.

27. Houck, *History of Missouri,* 3:34–36; Lemont Richardson, "Private Land Claims in Missouri, Part I," *Missouri Historical Review* 50, no. 2 (January 1956): 135–137; Timothy Flint, *Biographical Memoir of Daniel Boone, The First Settler of Kentucky: Interspersed With Incidents In the Early Annals of the Country* (Cincinnati: George Conclin, 1845), 246; Jay Feldman, *When the Mississippi Ran Backwards: Empire, Intrigue, Murder and the New Madrid Earthquakes* (New York: Free Press, 2005), 15, 136–143, 178.

28. R. Douglas Hurt, *Nathan Boone and the American Frontier* (Columbia: University of Missouri Press, 1998), 75–79, 82, 87–88, 91, 98–107; Aron, *American Confluence*, 152–155.

29. Timothy Flint, *Recollections of the Last Ten Years, Passed in Occasional Residences and Journeyings in the Valley of the Mississippi* (1826; repr., New York: DeCapo Press, 1968), 144–147; Rufus Babcock, ed., *Forty Years of Pioneer Life: The Memoir of John Mason Peck* (1864; repr., Carbondale: Southern Illinois University Press, 1965), 146; Aron, *American Confluence*, 158–169.

30. Malcolm J. Rohrbough, *The Land Office Business: The Settlement and Administration of American Public Lands, 1789–1837* (Oxford: Oxford University Press, 1968), 134–135; William E. Foley, *A History of Missouri*, vol. 1, *1673 to 1820* (Columbia: University of Missouri Press, 1999), 166–168; Henry Marie Brackenridge, *Views of Louisiana: Together with a Journal of a Voyage up the Missouri River, in 1811* (1814; repr., Chicago: Quadrangle Books, 1962), 113; Edwin James, *Part I of James's Account of S. H. Long's Expedition, 1819–1820*, in Thwaites, *Early Western Travels*, 14:158.

CHAPTER 2

1. Walter A. McDougall, *Freedom Just Around the Corner: A New American History, 1585–1828* (New York: Harper Collins Press, 2004), 5–7, 16–17; Gor-

don S. Wood, *The Radicalism of the American Revolution* (New York: Vintage Books, 1993), 6–8, 308–312, 336, 369; Gordon S. Wood, "The Significance of the Early Republic," *Journal of the Early Republic* 8, no. 1 (Spring 1988): 18–20.

2. Wood, "Significance of the Early Republic," 12–13; Wood, *Radicalism of the American Revolution*, 313; William G. Bek, "Nicholas Hesse, German Visitor to Missouri, 1835–1837, Part One," *Missouri Historical Review* 41, no. 1 (October 1946): 28, 34; Eduard Zimmerman, "Travel into Missouri in October, 1838," *Missouri Historical Review* 9, no. 1 (October 1914): 41.

3. McDougall, *Freedom Just Around the Corner*, 5–6, 16–18, 492–494; Wood, "Significance of the Early Republic," 18–20.

4. Alexis de Tocqueville, *Democracy in America* (1840; repr., New York: Perennial Classics, 2000), 54, 554.

5. Michael Merrill, "Cash Is Good to Eat: Self-Sufficiency and Exchange in the Rural Economy of the United States," *Radical History Review* 4, no. 1 (1977): 46, 53–55, 57–60, 64–66; James Henretta, "Families and Farms: *Mentalite* in Pre-Industrial America," in *The Origins of American Capitalism: Collected Essays* (Boston: Northeastern University Press, 1991), 75, 81–82, 84–87, 92–93, 97–98.

6. Winifred B. Rothenberg, "The Market and Massachusetts Farmers, 1750–1855," *Journal of Economic History* 41, no. 2 (June 1981): 288–298; Stephen Innes, *Creating the Commonwealth: The Economic Culture of Puritan New England* (New York: W. W. Norton, 1995), 44–45, 55–56. The literature on this topic is vast and briefly reviewed here.

7. Allan Kulikoff, "Households and Markets: Toward a New Synthesis of American Agricultural History," *William and Mary Quarterly*, 3rd Series, 50, no. 2 (April 1993): 344–355; James Henretta, "The 'Market' in the Early Republic," *Journal of the Early Republic* 18, no. 2 (Summer 1998): 294–296, 303–304; Robert A. Gross, "Culture and Cultivation: Agriculture and Society in Thoreau's Concord," *Journal of American History* 69, no. 1 (June 1982): 45–46, 53; Bushman, "Markets and Composite Farms," 364–366.

8. Christopher Clark, "Household Economy, Market Exchange and the Rise of Capitalism in the Connecticut Valley, 1800–1860," *Journal of Social History* 13, no. 2 (Winter 1979): 176–178; Lacy K. Ford, "Yeoman Farmers in the South Carolina Upcountry: Changing Production Patterns in the Late Antebellum Era," *Agricultural History* 60, no. 4 (Fall 1986): 29–31; Daniel Vickers, "Competency and Competition: Economic Culture in Early America," *William and*

Mary Quarterly, 3rd Series, 47, no. 1 (January 1990): 6.

9. J. Clemens to Joacher Pawling, October 4, 1816, Missouri History Envelope, MHM; Thomas Duggins to parents, June 12, 1840, Thomas Duggins Letters, Typescript Collection, vol. 3, no. 111, SHSM; S. E. Slater to John Slater, August 26, Missouri History Papers, MHM; Francis Fackler to Ann Burruss, February 13, 1834, Missouri History Collection, MHM; Mary Hardin to Charles Hardin, September 30, 1847, Duncan-Hardin-Jenkins Papers, SHSM. There is no date for Slater's letter, but it had to be written after St. Joseph was founded in 1842.

10. June 8, September 15, October 17, November 22, 1834, May 6, 1835, Frederick Steines's Letters, SHSM.

11. October 17, 1834, May 6, 1835, February 12, July 24, 1836, Frederick Steines's Letters, SHSM.

12. September 18, 1840, Frederick Steines's Letters, SHSM.

13. Malcolm J. Rohrbough, *The Trans-Appalachian Frontier: Peoples, Societies, and Institutions, 1775–1850* (Bloomington: Indiana University Press, 2008), 228–231, 272.

14. Burke, *On Slavery's Border*, 19, 25–28.

15. James Miller, *South by Southwest: Planter Emigration and Identity in the Slave South* (Charlottesville: University of Virginia Press, 2002), 15, 19–20, 74, 78; James Oakes, *The Ruling Race: A History of American Slaveholders* (New York: W. W. Norton, 1982), 69–72; James Solomon Otto, "The Migration of the Southern Plain Folk: An Interdisciplinary Synthesis," *Journal of Southern History* 51, no. 2 (May 1985): 192, 196–197; Joyce Oldham Appleby, *Inheriting the Revolution: The First Generation of Americans* (Cambridge, Mass.: Harvard University Press, 2001), 65; Susan Dunn, *Dominion of Memories: Jefferson, Madison and the Decline of Virginia* (New York: Basic Books, 2007), 20; John Mack Faragher, *Sugar Creek: Life on the Illinois Prairie* (New Haven, Conn.: Yale University Press, 1986), 49–50; Stephen Aron, *How the West Was Lost: The Transformation of Kentucky from Daniel Boone to Henry Clay* (Baltimore: Johns Hopkins University Press, 1996), 192–196.

16. Miller, *South by Southwest*, 63–64; Stephanie McCurry, *Masters of Small Worlds: Yeoman Households, Gender Relations and the Political Culture of the Antebellum South Carolina Low Country* (New York: Oxford University Press, 1997), 13–15, 19, 56; Steven Hahn, *The Roots of Southern Populism: Yeoman Farmers and the Transformation of the Georgia Upcountry, 1850–1890* (New York: Oxford University Press, 1983), 3, 50, 89; Dunn, *Dominion of Memories*, 21.

17. Oakes, *Ruling Race*, 72–75; Miller, *South by Southwest*, 5, 78, 125; Adam Rothman, *Slave Country: American Expansion and the Origins of the Deep South* (Cambridge, Mass.: Harvard University Press, 2005), 10–11, 183; Conevery Bolton Valencius, *The Health of the Country: How American Settlers Understood Themselves and Their Land* (New York: Basic Books, 2002), 43; Frank Lawrence Owsley, *Plain Folk of the Old South* (Chicago: Quadrangle Books, 1965), 24; John Inscoe, *Mountain Masters, Slavery, and the Sectional Crisis in Western North Carolina* (Knoxville: University of Tennessee Press, 1989), 12–14; John Grammar Tannor to Julia Tannor, September 9, 1844, John Grammar Tannor to William Font, January 12, 1852, Letters of John Grammar Tannor, St. Charles Collection, MHM.

18. Dunn, *Dominion of Memories*, 22–27; Avery Odelle Craven, *Soil Exhaustion as a Factor in the Agricultural History of Virginia and Maryland, 1606–1860* (1925; repr., Columbia: University of South Carolina Press, 2006), 24, 162.

19. Russell L. Gerlach, "Population Origins in Rural Missouri," *Missouri Historical Review* 71, no. 1 (October 1976): 8–9; Foley, *Genesis of Missouri*, 240; Stuart F. Voss, "Town Growth in Central Missouri, 1815–1880: An Urban Chaparral, Part I," *Missouri Historical Review* 64, no. 1 (October 1969): 64–65; James R. Shortridge, "The Expansion of the Settlement Frontier in Missouri," *Missouri Historical Review* 75, no. 1 (October 1980): 69–70; Hurt, *Nathan Boone*, 23, 33–34; John T. Schlebecker, *Whereby We Thrive: A History of American Farming, 1607–1972* (Ames: Iowa State University Press, 1975), 85.

20. Brackenridge, *Views of Louisiana*, 108–113, 203, 206.

21. Gerlach, "Population Origins in Rural Missouri," 6–9; Shortridge, "Expansion of the Settlement Frontier," 70–81; Foley, *Genesis of Missouri*, 240–241; Voss, "Town Growth in Central Missouri, Part I," 64–66.

22. Timothy R. Mahoney, *River Towns in the Great West: The Structure of Provincial Urbanization in the American Midwest, 1820–1870* (Cambridge: Cambridge University Press, 1990), 34–35, 42–51; Kim M. Gruenwald, *River of Enterprise: The Commercial Origins of Regional Identity in the Ohio Valley, 1790–1850* (Bloomington: Indiana University Press, 2002), 40–42; Robert P. Swierenga, *Pioneers and Profits: Land Speculation on the Iowa Frontier* (Ames: Iowa State University Press, 1968), 234–235; Robert B. Walz, "Migration into Arkansas, 1820–1880: Incentives and Means of Travel," *Arkansas Historical Quarterly* 17, no. 4 (Winter 1958): 315.

23. Brackenridge, *Views of Louisiana*, 117–118; James, *Part I of James's*

Account of S. H. Long's Expedition, 14:169–170; R. Douglas Hurt, "Planters and Slavery in Little Dixie," *Missouri Historical Review* 88, no. 4 (July 1994): 397–399; Milton D. Rafferty, "Agricultural Change in the Western Ozarks," *Missouri Historical Review* 69, no. 3 (April 1975): 300–301.

24. Babcock, *Forty Years of Pioneer Life*, 5–8, 101–103, 358–359. Babcock was a fellow Baptist minister and a friend of Peck who edited fifty-three volumes of diaries for publication after Peck died in 1857.

25. Babcock, *Forty Years of Pioneer Life*, 144–145.

26. Babcock, *Forty Years of Pioneer Life*, 145.

27. Henry R. Schoolcraft, *A Journal of A Tour Into the Interior of Missouri and Arkansaw From Potosi, or Mine a Breton, in Missouri Territory, in a Southwest Direction, toward The Rocky Mountains; Performed in the Years 1818 and 1819* (London: Sir Richard Phillips, 1821), 4, 28–37, 72–73; S. Charles Bolton, *Arkansas, 1800–1860: Remote and Restless* (Fayetteville: University of Arkansas Press, 1998), 6.

28. Hurt, *Agriculture and Slavery*, xi–xiii, 4–6, 64–69, 80, 90, 102.

29. Burke, *On Slavery's Border*, 33, 49–50, 57, 93–95; Craig T. Friend, *Along the Maysville Road: The Early American Republic in the Trans-Appalachian West* (Knoxville: University of Tennessee Press, 2005), 114–118.

30. Burke, *On Slavery's Border*, 49–51, 103, 111–112, 132–133, 141; Hurt, *Agriculture and Slavery*, 102–103, 215.

31. Phillip Scarpino, "Slavery in Callaway County, Missouri: 1845–1855," *Missouri Historical Review* 71, no. 1 (October 1976): 23, 37, 43; Burke, *On Slavery's Border*, 101; Hurt, *Agriculture and Slavery*, xii, 155, 215, 220; W. Darrell Overdyke, ed., "A Southern Family on the Missouri Frontier: Letters from Independence, 1843–1855," *Journal of Southern History* 17, no. 2 (May 1951): 225.

32. Burke, *On Slavery's Border*, 112–113, 137–139; Lewis E. Atherton, ed., "Life, Labor and Society in Boone County, Missouri, 1834–1852, As Revealed in the Correspondence of an Immigrant Slave Owning Family from North Carolina," Part 2, *Missouri Historical Review* 38, no. 4 (July 1944): 422.

33. Elizabeth A. Perkins, "The Consumer Frontier: Household Consumption in Early Kentucky," *Journal of American History* 78, no. 2 (September 1991): 486–495, 498–507; Craig T. Friend, "Merchants and Markethouses: Reflections on Moral Economy in Early Kentucky," *Journal of the Early Republic* 17, no. 4 (Winter 1997): 554; Donald L. Winters, *Tennessee Farming, Tennessee Farmers:*

Antebellum Agriculture in the Upper South (Knoxville: University of Tennessee Press, 1994), 48–54; John R. Finger, *Tennessee Frontiers: Three Regions in Transition* (Bloomington: Indiana University Press, 2001), 179–183; Lawrence H. Officer, "Dollar-Pound Exchange Rate from 1791," MeasuringWorth 2013, http://measuringworth.com/exchangepound/.

34. Wilma A. Dunaway, *The First American Frontier: The Transition to Capitalism in Southern Appalachia, 1700–1860* (Chapel Hill: University of North Carolina Press, 1996), 6, 16, 20, 125–127, 131–142, 145, 153–155; Inscoe, *Mountain Masters*, 52.

35. Hurt, *Agriculture and Slavery*, xi–xiii, 4–6; Friend, *Along the Maysville Road*, 105, 110–119, 124; Alphonso Wetmore, ed., *Gazetteer of the State of Missouri: With a map of the state. From the Office of the Surveyor-General, Including the Latest Additions and Surveys to Which Is Added An Appendix, Containing Frontier Sketches, and Illustrations of Indian Character* (St. Louis: C. Keemle, Harper and Brothers, Printers, 1837), 41, 86, 93.

CHAPTER 3

1. Christopher Clark, *Social Change in America: From the Revolution to the Civil War* (New York: Ivan R. Dee, 2007), 147–149; Vickers, "Competency and Competition," 4–6, 12, 25; Bushman, "Markets and Composite Farms," 365–366; J. Davis to Lewis Sawyer, September 25, 1837, St. Louis History Collection, MHM; Flint, *Recollections*, 129.

2. Nathan and Elizabeth Haines to brother and sisters, n.d., Haines Family Papers, folder 298, Missouri Collection, SHSM; Stephen Goddard to children, November 20, 1844, Goddard Family Papers, MHM; Lynn Morrow, "Dr. John Sappington: Southern Patriarch in the New West," *Missouri Historical Review* 90, no. 1 (October 1995): 38, 48, 60.

3. William D. Hoyt Jr., ed., "A Clay Countian's Letters of 1834," *Missouri Historical Review* 45, no. 4 (July 1951): 349–351; Louis W. Potts, "From Speculator to Gentleman: Waltus L. Watkins and the Case for Land Speculation on the Missouri Frontier," *Gateway Heritage* 13, no. 1 (Fall 1992): 47–48; Michael J. O'Brien, "The Roots of Frontier Expansion," in *Grassland, Forest and Historical Settlement: An Analysis of Dynamics in Northeast Missouri*, ed. Michael J. O'Brien (Lincoln: University of Nebraska Press, 1984), 85.

4. Joan E. Cashin, *A Family Venture: Men and Women on the Southern Frontier* (Baltimore: Johns Hopkins University Press, 1991), 32–35; George Bingham to Wyatt Bingham, October 19, 1826, Bingham Family Papers, SHSM.

5. Alan Taylor, *Liberty Men and Great Proprietors: The Revolutionary Settlement on the Maine Frontier, 1760–1820* (Chapel Hill: University of North Carolina Press, 1990), 8–9; Bushman, "Markets and Composite Farms," 365–371.

6. Jeremy Atack and Fred Bateman, *To Their Own Soil: Agriculture in the Antebellum North* (Ames: Iowa State University Press, 1987), 76–85. These authors count Missouri as a Northern state, because its slave population was relatively small, it lacked the dominant staple crop of other Southern states, and small-scale family farming dominated most of the state.

7. Bernard Bailyn, *Voyagers to the West: A Passage in the Peopling of America on the Eve of the Revolution* (New York: Vintage Books, 1986), 193–194, 233–237; Atack and Bateman, *To Their Own Soil*, 76; Friend, *Along the Maysville Road*, 220.

8. Hal S. Barron, *Those Who Stayed Behind: Rural Society in Nineteenth Century New England* (New York: Cambridge University Press, 1984), 32, 81, 87, 105; Richard A. Easterlin, "Population Change and Farm Settlement in the Northern United States," *Journal of Economic History* 36, no. 1 (March 1976): 66–68; Steven Herscovici, "Migration and Economic Mobility: Wealth Accumulation and Occupational Change among Antebellum Migrants and Persisters," *Journal of Economic History* 58, no. 4 (December 1998): 935, 938, 940

9. J. Davis to Lewis Sawyer, September 25, 1837, St. Louis History Collection, MHM; Joshua Belden to Dorothy Belden, July 13, 1830, St. Louis History Collection, MHM; J. H. Bronaugh, "Western Missouri in 1837," *Missouri Historical Review* 20, no. 3 (April 1926): 388–391. This short article includes a letter from her grandparents.

10. Carolyn Earle Billingsley, *Communities of Kinship: Antebellum Families and the Settlement of the Cotton Frontier* (Athens: University of Georgia Press, 2004), 18, 41–42, 52, 58, 63, 73; Faragher, *Sugar Creek*, 57–59; Edward E. Baptist, "The Migration of Planters to Antebellum Florida: Kinship and Power," *Journal of Southern History* 62, no. 3 (August 1996): 527, 531, 540–541; Faragher, *Daniel Boone*, 275–281.

11. Joshua Bradley to John McKown, March 14, 1857, John D. McKown Papers, SHSM.

12. Robert W. Frizzell, *Independent Immigrants: A Settlement of Hanoverian*

Germans in Western Missouri (Columbia: University of Missouri Press, 2007), 19–22, 29, 88; Paul C. Nagel, *The German Migration to Missouri: My Family's Story* (Kansas City, Mo.: Kansas City Star Books, 2002), 50–56; Walter D. Kamphoefner, *The Westfalians: From Germany to Missouri* (Princeton, N.J.: Princeton University Press, 1987), 38–39, 59, 66–69; Paul C. Nagel, *Missouri: A History* (Lawrence: University Press of Kansas, 1988), 96–98; Robyn Burnett and Ken Luebbering, *German Settlement in Missouri: New Land, Old Ways* (Columbia: University of Missouri Press, 1996), 7, 13; Kenneth Kronenberg, ed., *Lives and Letters of an Immigrant Family: The van Dreveldts' Experiences along the Missouri, 1844–1866* (Lincoln: University of Nebraska Press, 1998), 29–30; Gottfried Duden, *Report on a Journey to the Western States of North America and A Stay of Several Years Along the Missouri (During the Years 1824, '25, '26, 1827)*, ed. James W. Goodrich (1829; repr., Columbia: University of Missouri Press, 1980), 58, 67, 80, 217.

13. Nagel, *Missouri*, 96–98; Burnett and Luebbering, *German Settlement in Missouri*, 2–3, 13; Perry McCandless, *A History of Missouri*, vol. 2, *1820–1860* (Columbia: University of Missouri Press, 2000), 38–39.

14. Fred Gustorf, ed., *The Uncorrupted Heart: Journal and Letters of Frederick Gustorf, 1800–1845* (Columbia: University of Missouri Press, 1969), 135, 137, 139–140.

15. Ethelbert Lewis to William W. Lewis, January 20, 1837, Ethelbert Lewis Letters, SHSM; Samuel Sawyer to Aaron Sawyer, April 12, 1839, Samuel L. Sawyer Letters, SHSM; Thomas C. Lannan to George Peter, April 20, June 18, 1849, Thomas C. Lannan Letters, SHSM; Archy Kasson to Isaiah and John Townsend, January 17, 1831, Archy Kasson Letter, SHSM; J. R. Bohannon to Judith Clore, January 27, 1837, folder 209, Liliburn A. Kingsbury Collection, SHSM.

16. Samuel Sawyer to Aaron Sawyer, July 7, 1838, Samuel L. Sawyer Letters, SHSM.

17. William Powell to Henry A. Powell, January 1, July 1, 1839, November 10, 1840, William Powell Letters, SHSM; A. A. Edwards to Lewis Harvey, February 12, 1834, Harvey Family Papers, folder 1, SHSM.

18. Thomas Harvey to Susan Harvey, June 14, 1836, Harvey Family Papers, folder 1, SHSM; Samuel Sawyer to Aaron Sawyer, March 12, 1839, Samuel L. Sawyer Letters, SHSM; David Manchester to sister, April 19, 1819, David Manchester Letters, SHSM.

19. Wilson R. Smith to Henry W. Smith, November 26, 1838, folder 149, Liliburn A. Kingsbury Collection, SHSM; Jesse Mellon to Mary Evers, May 24, 1839, Jessie Mellon Letter, SHSM. See also Rebekah Myfanwy Kirstin Mergenthal, "Border Lines: The People of the Lower Missouri River Valley and the Expansion of the United States, 1803–1855" (Ph.D. diss., University of Chicago, 2008), 18–21, 28–45, for American reactions to Missouri.

20. October 17, 1834, April 30, May 6, 1835, Frederick Steines's Letters, SHSM.

21. A mattock is a tool for digging, like a hoe.

22. William A. Shelton, "A Pioneer Talks with Putnam's Eminent Men," Typescript Collection, vol. 13, no. 386, SHSM; J. T. Walker to Charly McWalker, May 8, 1842, folder 2, Berry-Thomson-Walker Family Papers, SHSM; Aron, *How the West Was Lost*, 194–198.

23. Thomas Dresser to Comfort Dresser, January 29, 1839, Thomas Dresser Letter, SHSM; Justus Post to John Post, December 5, 1817, Justus Post Letter, SHSM; W. R. Lenoir to William Lenoir, May 20, 1835, folder 2, Lenoir Family Letters, SHSM; William Powell to Henry A. Powell, July 1, 1839, January 28, 1840, William Powell Letters, SHSM; Wilson R. Smith to Henry W. Smith, November 26, 1838, folder 149, Liliburn A. Kingsbury Collection, SHSM; R. G. Smith to Henry W. Smith, August 13, 1840, folder 149, Liliburn A. Kingsbury Collection, SHSM; William Woods to G. W. Woods, July 4, 1836, Woods-Holman Family Papers, SHSM.

24. Wilson R. Smith to Henry W. Smith, November 26, 1838, folder 149, Liliburn A. Kingsbury Collection, SHSM; William Powell to Henry A. Powell, January 1, 1830, William Powell Letters, SHSM; Ethelbert Lewis to William W. Lewis, January 20, 1837, Ethelbert Lewis Letters, SHSM; J. R. Bohannon to Judith Clore, January 27, 1837, folder 209, Liliburn A. Kingsbury Collection, SHSM; Henretta, "Families and Farms," 87.

25. William Wood to D. G. Wood, April 16, 1831, C. Corwith Wagner Collection, MHM.

26. Justus Post to John Post, December 5, 1817, Justus Post Letters, SHSM; Samuel Sawyer to Aaron Sawyer, March 12, 1839, Samuel Sawyer Letter, SHSM.

27. Justus Post to John Post, August 2, 1816, December 5, 1817, Justus Post Letters, SHSM; Ethelbert Lewis to William W. Lewis, January 20, 1837, Ethelbert Lewis Letter, SHSM; William Powell to Henry A. Powell, November 10, 1840, William Powell Letters, SHSM; Thomas C. Lannan to George Peter, June 18,

1849, Thomas C. Lannan Letters, SHSM. Lewis did not provide a time frame for earning this amount, and his letter is often illegible.

28. J. Calvin Berry to John H. Marmmon, April 16, 1842, J. Calvin Berry Letter, SHSM; J. R. Bohannon to Judith Clore, January 27, 1837, folder 209, Liliburn A. Kingsbury Collection, SHSM; R. G. Smith to Henry W. Smith, August 13, 1840, folder 149, Liliburn A. Kingsbury Collection, SHSM; Archy Kasson to Isaiah and John Townsend, January 17, 1831, Archy Kasson Letters, SHSM; J. Clemens to Joacher Pawling, October 4, 1816, Missouri History Envelope, MHM.

29. Wilson R. Smith to Henry W. Smith, November 26, 1838, folder 149, Liliburn A. Kingsbury Collection, SHSM; J. R. Bohannon to Judith Clore, January 27, 1837, folder 209, Liliburn A. Kingsbury Collection, SHSM; Samuel Sawyer to Aaron Sawyer, April 12, 1839, Samuel Sawyer Letters, SHSM; Ethelbert Lewis to William W. Lewis, January 20, 1837, Ethelbert Lewis Letters, SHSM; William Powell to Henry A. Powell, July 1, 1839, William Powell Letters, SHSM.

30. J. Goodwin to Charles Custer, June 16, 1837, J. Goodwin Letter, SHSM; William A. Richards to Charles Richards, November 9, 1841, April 8, 1842, William A. Richards Letters, SHSM. See also Durward T. Stokes, "The Wilson Letters, 1833–1849," *Missouri Historical Review* 60, no. 4 (July 1966): 497–502, for the commercial interests of settlers.

31. Archy Kasson to Isaiah and John Townsend, January 17, 1831, Archy Kasson Letter, SHSM; W. R. Lenoir to William Lenoir, May 20, 1835, Lenoir Family Letters, SHSM.

32. Patricia Nelson Limerick, *The Legacy of Conquest: The Unbroken Past of the American West* (New York: W. W. Norton, 1987), 67–68; Rohrbough, *Land Office Business*, xii–xiii; North, *Economic Growth of the United States*, 182–185, 198–208.

33. Foley, *Genesis of Missouri*, 250; St. Louis *Missouri Gazette*, October 26, 1816.

34. Jonathan Hughes, "The Great Land Ordinances: Colonial America's Thumbprint on History," in *Essays on the Economy of the Old Northwest*, ed. David C. Klingman and Richard K. Vedder (Athens: Ohio University Press, 1987), 1–15; Foley, *Genesis of Missouri*, 250–253; Hurt, *Agriculture and Slavery*, 46–48; Atack and Passell, *New Economic View of American History*, 257.

35. James E. Davis, *Frontier Illinois* (Bloomington: Indiana University Press, 1998), 209–213; Flint, *Recollections*, xvi–xxi, 135–136, 145, 199; Hurt, *Agri-*

culture and Slavery, 47.

36. Flint, *Recollections*, 186, 198–199; David Manchester to sister, April 19, 1819, David Manchester Letters, SHSM.

37. Thomas Harrison to children, June 20, 1831, Thomas Harrison Letters, SHSM; Atack and Passell, *New Economic View of American History*, 269. Long-term landholding could be very profitable. Speculator Matthew Scott purchased 42,000 acres of land in Illinois and held on to it for decades. He sold his lands in the 1850s for between \$6 and \$10 an acre. In the 1860s, most of his land sold for \$10 to \$12 an acre, while he earned at least \$20 an acre in the 1870s. See Paul Wallace Gates, *Frontier Landlords and Pioneer Tenants* (Ithaca, N.Y.: Cornell University Press, 1945), 25–26.

38. Lewis E. Atherton, ed., "Life, Labor and Society in Boone County, Missouri, 1834–1852, As Revealed in the Correspondence of an Immigrant Slave Owning Family from North Carolina," Part 1, *Missouri Historical Review* 38, no. 3 (April 1944): 277–282; W. R. Lenoir to William Lenoir, November 26, December 30, 1834, May 20, 1835, Lenoir Family Letters, SHSM.

39. James Riggs Memoir, 3–7, Missouri Collection, SHSM. This memoir was written in 1877.

40. James Riggs Memoir, SHSM, 8–18.

41. Herbert S. Jones, "Missouri–A Promised Land," SHSM. See Jason H. Combs, "Early Settlement of a Frontier Community: The Platte Purchase, 1836–1850" (Ph.D. diss., University of Nebraska, 2000), chapters 3 and 5, for a good survey of the region.

42. John Bidwell, "The First Emigrant Train to California," *Century Illustrated Monthly Magazine* 41, no. 1 (November 1890): 106–110. See also the George F. and Ursula Terry Letters, SHSM, regarding fraud, hard times, and tragedy in the early 1840s,.

43. Justus Post to John Post, August 19, September 10, November 9, 1815, Justus Post Letters, MHM; William E. Foley, "Justus Post: Portrait of a Frontier Land Speculator," *Missouri Historical Society Bulletin* 36, no. 1 (October 1979): 19–25.

44. Justus Post to John Post, Justus Post Letters, December 10, 24, 1815, January 22, 1816, MHM.

45. Justus Post Letters, December 10, 24, 1815, January 22, 1816, MHM.

46. Justus Post to John Post, May 12, June 3, August 19, September 22, October 28, 1816, Justus Post Letters, MHM.

47. Justus Post to John Post, February 4, 1816, Justus Post Letters, SHSM; Justus Post to John Post, May 12, July 14, 1816, February 1, December 5, 1818, March 15, 1819, Justus Post Letters, MHM.

48. Barney, *Passage of the Republic*, 131; McCandless, *History of Missouri*, 2:23–24; Dorothy B. Dorsey, "The Panic of 1819 in Missouri," *Missouri Historical Review* 29, no. 2 (January 1935): 79–91; Sam Rezneck, "The Depression of 1819–1822: A Social History," *American Historical Review* 39, no. 1 (October 1933): 28–33; Justus Post to John Post, Justus Post Letters, December 18, 1820, June 28, 1821, MHM.

49. This information is from the "Forward to Justus Post Letters" and a biographical sketch of Post written by Elizabeth Gentry Sayad. Justus Post Letters, MHM; Foley, "Justus Post," 23–25.

CHAPTER 4

1. Walter A. Schroeder, "The Spread of Settlement in Howard County, Missouri, 1810–1859," *Missouri Historical Review* 63, no. 1 (October 1968): 2–5; Bek, "Nicholas Hesse," 25–28; R. Douglas Hurt, "Seeking Fortune in the Promised Land: Settling the Boon's Lick Country, 1808–1825," *Gateway History* 13, no. 1 (Summer 1992): 6.

2. Hurt, *Agriculture and Slavery*, 6–7, 64–65; Inscoe, *Mountain Masters*, 53, 57; Morris Birkbeck, *Notes On A Journey In America, From the Coast of Virginia To the Territory of Illinois* (London: Severa, 1818), 91.

3. W. W. Lester, *Decisions of the Interior Department In Public Land Cases and Land Laws Passed By The Congress of the United States; Together With The Regulations Of the General Land Office* (Philadelphia: H. P. & R. H. Small, 1860), 355–356, 576–580; R. Douglas Hurt, *The Ohio Frontier: Crucible of the Old Northwest, 1720–1830* (Bloomington: Indiana University Press, 1996), 144–145; Rohrbough, *Land Office Business*, 103; Mark Wyman, *The Wisconsin Frontier* (Bloomington: Indiana University Press, 1998), 176.

4. Lester, *Decisions of the Interior Department*, 355–361; Rohrbough, *Land Office Business*, 60–61, 103, 201; R. Douglas Hurt, *American Agriculture: A Brief History* (West Lafayette, Ind.: Purdue University Press, 2002), 132. The first federal preemption law was passed in 1830, with additional legislation in 1832, 1834, and 1841.

5. Maria R. Audubon, ed., *Audubon and His Journals* (New York: Charles Scribner's Sons, 1897), 2:443–445.

6. John Mason Peck and Nicholas Patterson, "The Boon's Lick Country: Two Gospel Preachers Explore a New Settlement," *Missouri Historical Society Bulletin* 6, no. 4 (July 1950): 443–444, 459–461; Massena Moreau McCormick Deposition, Mamie J. McCormick Papers, SHSM; Babcock, *Forty Years of Pioneer Life*, 144; Robert Leslie Jones, *History of Agriculture in Ohio to 1880* (Kent, Ohio: Kent State University Press, 1983), 22.

7. Danbom, *Born in the Country*, 70–71; Atack and Bateman, *To Their Own Soil*, 111; Hurt, *Agriculture and Slavery*, 63–64; Robert E. Ankli, "Farm-Making Costs in the 1850s," *Agricultural History* 48, no. 1 (January 1974): 51–52.

8. Danbom, *Born in the Country*, 71–72; Paul Salstrom, *From Pioneering to Persevering: Family Farming in Indiana to 1880* (West Lafayette, Ind.: Purdue University Press, 2007), 41, 111; Atack and Bateman, *To Their Own Soil*, 111–112; Hurt, *Agriculture and Slavery*, 49–50, 62–64.

9. Richard A. Bartlett, *The New Country: A Social History of the American Frontier, 1776–1890* (Oxford: Oxford University Press, 1974), 176–181; Bidwell and Falconer, *History of Agriculture*, 162.

10. Bartlett, *New Country*, 180–182; Clarence H. Danhof, *Change in Agriculture: The Northern United States, 1820–1870* (Cambridge, Mass.: Harvard University Press, 1969), 117–120; Hurt, *Agriculture and Slavery*, 62.

11. Bek, "Nicholas Hesse," 20, 37–38.

12. Philander Draper, "Farming in Missouri in Early Days," folder 90, Draper-McClurg Family Papers, SHSM.

13. Bek, "Nicholas Hesse," 39–40; Faragher, *Sugar Creek*, 71–72; Lewis Cecil Gray, *History of Agriculture in the Southern United States to 1860* (Gloucester, Mass.: Peter Smith, 1958), 2:441.

14. John Woods, *Two Years Residence In The Settlement On The English Prairie In the Illinois Country, United States. With An Account Of Its Animal And Vegetable Productions, Agriculture, &c. &c. A Description Of the Principal Towns, Villages, &c. &c. With The Habits And Customs Of The Back-Woodsmen* (London: Longman, Hurst, Rees, Orme, and Brown, 1822), 168–175; Edmund Flagg, *The Far West, Or A Tour Beyond the Mountains, Embracing Outlines of Western Life and Society: Sketches of the Prairies, Rivers, Ancient Mounds, Early Settlements of the French, Etc., Etc.* (New York: Harper and Brothers, 1838), 187–189.

15. July 21, December 17, 1835, October 13, 1838, June 12, 22, 23, 1839, Jacob Lanius Diary, SHSM. Steamboats made regular trips up the Osage River, starting in the late 1830s. See James Sterling Pope, "A History of Steamboating on the Lower Missouri: 1838–1849, St. Louis to Council Bluffs, Iowa Territory" (Ph.D. diss., St. Louis University, 1984), 17–18.

16. James Bumgardner Jr., "Reminiscences," Typescript Collection, vol. 1, no. 25, SHSM.

17. Bumgardner, "Reminiscences."

18. Eliza Dyer Price, "Recollections of My Father," Typescript Collection, vol. 12, no. 276, SHSM; Lucy Blythe, "The Early Settlers of Missouri," Typescript Collection, vol. 13, no. 351, SHSM.

19. Gerald Grob, *The Deadly Truth: A History of Disease in America* (Cambridge, Mass.: Harvard University Press, 2002), 65, 128–131; Sonia Shah, *The Fever: How Malaria Has Ruled Humankind for 500,000 Years* (New York: Farrar, Strauss and Giroux, 2010), 38–40, 60–61, 70; Valencius, *Health of the Country*, 79–82.

20. Grob, *Deadly Truth*, 65–66, 87, 131–132; M. H. Dunlop, *Sixty Miles from Contentment: Traveling the Nineteenth-Century American Interior* (Boulder, Colo.: Westview Press, 1998), 182–184; Shah, *Fever*, 70–73; May 4, August 24, September 4, 1819, "John C. Bush's Book of Travels," Bush Family Papers, SHSM; July 6, 1846, Charles Peabody Diary, Journals and Diaries Collection, MHM.

21. Dunlop, *Sixty Miles from Contentment*, 183; Faragher, *Sugar Creek*, 90; Edward D. Jervey and James E. Moss, eds., "From Virginia to Missouri in 1846: The Journal of Elizabeth Ann Cooley," *Missouri Historical Review* 60, no. 2 (January 1966): 162–171, 192–206; John Grammar Tannor to Julia G. Tannor, May 25, July 18, 1845, Letters from Dr. John Grammar Tannor, St. Charles Collection, MHM; Sewell Hepbron to Thomas Hepbron, October 11, 1848, Sewell Hepbron Letters, Missouri Collection, SHSM.

22. Elliott West, *Growing Up with the Country: Childhood on the Far Western Frontier* (Albuquerque: University of New Mexico Press, 1989), 217; Grob, *Deadly Truth*, 104–106; Jared Diamond, *Guns, Germs and Steel: The Fates of Human Societies* (New York: W. W. Norton, 1999), 199.

23. Patrick E. McLear, "The St. Louis Cholera Epidemic of 1849," *Missouri Historical Review* 63, no. 2 (January 1969): 176–179; Grob, *Deadly Truth*, 106–107; Niklaus to William Waye, September 10, 1852, William Waye Papers, SHSM.

24. September 15, 1834, Frederick Steines's Letters, SHSM.

25. Grob, *Deadly Truth*, 53, 84–86, 134–135.

26. Grob, *Deadly Truth*, 83–84, 101; Sewell Hepbron to Thomas Hepbron, April 14, 1843, August 30, 1848, Sewell Hepbron Letters, Missouri Collection, SHSM.

27. Jonathan Harris to brother, mother, and sister, May 26, 1843, Jonathan Harris Letters, Missouri Collection, SHSM; Nathan Haines to son, April 27, 1845, June 1, 1846, Haines Family Letters, Missouri Collection, SHSM. The Harris's child may have died from diphtheria, which can infect tonsils; see Grob, *Deadly Truth*, 80–82. For a description of measles, see June 19, 1837, John Geiger Diary, Journals and Diaries Collection, MHM.

28. July 2, July 3, 1846, Charles Peabody Diary, Journals and Diaries Collection, MHM; William A. Schutt Jr., *Dark Banquet: Blood and the Curious Lives of Blood-Feeding Creatures* (New York: Harmony Books, 2008), 195, 199, 204–207, 211.

29. July 3, July 6, 1846, Charles Peabody Diary, Journals and Diaries Collection, MHM.

30. Solomon Eby to friends, May 23, 1847, Solomon Eby Letter, Cooper County Collection, MHM; Frederick S. Klein, ed., "Letters of a Young Surveyor, 1828–1829," *Missouri Historical Review* 23, no. 1 (October 1928): 75, 81; Joel Palmer, *Journal of Travels Over the Rocky Mountains, to the Mouth of the Columbia River; Made During the Years 1845 and 1846: Containing Mining Descriptions of the Valleys of the Willamette, Umpqua, And Clamet: A General Description of the Oregon Territory; Its Inhabitants, Climate, Soil, Productions, Etc., Etc.; A List of Necessary Outfits For Emigrants; And A Table of Distances from Camp to Camp on the Platte* (1847; repr., Fairfield, Wash.: Ye Galleon Press, 1983), 12.

31. July 18, September 16, December 12, 26, 28, 1819, "John C. Bush's Book of Travels," Bush Family Papers, SHSM; "Memoirs of Dr. William Allen Wilcox," St. Louis History Collection, MHM; R. Rowland to Mary Ann Rowland, November 25, 1840, R. Rowland Letter, Western Travel Collection, MHM; November 24, 1835, December 26, 30, 1838, January 8, 1839, April 25, 26, 1840, Jacob Lanius Diary, SHSM.

32. Terry G. Jordan and Matt Kaups, *The American Backwoods Frontier: An Ethnic and Ecological Interpretation* (Baltimore: Johns Hopkins University Press, 1989), 224–226.

33. John Lewis Peyton, *Over the Alleghanies and Across the Prairies: Personal Recollections of the Far West, One and Twenty Years Ago* (London: Simpkin, Marshall, 1869), xiv–xv, 288–292.

34. October 17, 1834, July 19, 1835, Frederick Steines's Letters, SHSM; David William Graves Autobiography, 21–24, SHSM.

35. Henry S. Kelley Autobiographical Sketch, 2–5, SHSM.

36. Wilson R. Smith to Henry W. Smith, November 26, 1838, folder 149, Liliburn A. Kingsbury Collection, SHSM; R. G. Smith to Henry W. Smith, August 13, 1840, folder 149, Liliburn A. Kingsbury Collection, SHSM; James, *Part I of James's Account of S. H. Long's Expedition*, 14:166.

37. Henry S. Kelley Autobiographical Sketch, 2–6, SHSM; Wetmore, *Gazetteer of the State of Missouri*, 29–30; Massena McCormick Deposition, Mamie J. McCormick Papers, SHSM; Allan W. Eckhert, *The Silent Sky: The Incredible Extinction of the Passenger Pigeon* (Lincoln, Neb.: iUniverse.com, 2000), 241–242.

38. Jordan and Kaups, *American Backwoods Frontier*, 121; Thomas Beckwith, "Early Customs," Missouri History Collection, MHM.

39. Bartlett, *New Country*, 198–201.

40. Paul W. Gates, *The Farmer's Age: Agriculture, 1815–1860* (New York: Holt, Rinehart and Winston, 1960), 169–170; Hurt, *American Agriculture*, 111, 120; Allan G. Bogue, *From Prairie to Corn Belt: Farming on the Illinois and Iowa Prairies in the Nineteenth Century* (Chicago: University of Chicago Press, 1963), 132–133; Jordan and Kaups, *American Backwoods Frontier*, 115.

41. Gates, *Farmer's Age*, 170; John Mack Faragher, *Women and Men on the Overland Trail* (New Haven, Conn.: Yale University Press, 2000), 53; Jordan and Kaups, *American Backwoods Frontier*, 115; Charles D. Drake, ed., *Pioneer Life in Kentucky: A Series of Reminiscential Letters From Daniel Drake, M.D., of Cincinnati, to His Children* (Cincinnati: Robert Clarke, 1870), 49–51; Bek, "Nicholas Hesse," 39–42.

42. Gates, *Farmer's Age*, 170–172; Jordan and Kaups, *American Backwoods Frontier*, 115–116; Bek, "Nicholas Hesse," 39–43.

43. Babcock, *Forty Years of Pioneer Life*, 144; Faragher, *Women and Men on the Overland Trail*, 50–51; July 8, 1835, Frederick Steines's Letters, SHSM; Woods, *Two Years Residence*, 214–215, 223–226.

44. Gates, *Farmer's Age*, 217–218; John C. Hudson, *Making the Corn Belt: A Geographical History of Middle-Western Agriculture* (Bloomington: Indiana

University Press, 1994), 74, 80–83, 96, 116; Foley, *Genesis of Missouri*, 241–243; Jordan and Kaups, *American Backwoods Frontier*, 120–121; Shelton, "Pioneer Talks with Putnam's Eminent Men"; Bumgardner, "Reminiscences."

45. Hudson, *Making the Corn Belt*, 80–83; Salstrom, *From Pioneering to Persevering*, 43; December 10, 1829, William Nash Diary, MHM.

46. Wiley Britton, "Pioneer Life in Southwest Missouri," *Missouri Historical Review* 16, no. 1 (October 1921): 65–68, 84; Daniel McKinley, "White Man's Fly on the Frontier," *Missouri Historical Review* 58, no. 4 (July 1964): 448–451; Jones, "Missouri"; W. L. Irwin to brother, June 9, 1859, W. L. Irwin Letter, SHSM; Faragher, *Sugar Creek*, 75; James W. Goodrich and Lynn Wolf Gentzler, eds., "'I Well Remember': David Holms Conrad's Recollections of St. Louis, 1819–1823," *Missouri Historical Review* 90, no. 1 (October 1995): 37; M. J. Morgan, *Land of Big Rivers: French and Indian Illinois, 1699–1778* (Carbondale: Southern Illinois University Press, 2010), 31, 36.

47. Drake, *Pioneer Life in Kentucky*, 134–136.

48. Faragher, *Sugar Creek*, 3, 15–17; W. R. Lenoir to Edmond Jones, December 30, 1834, Walter R. Lenoir Letter, SHSM; Drake, *Pioneer Life in Kentucky*, 85–86.

49. Jones, *History of Agriculture in Ohio*, 44–48.

50. Jones, *History of Agriculture in Ohio*, 48.

51. Flint, *Recollections*, 129; December 28, 1838, Jacob Lanius Diary, SHSM.

52. For an introduction to the environmental costs of settlement, see F. Terry Norris, "Where Did the Villages Go? Steamboats, Deforestation and Archaeological Loss in the Mississippi Valley," in *Common Fields: An Environmental History of St. Louis*, ed. Andrew Hurley (St. Louis: Missouri Historical Society, 1997), 79–82.

CHAPTER 5

1. Clarinda P. Tate to Jane Tate, April 24, October 1, December 14, 1823, Missouri History Papers, MHM.

2. Danbom, *Born in the Country*, 90–91; Burke, *On Slavery's Border*, 134.

3. Andrew Cayton and Peter Onuf have contended that the argument that "settlers were ever fully self-sufficient is now generally discredited." Andrew R. L. Cayton and Peter S. Onuf, *The Midwest and the Nation: Rethinking the*

History of an American Region (Bloomington: Indiana University Press, 1990), 35; October 17, 1834, Frederick Steines's Letters, SHSM.

4. Bettye Hobbs Pruitt, "Self-Sufficiency and the Agricultural Economy of Eighteenth-Century Massachusetts," *William and Mary Quarterly*, 3rd Series, 41, no. 3 (July 1984): 333–338, 348–352.

5. Pruitt, "Self-Sufficiency," 338, 348–356, 364; Carole Shammas, "How Self-Sufficient Was Early America?" *Journal of Interdisciplinary History* 13, no. 2 (Autumn 1982): 247, 252–257, 260–268.

6. Charles Joseph Latrobe, *The Rambler in North America, 1832–1833* (London: R. G. Seeley and W. Burnside, 1835), 135–137.

7. Robert V. Hine, *Community on the American Frontier: Separate But Not Alone* (Norman: University of Oklahoma Press, 1980), 104; Faragher, *Sugar Creek*, 131–136; Nancy Grey Osterud, *Bonds of Community: The Lives of Farmwomen in Nineteenth Century New York* (Ithaca, N.Y.: Cornell University Press, 1991), 216–218.

8. Bradbury, *Travels in the Interior of America*, 5:282–283; August 23, September 1, 21, 24, 28, November 11, 12, 16, 19, 1844, Archibald Little Hager Diary, SHSM. Hager, who lived in Perry County, about sixty miles south of St. Louis, is technically outside the regional bounds of this study. Hager does provide a useful estimate of the regularity of such neighborhood assistance, though.

9. Everett Dick, *The Dixie Frontier: A Social History* (Norman: University of Oklahoma Press, 1993), 125–127.

10. W. J. Rorabaugh, *The Alcoholic Republic: An American Tradition* (Oxford: Oxford University Press, 1979), 7–14, 18–19, 95–97; Jordan and Kaups, *American Backwoods Frontier*, 118; Bidwell and Falconer, *History of Agriculture*, 169; Reginald Horsman, *Feast or Famine: Food and Drink in American Westward Expansion* (Columbia: University of Missouri Press, 2008), 30, 35–36; Drake, *Pioneer Life in Kentucky*, 188; Woods, *Two Years Residence*, 30.

11. Ovid Bell, "Pioneer Life in Callaway County," *Missouri Historical Review* 21, no. 2 (January 1927): 162–163; Bidwell and Falconer, *History of Agriculture*, 169; Palmer, *Journal of Travels Over the Rocky Mountains*, 13; William S. Bryant and Robert Rose, *A History Of The Pioneer Families Of Missouri, With Numerous Sketches, Anecdotes, Adventures, Etc., Relating To Early Days In Missouri. Also The Lives Of Daniel Boone And The Celebrated Indian Chief Black Hawk, With Numerous Biographies And Histories Of Primitive Institu-*

tions (St. Louis: Bryan, Brand, 1876), 71–72; Drake, *Pioneer Life in Kentucky*, 82–83; Sam L. Wilson to Joseph Winston, June 12, 1827, folder 2, Winston Family Papers, SHSM.

12. Drake, *Pioneer Life in Kentucky*, 189–190; Fortescue Cuming, *Sketches of a Tour to the Western Country: Through the States of Ohio and Kentucky; a Voyage down the Ohio and Mississippi rives and a Trip through the Mississippi Territory and part of West Florida. Commenced at Philadelphia in the Winter of 1807, and concluded in 1809*, in Thwaites, *Early Western Travels*, 4:135–136.

13. March 26, 1851, Archibald Little Hager Diary, SHSM; January 27, April 12, August 4, 1858, Charles Wesley Gilliam Diary, SHSM.

14. Alonzo M. Swan, *Canton: Its Pioneers and History. A Contribution to the History of Fulton County* (Peoria, Ill.: N. C. Mason, 1871), 70–72; Drake, *Pioneer Life in Kentucky*, 54–56; David William Graves Autobiography, 25, SHSM.

15. July 8, 1835, Frederick Steines's Letters, SHSM.

16. Draper, "Farming in Missouri"; Arthur G. Draper, ed., "Farming on the Missouri Frontier: Essays by Philander Draper," *Missouri Historical Review* 87, no. 1 (October 1992): 18–21.

17. William G. Bek, "The Followers of Duden: The American as Neighbor," *Missouri Historical Review* 16, no. 3 (April 1922): 345; Ethel Grant Inman, "Pioneer Days in Northwest Missouri—Harrison County, 1837–1873," *Missouri Historical Review* 22, no. 3 (April 1928): 316–319; William G. Bek, "The Followers of Duden: Gert Goebel," *Missouri Historical Review* 16, no. 2 (January 1922): 289–290.

18. October 29, November 6, 1855, June 28, 1856, March 1, July 20, August 10, September 10, 23, October 12, 20, November 5, 26, December 16, 1857, folder 17, Mary Ann Kitzmillen Diary, Fannie Blair Long Papers, SHSM.

19. November 20, 1823, July 3, 1824, May 28, 1828, March 15, 1831, August 10, 1832, October 1, 1833, May 11, 1836, June 25, July 12, September 19, October 1, 1837, June 2, 1838, January 11, February 8, 1839, William Nash Diary, MHM.

20. August 14, 15, 23, September 5, 11, 14, 18, 27, 28, October 12, 15, 1835, January 29, 1836, Thomas Keyes Humphreys Diary, MHM.

21. January 14, February 16, 17, 24, March 2, April 19, 26, 30, May 13, 17, 18, 21, 31, June 8, 20, 27, 1836, Thomas Keyes Humphreys Diary, MHM.

22. December 8, 1836, January 23, February 2, 4, 8, 23, March 9, 15, 22, 28,

April 7, 15, May, 15, 19, September 1, 2, 26, 1837, Thomas Keyes Humphreys Diary, MHM.

23. May 21, 27, August 5, October 22, November 17, 20, 1855, January 6, May 4, 1856, August 26, 1858, Pauline Stratton Diary, Pauline H. Stratton Papers, SHSM.

24. Danbom, *Born in the Country*, 91–92.

25. Karen V. Hansen, *A Very Social Time: Crafting Community in Antebellum New England* (Berkeley: University of California Press, 1994), 79–84, 106–109.

26. Drake, *Pioneer Life in Kentucky*, 183–184; Mildred Arrington Huckstep Gillum to Christina Jones, June 4, 1839, Missouri History Papers, MHM.

27. January 19, 23, 25, 27, 29, 30, February 16, 17, 18, 20, 21, 22, 24, 26, 27, 28, 1859, Franklin Burt Diary, Franklin Burt Papers, SHSM; September 21, November 17, 1857, January 10, 16, 25, 1858, March 13, 14, 23, April 18, May 2, June 21, 22, 23, 26, 1858, Charles Wesley Gilliam Diary, SHSM.

28. Thomas J. McCormack, ed., *Memoirs of Gustave Koerner, 1809–1896: Life Sketches Written at the Suggestion of His Children* (Cedar Rapids, Iowa: Torch Press, 1909), 1:311, 315, 319, 321–322.

29. April 17, 26, 29, May 9, June 13, 1857, Martha J. Woods Diary, Arrow Rock Tavern Board Papers, SHSM.

30. William Graham Johnston, *Experiences of a Forty-Niner* (Pittsburgh: n.p., 1892), 25; Klein, "Letters of a Young Surveyor," 61–62, 74.

31. McCandless, *History of Missouri*, 2:33–37.

CHAPTER 6

1. Carol K. Coburn, *Life at Four Corners: Religion, Gender and Education in a German-Lutheran Community, 1868–1948* (Lawrence: University Press of Kansas, 1992), 86, 155, 159; Joan M. Jensen, *Loosening the Bonds: Mid-Atlantic Farm Women, 1750–1850* (New Haven, Conn.: Yale University Press, 1986), 91, 116; McCandless, *History of Missouri*, 2:31, 136–138; Glenda Riley, *Frontierswomen: The Iowa Experience* (Ames: Iowa State University Press, 1994), 58; Paul E. Johnson, *The Early American Republic, 1789–1829* (New York: Oxford University Press, 2007), 64–67; Raymond D. Thomas, "Missouri Valley Settlement: St. Louis to Independence," *Missouri Historical Review* 21, no. 1 (October 1926): 40; Nancy Grey Osterud, "Gender and the Transition

to Capitalism in Rural America," *Agricultural History* 67, no. 2 (Spring 1993): 22–23; Eliza Wallace to Kitty Hinde, July 2, 1849, Hinde Family Papers, SHSM.

2. For a good summary of the role of women in Missouri history, see Mary K. Dains, "Missouri Women in Historical Writing," *Missouri Historical Review* 83, no. 4 (July 1989): 417–428. The most useful work on nineteenth-century women is Carla Waal and Barbara Oliver Korner, eds. *Hardship and Hope: Missouri Women Writing About Their Lives, 1820–1920* (Columbia: University of Missouri Press, 1997). See also Burke, *On Slavery's Border*, 55, 69, 105, 134–138.

3. Laurel Thatcher Ulrich, *A Midwife's Tale: The Life of Martha Ballard, Based on Her Diary, 1785–1812* (New York: Vintage Books, 1990), 29–30, 76–77, 84; Linda Schelbitzki Pickle, *Contented among Strangers: Rural German-Speaking Women and Their Families in the Nineteenth-Century Midwest* (Urbana: University of Illinois Press, 1996), 56.

4. Susan Sessions Rugh, *Our Common Country: Family Farming, Culture, and Community in the Nineteenth-Century Midwest* (Bloomington: Indiana University Press, 2001), 65–66; Jeanne Boydston, *Home and Work: Housework, Wages, and the Ideology of Labor in the Early Republic* (Oxford: Oxford University Press, 1990), 11–13, 97.

5. Sarah Elbert, "The Farmer Takes a Wife: Women in America's Farming Families," in *Women, Households and the Economy*, ed. Lourdes Beneria and Catharine R. Stimpson (New Brunswick, N.J.: Rutgers University Press, 1987), 174, 184; Christopher Phillips and Jason C. Pendleton, eds., *The Union on Trial: The Political Journals of Judge William Barclay Napton, 1829–1883* (Columbia: University of Missouri Press, 2005), 27–35.

6. May 22–29, 1855, folder 17, Mary Ann Kitzmillen Diary, Fannie Blair Long Papers, SHSM; Riley, *Frontierswomen*, 64–65. Kitzmillen and her family lived near Lewistown in southwest Lewis County in northeast Missouri.

7. October 4, 7, 13, 15, 16, 17, 19, 22, 23, 27, 30, November 5, 7, 13, 16, December 8, 20, 23, 1855, folder 17, Mary Ann Kitzmillen Diary, Fannie Blair Long Papers, SHSM.

8. Faragher, *Women and Men on the Overland Trail*, 52–53; Osterud, *Bonds of Community*, 169–171; Sara Lockwood Williams, "Pioneer Days in 'Old Sparta,'" *Missouri Historical Review* 25, no. 4 (July 1931): 551–552, 554. The article is mostly a reminiscence by the author's aunt, set in the 1850s.

9. Faragher, *Women and Men on the Overland Trail*, 50–51; Jack Larkin, *The*

Reshaping of Everyday Life, 1790–1840 (New York: Harper and Row, 1988), 15–17; Edith Burris, "Patsy the Pioneer," SHSM.

10. West, *Growing Up with the Country*, 73–75, 97–98.

11. Faragher, *Sugar Creek*, 100; Drake, *Pioneer Life in Kentucky*, 35–36, 47–48, 64–68, 70, 72, 76, 91–93.

12. West, *Growing Up with the Country*, 76–78, 82–88.

13. Glenda Riley, *The Female Frontier: A Comparative View of Women on the Prairie and the Plains* (Lawrence: University Press of Kansas, 1988), 52, 84–85; Rugh, *Our Common Country*, 20–21.

14. Burris, "Patsy the Pioneer"; Faragher, *Women and Men on the Overland Trail*, 51–53; Larkin, *Reshaping of Everyday Life*, 17–18, 27–30; Adolf E. Schroeder and Carla Schulz-Geisberg, eds., *Hold Dear, As Always, Jette: A German Immigrant Life in Letters* (Columbia: University of Missouri Press, 1988), 34, 51, 79, 86, 91–92, 127.

15. Schroeder and Schulz-Geisberg, *Hold Dear*, 7–9, 69–70. Dr. Bruns was inspired to immigrate to the United States by Gottfried Duden's book about his three years of farming in central Missouri. See Duden, *Report on a Journey to the Western States*.

16. Schroeder and Schulz-Geisberg, *Hold Dear*, 9–13, 73–79, 83, 85, 89, 91–93. For further biographical information on Bruns, see Margaret Baker Graham, ed., "Stories of Everyday Living: The Life and Letters of Margaret Bruin Machette," *Missouri Historical Review* 93, no. 4 (July 1999): 367–385.

17. Schroeder and Schulz-Geisberg, *Hold Dear*, 28, 92, 105–107, 109, 111, 127.

18. Schroeder and Schulz-Geisberg, *Hold Dear*, 13–15, 159, 165.

19. See the Day Book of Natalie Kuemmel, Natalie Wagner Kuemmel Notebook, SHSM, for a detailed example of how much sewing and mending she completed. In eleven days at the start of January 1861, Kuemmel mended, sewed, or made twenty-six pieces of clothing, sheets, gloves, or neckerchiefs. There was a list of fifty items on her "Make and Mend" list, including shirt collars, pants, gloves, dresses, stockings, shirts, and socks.

20. "Autobiography of J. A. Ward," James Alexander Ward Memoir, SHSM; Williams, "Pioneer Days," 553–554; Rugh, *Our Common Country*, 17–20; Faragher, *Sugar Creek*, 99–105; Osterud, *Bonds of Community*, 12, 147–150; Faragher, *Women and Men on the Overland Trail*, 50–51; Burnett and Luebbering, *German Settlement in Missouri*, 55–56.

21. Memoirs of Martha Tyler Overall, 6–9, folder 440, Missouri Collection, SHSM. Her reminiscences were written between 1922 and 1924.

22. Memoirs of Martha Tyler Overall, 16, 29, 32, 36, 48, folder 440, Missouri Collection, SHSM.

23. Linda Schelbitzki Pickle, "German-Speaking Women in Nineteenth Century Missouri: The Immigrant Experience," in *Women in Missouri History: In Search of Power and Influence*, ed. LeeAnn Whites, Mary C. Neth, and Gary R. Kremer (Columbia: University of Missouri Press, 2004), 59–60.

24. Sarah J. Gregory, ed., "Pioneer Housewife: The Autobiography of Sally Dodge Morris," *Gateway Heritage* 3, no. 4 (Spring 1983): 25–27, 32–33. Morris died in California in 1902 at the age of ninety-one.

25. Elise Dubach Isley, *Sunbonnet Days, by Elise Dubach Isley, as Told to Her Son, Bliss Isley* (Caldwell, Idaho: Caxton Printers, 1935), 7–8, 59–80.

26. Isley, *Sunbonnet Days*, 65, 86, 94.

27. James Williams, *75 Years on the Border* (Kansas City, Mo.: Press of Standard Printing, 1912), 2–3, 5, 59–61.

28. January 12, 14, 20, 27, March 10, April 10, May 1, October 5, 1856, Pauline Stratton Diary, Pauline H. Stratton Papers, SHSM; 1860 Slave Census for Cooper County, Missouri; 1860 Population Census, Missouri; *Agriculture of the United States in 1860: Complied From The Original Returns of the Eighth Census* (Washington, D.C.: Government Printing Office, 1864), 233–234; Hurt, *Agriculture and Slavery*, 221; Burke, *On Slavery's Border*, 134–136.

29. July 6, December 4, 1856, November 28, 1857, April 21, May 8, 1859, Pauline Stratton Diary, Pauline H. Stratton Papers, SHSM; 1860 Population Census.

30. Burke, *On Slavery's Border*, 135–138.

31. February 16, April 6, July 20, 1856, January 18, February 17, 22, April 23, 1857, June 12, August 27, 1859, Pauline Stratton Diary, Pauline H. Stratton Papers, SHSM.

32. January 12, 14, February 16, March 2, 14, 28, April 6, 30, June 2, 9, July 20, September 23, October 5, December 24, 1856, Pauline Stratton Diary, Pauline H. Stratton Papers, SHSM.

33. Early February, February 22, mid-March (n.d.), April 1, 23, November 27, mid-December, late December 1857, Pauline Stratton Diary, Pauline H. Stratton Papers, SHSM. See the list following the April 1861 entries (no exact date) for sales in 1860–1861. The $22 income estimate is a conservative

one, based on a price of fifteen cents per pound of butter, an average price she received.

34. *Agriculture of the United States in 1860*, lxxxii; 1860 Population Census for Cooper County. Neither the 1850 nor the 1860 census recorded information on egg production. Cooper County had 13,528 white residents in 1860. See the *Seventh Census of the United States, 1850* (Washington, D.C.: Robert Armstrong, Public Printer, 1853) for information on Missouri's farm production.

35. The Strattons earned six-and-a-half cents per pound for a large, 200-pound hog, or approximately $13 each. Pauline earned $1.50 for a dozen chickens on July 22, 1860, and this price is used when no price is provided to estimate income for the year. A price of ten cents per dozen eggs is used, as this is a common price she earned for this product. Fifteen cents per pound of butter is a common price, used here when no other price is given. A price of ten cents per pound for bacon is assumed (no price given in diary), and this seems to be a low price for Missouri about 1860. The price for bacon in Platte County, Missouri, in May 1857 was thirteen cents a pound, while the average wholesale price of bacon in New Orleans in 1859–1860 was eleven cents per pound. See Roger L. Ransom and Richard Sutch, *One Kind of Freedom: The Economic Consequences of Emancipation* (London: Cambridge University Press, 1977), 218; William McClurg Paxton, *Annals of Platte County, Missouri, From Its Exploration Down To June 1, 1897: With Genealogies of Its Noted Families and Sketches of Its Pioneer and Distinguished People* (Kansas City, Mo.: Hudson-Kimberly, 1897), 236; November 21, 1858, April 28, June 12, August 27, 1859, January 16, February 27, March 7, April 22, May 1, June 1, July 22, August 14, 23, October 27, 28, November 11, 17, 29, 1860, Pauline Stratton Diary, Pauline H. Stratton Papers, SHSM. There is a chart, "May 1860," on pages 11 and 12 in the diary that also lists sales of butter for 1860. The sale of seventeen pounds of butter in August and twenty-one pounds of butter in November is replicated in her diary and not included in these calculations.

36. Faragher, *Sugar Creek*, 96–105; Riley, *Frontierswomen*, 56–58, 69–77; Osterud, *Bonds of Community*, 1–5, 147–152, 179–180; Christopher Morris, *Becoming Southern: The Evolution of a Way of Life, Warren County and Vicksburg, Mississippi, 1770–1860* (New York: Oxford University Press, 1995), 45–47.

CHAPTER 7

1. Danbom, *Born in the Country*, 75.

2. Flint, *Recollections*, xiv–xvi, xxii, 76–78; Marie George Windell, ed., "The Road West in 1818, The Diary of Henry Vest Bingham, Part II," *Missouri Historical Review* 40, no. 2 (January 1946): 189.

3. Flint, *Recollections*, 78–80; Christian Schultz, *Travels On an Inland Voyage Through the States of New York, Pennsylvania, Virginia, Ohio, Kentucky and Tennessee, And Through the Territories of Indiana, Louisiana, Mississippi and New-Orleans: Performed In the Years 1807 and 1808; Including A tour of Nearly Six Thousand Miles* (New York: Isaac Riley, 1810), 1:116; Beckwith, "Early Customs."

4. Basil Hall, *Travels in North America, in the Years 1827, 1828* (Edinburgh: Simpkin and Marshall, 1830), 3:348–350; Peyton, *Over the Alleghanies*, 263–264; James E. Fickle, *Mississippi Forests and Forestry* (Jackson: University Press of Mississippi, 2001), 48–49; Adam I. Kane, *The Western River Steamboat* (College Station: Texas A&M Press, 2004), 23–24; Charles MacKay, *Life and Liberty in America: Sketches of a Tour in the United States and Canada in 1857–1858* (New York: Harper and Brothers, 1859), 155. Peyton complained of frequent delays when wood was loaded for fuel. A cord of wood is a stack eight feet long, four feet wide, and four feet high.

5. Beckwith, "Early Customs"; Hall, *Travels in North America*, 3:348; Beckwith's collected writings, cobbled together here in "Early Customs," were copied from his notebook in 1910. According to Hall, $2.50 to $3.00 was a regular price for a cord of wood.

6. Michael Allen, *Western Rivermen, 1763–1861: Ohio and Mississippi Boatmen and the Myth of the Alligator Horse* (Baton Rouge: Louisiana State University Press, 1990), 147–150; Eric Rutkow, *American Canopy: Trees, Forests and the Making of a Nation* (New York: Scribner, 2012), 110.

7. Lewis Atherton, *The Frontier Merchant in Mid-America* (Columbia: University of Missouri Press, 1971): 45–47; Paul J. Uselding, "Peddling in the Antebellum Economy: Precursor of Mass-Marketing or a Start in Life?" *American Journal of Economics and Sociology* 34, no. 1 (January 1975): 57–62.

8. Bryan and Rose, *History Of The Pioneer Families of Missouri*, 78–79.

9. Atherton, *Frontier Merchant*, 45–48; Charles J. Farmer, *In the Absence of Towns: Settlement and Country Trade in Southside Virginia, 1730–1800* (Lanham,

Md.: Rowman and Littlefield, 1993), 139–142; Joseph T. Rainer, "The 'Sharper' Image: Yankee Peddlers, Southern Consumers and the Market Revolution," in *Cultural Change and the Market Revolution in America, 1789–1860*, ed. Scott C. Martin (Lanham, Md.: Rowman and Littlefield, 2005), 89–97, 107–108; Uselding, "Peddling in the Antebellum Economy," 63; *Michigan Farmer* (January 1855), 245.

10. Thomas D. Clark, "Manners and Humors of the American Frontier," *Missouri Historical Review* 35, no. 1 (October 1940): 22–23; John Ludlum McConnel, *Western Characters: Or, Types of Border Life in Western States* (New York: Redfield, 1853), 279–282; *Laws of the State of Missouri, Passed at the First Session of the Twentieth General Assembly* (Jefferson City: C. J. Corwin, Public Printer, 1859), 300.

11. Atherton, *Frontier Merchant*, 46–47; John James Audubon, *The Life of John James Audubon, The Naturalist* (New York: G. P. Putnam's Sons, 1873), 35–36, 40, 45. This incident occurred about 1807, for Audubon claimed to have met a returning French member of the Lewis and Clark expedition.

12. McCormack, *Memoirs of Gustave Koerner*, 1:314; Cayton and Onuf, *Midwest and the Nation*, 30–36.

13. Hurt, "Seeking Fortune," 8–9; Cayton and Onuf, *Midwest and the Nation*, 30–36; Davis, *Frontier Illinois*, 104–105, 171; Peter Hardeman Burnett, *Recollections and Opinions of an Old Pioneer* (New York: D. Appleton, 1880), 9; "For the Brunswicker," 5, Lisbon Applegate Collection, SHSM.

14. Taylor, *Transportation Revolution*, 15–16, 56; Stuart F. Voss, "Town Growth in Central Missouri: An Urban Chaparral, Part III," *Missouri Historical Review* 64, no. 3 (April 1970): 323; Cayton and Onuf, *Midwest and the Nation*, 39; McCandless, *History of Missouri*, 2:31, 137–139.

15. March 18, 25, May 31, 1852, Lisbon Basye Diary, Typescript Collection, vol. 1, no. 4, SHSM.

16. Taylor, *Transportation Revolution*, 56; Erik F. Haites, James Mak, and Gary M. Walton, *Western River Transportation: The Era of Early Internal Development, 1810–1860* (Baltimore: Johns Hopkins University Press, 1975), 11, 14–15; Donald T. Zimmer, "The Ohio River: Pathway to Settlement," in *Transportation and the Early Nation* (Indianapolis: Indiana Historical Society, 1982), 64; George Lewis Prentiss, ed., *A Memoir of S. S. Prentiss* (New York: Charles Scribner, 1856), 1:182–183.

17. James Hall, *The West: Its Commerce and Navigation* (Cincinnati: H. W.

Derby, 1848), 166; Latrobe, *Rambler in North America*, 112–113; Timothy Flint, *The History and Geography of the Mississippi Valley. To Which Is Appended A Condensed Physical Geography of the Atlantic United States, And the Whole American Continent* (Cincinnati: E. H. Flint, 1833), 1:156–157.

18. Taylor, *Transportation Revolution*, 57–58, 63–64; Haites, Mak, and Walton, *Western River Transportation*, 15–17; Zimmer, "Ohio River," 64–65, 74. For an excellent account of flatboat life, see Michael Allen, ed., "Reminiscences of a Common Boatman (1849–1851)," *Gateway Heritage* 5, no. 2 (Fall 1984): 36–49.

19. F. A. Sampson, "Washington Irving: Travels in Missouri and the South," *Missouri Historical Review* 5, no. 1 (October 1910): 17–18; Washington Irving, *The Works of Washington Irving*, vol. 8, *Astoria: Or Anecdotes Of An Enterprise Beyond the Rocky Mountains* (New York: G. P. Putnam, 1861), 136–137; John B. Wyeth, *Oregon: Or A Short History Of A Long Journey From The Atlantic Ocean To The Region Of The Pacific, By Land*, in Thwaites, *Early Western Travels*, 21:46–47.

20. Haites, Mak, and Walton, *Western River Transportation*, 17–20; Zimmer, "Ohio River," 74–75; James Mak and Gary M. Walton, "Steamboats and the Great Productivity Surge in River Transportation," *Journal of Economic History* 32, no. 3 (September 1972): 619–620; Erik F. Haites and James Mak, "Steamboating on the Mississippi, 1810–1860: A Purely Competitive Industry," *Business History Review* 45, no. 1 (Spring 1971): 52–53.

21. Haites, Mak, and Walton, *Western River Transportation*, 18–19; Haites and Mak, "Steamboating on the Mississippi," 52–54; Jeremy Atack and Fred Bateman, "Marketable Farm Surpluses: Northeastern and Midwestern United States, 1859 and 1860," *Social Science History* 8, no. 4 (August 1984): 372–373, 383; Kane, *Western River Steamboat*, 127–128.

22. Taylor, *Transportation Revolution*, 3–9, 29, 32–47, 396–398; Johnson, *Early American Republic*, 55–56, 64–67; Wyman, *Wisconsin Frontier*, 128–129; Gregory H. Nobles, "Commerce and Community: A Case Study of the Rural Broom-making Business in Antebellum Massachusetts," *Journal of the Early Republic* 4, no. 3 (Autumn 1984): 295–296; Paul Wallace Gates, "The Railroads of Missouri, 1850–1870," *Missouri Historical Review* 26, no. 2 (January 1932): 129–130, 132–138. There were only 689 miles of track in the state by January 1, 1860, mostly built in the late 1850s.

23. Hunter, *Steamboats on Western Rivers*, 12–13, 21, 38, 47; Zimmer, "Ohio

River," 68; Franklin *Missouri Intelligencer*, May 28, 1819, June 16, 1826; Fayette *Missouri Intelligencer*, March 21, 1828, January 29, 1830; Dorothy Dorsey, "The Panic and Depression of 1837–1843 in Missouri," *Missouri Historical Review* 30, no. 2 (January 1936): 134; David Dary, *The Santa Fe Trail: Its History, Legends, and Lore* (New York: Penguin Books, 2000), 65.

24. Taylor, *Transportation Revolution*, 63–65; Haites, Mak, and Walton, *Western River Transportation*, 18–21, 32, 49; Primm, *Lion of the Valley*, 134–135; Johnson, *Early American Republic*, 65–66; Davis, *Frontier Illinois*, 169–170; Robert Baird, *View of the Valley of the Mississippi, Or the Emigrants' and Traveller's Guide To The West. Containing A General Description of That Entire Country: And Also Notices of the Soil, Productions, Rivers, and Other Channels of Intercourse and Trade: And Likewise of the Cities and Towns, Progress of Education, &c. of Each State and Territory* (Philadelphia: H. S. Tanner, 1834), 340–342.

25. Haites, Mak, and Walton, *Western River Transportation*, 49–50; McCandless, *History of Missouri*, 2:137; R. Rowland to Mary Ann Rowland, November 25, 1840, R. Rowland Letter, Western Travel Collection, MHM; Columbia *Patriot*, March 19, 1842.

26. Haites and Mak, "Steamboating on the Mississippi," 54–55, 61, 62, 70; Mak and Walton, "Steamboats and the Great Productivity Surge," 625–626, 628–629, 631; Liberty *Weekly Tribune*, May 6, 1853, April 7, 1854, April 4, 1856, November 6, 1857, September 1, 1859.

27. Melinda Houston Estes, "Old Memories," Typescript Collection, vol. 20, no. 548, SHSM.

28. Hurt, *Agriculture and Slavery*, 65–66; Primm, *Lion of the Valley*, 134–135; July 21, 1835, Frederick Steines's Letters, SHSM; William E. Lass, "Tourists' Impressions of St. Louis, 1763–1859, Part II," *Missouri Historical Review* 53, no. 1 (October 1958): 16.

29. George W. C. Huse to Carr Huse, July 22, 1846, St. Louis History Collection, MHM; William F. Switzler, "A Trip to the South," 23, Switzler Family Papers, MHM; Zimmerman, "Travel into Missouri," 34; James S. Cowan to John W. Ellis, June 25, 1847, James S. Cowan Letter, SHSM. For an account of a steamboat wreck and the great Missouri flood of 1844, see Ralph Gregory, ed., "The Autobiography of Henry Wellenkamp, 1822–1907," *Missouri Historical Society Bulletin* 19, no. 4 (July 1963): 319–324.

30. Voss, "Town Growth in Central Missouri, Part I," 65; McCandless, *History of Missouri*, 2:131; Gustorf, *Uncorrupted Heart*, 122.

31. Peyton, *Over the Alleghanies*, 269–270.

32. Voss, "Town Growth in Central Missouri, Part III", 323; Voss, "Town Growth in Central Missouri, Part I," 65–67, 76–80; Schroeder, "Spread of Settlement," 18–19; Hurt, "Seeking Fortune," 9–12; Jonas Viles, "Old Franklin: A Frontier Town of the Twenties," *Mississippi Valley Historical Review* 9, no. 4 (March 1923): 269–275; Fayette *Missouri Intelligencer*, May 2, 1828,; Dary, *Santa Fe Trail*, 108.

33. Hurt, *Agriculture and Slavery*, 103, 109–110; Miles W. Eaton, "The Development and Later Decline of the Hemp Industry in Missouri," *Missouri Historical Review* 43, no. 4 (July 1949): 344–346, 349, 351; Scarpino, "Slavery in Callaway County," 24–25, 32; Aron, *How The West Was Lost*, 128–129.

34. Hurt, "Seeking Fortune," 11; Eldon Hattervig, "Jefferson Landing: A Commercial Center of the Steamboat Era," *Missouri Historical Review* 74, no. 3 (April 1980): 277–278; Stephen G. Hyslop, *Bound for Santa Fe: The Road to New Mexico and the American Conquest, 1806–1848* (Norman: University of Oklahoma Press, 2002), 109; McCandless, *History of Missouri*, 2:132; Inscoe, *Mountain Masters*, 30–31, 37–38; J. A. Pritchard, "Diary of a Journey from Kentucky to California in 1849," *Missouri Historical Review* 18, no. 4 (July 1924): 541.

35. Josiah Gregg, *The Commerce of the Prairies*, ed. Milo Milton Quaife (1844; repr., Lincoln: University of Nebraska Press, 1967), 20–22; Bidwell and Falconer, *History of Agriculture*, 308; Dary, *Santa Fe Trail*, 107–110.

36. Hyslop, *Bound for Santa Fe*, 37–43; David J. Weber, *The Mexican Frontier, 1821–1846: The American Southwest under Mexico* (Albuquerque: University of New Mexico Press, 1982), 125, 128–129; McCandless, *History of Missouri*, 2:128–130.

37. McCandless, *History of Missouri*, 2:119, 128–131; Hyslop, *Bound for Santa Fe*, 40–50; Gregg, *Commerce of the Prairies*, 6–10; Authorene Wilson Phillips, *Arrow Rock: The Story of a Missouri Village* (Columbia: University of Missouri Press, 2005), 35–40; Franklin *Missouri Intelligencer*, October 28, 1823; Dary, *Santa Fe Trail*, 84–85.

38. Richard Gentry to wife, July 4, 1830, Richard Gentry to Richard Gentry, Sr., November 4, 1830, Richard Gentry Letters, Typescript Collection, vol. 2, no. 36, SHSM.

39. James Josiah Webb, *Adventures in the Santa Fe Trade, 1844–1847* (1931; repr., Lincoln: University of Nebraska Press, 1995), 23–28, 42–45, 127–129;

F. F. Stephens, "Missouri and the Santa Fe Trade," *Missouri Historical Review* 11, nos. 3–4 (April–July 1917): 295–300, 304–306, 309–310; Fayette *Missouri Intelligencer*, August 21, 1829; Columbia *Missouri Intelligencer*, April 2, 1831.

40. Dorsey, "Panic and Depression," 133–135; F. F. Stephens, ed., "Major Alphonso Wetmore's Diary of a Journey to Santa Fe, 1828," *Missouri Historical Review* 8, no. 4 (July 1914): 177–178, 183; Septimus Scholl to children, April 23, 1848, Hinde Family Papers, SHSM.

41. D. W. Meinig, *The Shaping of America*, vol. 2, *Continental America, 1800–1867* (New Haven, Conn.: Yale University Press, 1993), 101, 113; Francis Parkman, *The Oregon Trail* (1847; repr., New York: Library of America/Viking Press, 1991), 9–13; Howe, *What Hath God Wrought*, 717.

42. Malcolm J. Rohrbough, *Days of Gold: The California Gold Rush and the American Nation* (Berkeley: University of California Press, 1997), 1, 28, 31, 33, 56–61; Walker D. Wyman, ed., "California Emigrant Letters," *California Historical Society Quarterly* 24, no. 1 (March 1945): 27; Charles W. Bryan Jr., ed., "From Marthasville to Marysville in 1850," *Missouri Historical Society Bulletin* 19, no. 2 (January 1963): 115–116.

43. John D. Unruh Jr., *The Plains Across: The Overland Emigrants and the Trans-Mississippi West, 1840–1860* (Urbana: University of Illinois Press, 1979), 68, 73; Louise Barry, ed., "Overland to the Gold Fields of California in 1852: The Journal of John Hawkins Clark," *Kansas Historical Quarterly* 11, no. 3 (August 1942): 232; Edwin Bryant, *What I Saw in California: Being the Journal of A Tour By the Emigrant Route And South Pass of the Rocky Mountains, Across the Continent of North America, The Great Desert Basin And Through California, In the Years 1846, 1847* (New York: D. Appleton, 1849), 14.

44. William Kelly, *An Excursion to California Over The Prairie, Rocky Mountains, And Great Sierra Nevada. With A Stroll Through The Diggings And Ranches Of That Country* (London: Chapman and Hall, 1851), 1:31–33, 37, 41–43; Sam Wilson to mother, April 17, 1849, Sam S. Wilson Letter, SHSM.

45. John Evans Brown, *Memoirs of a Forty-Niner* (New Haven, Conn.: Associated Publishers of American Records, 1907), 5–6; Joseph Sedgley, *Overland to California in 1849* (Oakland, Calif.: Butler and Bowman, 1877), 10–13; Johnston, *Experiences of a Forty-Niner*, 25, 30, 42–44; Barry, "Overland to the Gold Fields," 232; J. S. Holliday, *The World Rushed In: The California Gold Rush Experience* (Norman: University of Oklahoma Press, 2002), 76–78, 88–89.

46. Walker D. Wyman, "The Outfitting Posts," *Pacific Historical Review* 18,

no. 1 (February 1949): 15–16; Kate L. Gregg, "Boonslickers in the Gold Rush to California," *Missouri Historical Review* 41, no. 4 (July 1947): 358; April 11, 14, 18, 27, 1849, John A. Stauder Diary, SHSM; Septimus Scholl to children, April 23, 1848, June 7, 1849, Hinde Family Papers, SHSM; April 24, 1849, James A. Tate Diary, SHSM.

47. "Farming in Missouri, &c," *Cultivator* 6 (October 1849): 302–303; Edward Bode, ed., "Charles Kleinsorge: Missouri to California in 1854," *Missouri Historical Review* 76, no. 4 (July 1982): 421–422, 427; *Report of the Commissioner of Patents For the Year 1853: Agriculture* (Washington, D.C.: A. O. P. Nicholson Printer, 1854), 11–12.

48. Elliott West, *The Contested Plains: Indians, Goldseekers, and the Rush to Colorado* (Lawrence: University Press of Kansas, 1998), 102–105, 120–122; Westport *Weekly Border State*, March 31, 1860; Clifford D. Carpenter, "The Early Cattle Industry in Missouri," *Missouri Historical Review* 47, no. 3 (April 1953): 202–204; April 19, 20, 22, 23, 26, 1859, William Yates Diary, SHSM. Merchants in Springfield, Missouri, in the southwest corner of the state, also advertised outfits for the Pike's Peak rush; see, for example, the Springfield *Mirror*, April 30, 1859.

49. Johnson, *Early American Republic*, 67; Davis, *Frontier Illinois*, 104–105, 113, 133–134; Cayton and Onuf, *Midwest and the Nation*, 29, 42; Rohrbough, *Trans-Appalachian Frontier*, 156, 207, 234; Ray Allen Billington, *Westward Expansion: A History of the American Frontier* (New York: Macmillan, 1960), 468–469; McCandless, *History of Missouri*, 2:31–35, 119.

CHAPTER 8

1. Duden, *Report on a Journey to the Western States*, xii–xiii, 52–57, 66–67, 176.

2. Duden, *Report on a Journey to the Western States*, 256–257; St. Louis *Daily Missouri Republican*, May 26, 1856. *Hunt's Merchant Magazine and Commercial Review* 22 (January 1850) listed goods and materials received in St. Louis in 1849. These included tobacco, hemp, corn, beef, and oats, as well as other items produced in rural areas and exported downriver to the city, such as brooms, hides, eggs, and bagging.

3. John G. Clark, "The Antebellum Grain Trade of New Orleans: The

Changing Patters in the Relations of New Orleans with the Old Northwest," *Agricultural History* 38, no. 3 (July 1964): 134–136; Warren R. Hofstra and Robert D. Mitchell, "Town and Country in Backcountry Virginia: Winchester and the Shenandoah Valley, 1730–1800," *Journal of Southern History* 59, no. 4 (November 1993): 621, 634–637, 642.

4. Hofstra and Mitchell, "Town and Country," 621, 642; Andrew H. Baker and Holly V. Izard, "New England Farmers and the Marketplace, 1780–1865," *Agricultural History* 65, no. 3 (Summer 1991): 29–30; Christopher Clark, *The Roots of Rural Capitalism: Western Massachusetts, 1780–1860* (Ithaca, N.Y.: Cornell University Press, 1990), 84–85; Clark, "Antebellum Grain Trade," 136; Boonville *Weekly Observer*, November 22, December 6, 13, 1856. One saloon even sold fresh oysters, "packed in ice," along with imported liquors and cigars; businesses also offered soap, tobacco, whiskey, salt, and other items to replace home production. See Boonville *Weekly Observer*, December 6, 1856.

5. Franklin *Missouri Intelligencer*, September 3, 1819, March 13, 1824; Dewitt Clinton Basey, "My Early Recollections of Brunswick," Typescript Collection, vol. 8, no. 347, SHSM; Burke, *On Slavery's Border*, 93.

6. Carr Waller Pritchett, "Memorabilia, 1904," Typescript Collection, vol. 8, no. 400, SHSM.

7. Mahoney, *River Towns of the Great West*, 44–49; Gruenwald, *River of Enterprise*, 28; Faragher, *Women and Men on the Overland Trail*, 42; Hurt, *Agriculture and Slavery*, 64–66; Klein, "Letters of a Young Surveyor," 83.

8. Schroeder, "Spread of Settlement," 15–20; Hurt, "Seeking Fortune," 9–15; Walter H. Ryle, "A Study of Early Days in Randolph County, 1818–1860," *Missouri Historical Review* 24, no. 2 (January 1930): 231–232.

9. Hurt, *Agriculture and Slavery*, 100–101; James William McGettigan Jr., "Boone County Slaves: Sales, Estate Divisions and Families, 1820–1865, Part 1," *Missouri Historical Review* 72, no. 2 (January 1978): 176, 180; Gates, *Farmer's Age*, 102–103.

10. Gert Goebel, *Longer Than a Lifetime*, ed. Martin W. Heinrichsmeyer (1877; repr., St. Louis: Missouri Historical Society, 1956), 83; Lucy Routt Bradford Duncan, "Early Days in Phelps County," *Missouri Historical Review* 19, no. 1 (October 1924): 99–100. Duncan's article is an autobiographical reminiscence.

11. Lewis E. Atherton, "The Services of the Frontier Merchant," *Mississippi Valley Historical Review* 24, no. 2 (September 1937): 156–163; Gruenwald, *River of Enterprise*, 4; David Blanke, *Sowing the American Dream: How Consumer*

Culture Took Root in the Rural Midwest (Athens: Ohio University Press, 2000), 67; Basey, "Early Recollections of Brunswick"; Liberty *Far Western*, September 8, October 6, 1836. The October 6 paper carried an advertisement for "wife wanted." A man requested a female companion who could "do everything well, but scold well."

12. Martin Bruegel, *Farm, Shop, Landing: The Rise of a Market Society in the Hudson Valley, 1780–1860* (Durham, N.C.: Duke University Press, 2002), 56, 162; Gruenwald, *River of Enterprise*, xii, 4, 42, 100; Atherton, "Services of the Frontier Merchant," 159–162.

13. Gruenwald, *River of Enterprise*, 28–31, 117; Blanke, *Sowing the American Dream*, 72; Larkin, *Reshaping of Everyday Life*, 133–145; Sarah Randleman Holcomb Barnes Reminiscence, SHSM.

14. John Barber White, "The Missouri Merchant One Hundred Years Ago," *Missouri Historical Review* 13, no. 2 (January 1919): 109–111. Bonnets were still popular in the late 1850s, see the California (Mo.) *Weekly California News*, November 6, 1858, July 2, 1859. Some merchants marketed directly to women, advertising satin, calico, scarfs, shawls, and hosiery. See *Weekly California News*, November 6, 1858, July 2, 1859, and Fayette *Boon's Lick Times*, April 12, 1845, May 8, 1847.

15. Luke Shortfield, *The Western Merchant, A Narrative, Containing Useful Instruction for the Western Man of Business Who Makes His Purchases in the East; Also, Information for the Eastern Man Whose Customers Are In the West; Likewise, Hints For Those Who Design Emigration to the West. Deduced From Actual Experience* (Philadelphia: Gregg, Elliot, 1849), 29, 40–49, 63, 123.

16. Inman, "Pioneer Days," 314.

17. Inman, "Pioneer Days," 314–315.

18. Ruth Ralls Fisher, "Record of the Haley Family in Missouri," Typescript Collection, vol. 13, no. 612, SHSM.

19. W. L. Irwin to brother, June 9, 1859, W. L. Irwin Letter, SHSM; Clark, "Household Economy," 172–174; Michael Shirley, "The Market and Community Culture in Antebellum North Carolina," *Journal of the Early Republic* 11, no. 2 (Summer 1991): 220–221, 227–229.

20. Farmer, *In the Absence of Towns*, 159–167; James R. Wettstaed, "A Look at Early Nineteenth Century Life in an Ozarks Mining Town: The View from the Company Store," *Plains Anthropologist* 45, no. 171 (February 2000): 89–90, 92, 93; Westport *Weekly Border State*, October 1, 1859. See the January 1848

entries, Hugh Elliott Account Book, vol. 4, Newton G. Elliott Papers, MHM, for examples of the variety of goods available, including tea, cambric, red flannel, lamp oil, nutmeg, rice, and pepper.

21. Mary Alice Kennedy, "The Business Career of Moses U. Payne, 1828–1870" (Master's thesis, University of Missouri, 1944), 5, 9, 12–16, 22–26; collection description for Payne-Broadwell Family Papers, SHSM.

22. Atherton, *Frontier Merchant*, 146; Kennedy, "Business Career of Moses U. Payne," 25–26, 33–36; J. M. and A. M. Payne Day Book, 1830–1831, vols. 3–4, Payne-Broadwell Family Papers, SHSM; Jacob Payne to Moses Payne, December 20, 1831, folder 6, Payne-Broadwell Family Papers, SHSM; O. Williams to Moses Payne, July 1832 (exact date illegible), folder 7, Payne-Broadwell Family Papers, SHSM; December 8, 1832, bill from Jacob Payne to Moses Payne, folder 7, Payne-Broadwell Family Papers, SHSM; MacKay Morton to Moses Payne, August 5, 1854, folder 18, Payne-Broadwell Family Papers, SHSM.

23. Kennedy, "Business Career of Moses U. Payne," 32–35, 38, 39–41, 47–50; Mauthe's Store Account Book, April 1 to July 31, 1859, sales, MHM. The Franklin business was Mauthe's store. George W. Walker and Hinton and Walker Account Book, 1855–1856, vol. 12, James Keyte Collection, SHSM, shows that this firm in Rocheport shipped large amounts of hemp, wheat, flour, tobacco, bacon, and lard to St. Louis between June 1855 (no exact date) and September 25, 1855. The firm must have collected foodstuffs from farmers in payment for goods bought at the store. On March 22, 1856, for example, it shipped lard, dried fruit, and wheat downriver.

24. Vol. 25, Aull Family Business Records, SHSM.

25. Lewis E. Atherton, "James and Robert Aull: A Frontier Missouri Mercantile Firm," *Missouri Historical Review* 93, no. 1 (October 1998): 27–28, 31, 40–41, 46–47; Atherton, "Services of the Frontier Merchant," 164; vol. 4, Aull Family Business Records, SHSM. The total value of the inventory was $8,777.74.

26. Gross, "Culture and Cultivation," 50; June 17 to July 10, Daybook of Store, 1839–1840, vol. 1, Aull Family Business Records, SHSM.

27. September 1 to September 30, 1854, vol. 7, Aull Family Business Records, SHSM.

28. December 14, 1819, to August 2, 1820, Jacob Wyan Day Book, Jacob Wyan Collection, MHM.

29. September 24, 1838, to June 1, 1839, Irwin Hockaday Account Book, Hockaday Family Papers, MHM. The Yates Account Book, T. S. Yates Account

Books, vol. 2 (July 7 to October 1, 1831, sample), SHSM, also shows this same pattern of consumption. Customers purchased mostly coffee, sugar, and various types of cloth, followed by salt, indigo, shoes, hats, nails, and tea. Merchants could be left with a surplus of goods, of course. Christian Wilt, who managed a store in St. Louis in the 1810s, complained that he had far more copies of *Love's Labor Lost* than he could sell in fifty years. Christian Wilt to Joseph Hertzog, September 18, 1813, Christian Wilt Papers, MHM.

30. Clark, *Roots of Rural Capitalism*, 170–171; Bruegel, *Farm, Shop, Landing*, 58–59; John Lauritz Larson, *The Market Revolution in America: Liberty, Ambition and the Eclipse of the Common Good* (New York: Cambridge University Press, 2010), 29, 57–58, 87–88, 167; Daniel Dupre, "Ambivalent Capitalists on the Cotton Frontier: Settlement and Development in the Tennessee Valley of Alabama," *Journal of Southern History* 56, no. 2 (May 1990): 235.

31. Clark, *Roots of Rural Capitalism*, 166–167; Atherton, "James and Robert Aull," 46–47; Aull Letter Book II, 210, 213, Aull Letter Book IV, 28, 79–80, Box 1, Ernestine Selter Collection, SHSM.

32. Aull Letter Book II, 201, 210–211, 213, 217, 221, Aull Letter Book IV, 50, 56, 63, 70, Box 1, Ernestine Selter Collection, SHSM; Columbia *Missouri Intelligencer*, October 27, 1832.

33. March 1831 bill from "C. & M. C. Cope," folder 56, Payne-Broadwell Family Papers, SHSM; March 1831 bill from "Busby & Sprague," folder 56, Payne-Broadwell Family Papers, SHSM; March 14, 1831, shipping bill, folder 56, Payne-Broadwell Family Papers, SHSM; undated bill from "Wood & Oliver," folder 56, Payne-Broadwell Family Papers, SHSM; March 10, 1831, shipping bill (name illegible), folder 56, Payne-Broadwell Family Papers, SHSM; James A. Ramage, *John Wesley Hunt: Pioneer Merchant, Manufacturer and Financier* (Lexington: University Press of Kentucky, 1974), 24–26; Atherton, *Frontier Merchant*, 66; Fayette *Boon's Lick Times*, September 26, October 3, 1840.

34. Good and bad debts, vol. 4, Aull Business Records, 1838, SHSM; Aull Business Records, vol. 10, SHSM; Gregory Nobles, "The Rise of Merchants in Rural Market Towns: A Case Study of Eighteenth-Century Northampton, Massachusetts, " *Journal of Social History* 24, no. 1 (Fall 1990): 9; Atherton, *Frontier Merchant*, 146–147.

35. William J. Bernstein, *A Splendid Exchange: How Trade Shaped the World* (New York: Grove Press, 2008), 339–340, 375; William E. Lass, *Navigating the Missouri: Steamboating on Nature's Highway, 1819–1935* (Norman: Uni-

versity of Oklahoma Press, 2007), 72–73, 77, 85, 91, 93, 128–131; Craig T. Friend, *Kentucke's Frontiers* (Bloomington: Indiana University Press, 2010), 240–244; Ann Smart Martin, *Buying into the World of Goods: Early Consumers in Backcountry Virginia* (Baltimore: Johns Hopkins University Press, 2008), 6–8, 54–56, 75–85.

36. Ford, "Yeoman Farmers," 29–32; Clark, "Household Economy," 176–177, 180–181; Nobles, "Rise of Merchants," 18; February 15, 1836, Frederick Steines's Letters, SHSM.

37. Bruegel, *Farm, Shop, Landing,* 218, 222–226.

CONCLUSION

1. Gruenwald, *River of Enterprise,* 4, 13, 114.

2. Faragher, *Sugar Creek,* 130–136, 181; Davis, *Frontier Illinois,* 349–351.

3. Rugh, *Our Common Country,* 16–23.

4. Danbom, *Born in the Country,* 75–77.

5. Clark, *Roots of Rural Capitalism,* 170, 280.

6. William E. Parrish, *A History of Missouri,* vol. 3, *1860 to 1875* (Columbia: University of Missouri Press, 1975), v, 59–62, 70, 79–80, 198–199, 210–212, 219–222.

7. Parrish, *History of Missouri,* 3:281–283, 287; Danbom, *Born in the Country,* 134, 152–153; David Thelen, *Paths of Resistance: Tradition and Dignity in Industrializing Missouri* (New York: Oxford University Press, 1986), 3–6, 44–45.

8. Thelen, *Paths of Resistance,* 44–46, 51–52.

9. *Report on the Productions of Agriculture As Reported In The Tenth Census* (Washington, D.C.: Government Printing Office, 1883), 13; Mary Eschelbach Hansen, "Land Ownership, Farm Size, and Tenancy after the Civil War," *Journal of Economic History* 58, no. 3 (September 1998): 822–824. The north-central region included states and territories from Ohio to Nebraska and Dakota.

10. Atack and Passell, *New Economic View of American History,* 423–424; Thelen, *Paths of Resistance,* 86–87, 92–99, 205–216.

11. Salstrom, *From Pioneering to Persevering,* 76–80, 125; Hurt, *American Agriculture,* 165, 172.

BIBLIOGRAPHY

UNPUBLISHED PRIMARY SOURCES

State Historical Society of Missouri, University of Missouri, Columbia

Lisbon Applegate Collection
Arrow Rock Tavern Board Papers
Aull Business Records
Aull Family Business Records
Sarah Holcomb Randleman Barnes Reminiscence
J. Calvin Berry Letter
Berry-Thomson-Walker Family Papers
Bingham Family Papers
Edith Burris, "Patsy the Pioneer"
Franklin Burt Papers
Bush Family Papers
James S. Cowan Letter
Draper-McClurg Family Papers
Theodore Dresser Letter
Duncan-Hardin-Jenkins Family Papers
Charles Wesley Gilliam Diary
J. Goodwin Letter
David William Graves Autobiography
Archibald Little Hager Diary
Thomas Harrison Letters
Harvey Family Papers
Hinde Family Papers
W. L. Irwin Letter

Herbert S. Jones, "Missouri–A Promised Land"
Archy Kasson Letter
Henry S. Kelley Autobiographical Sketch
Kensinger Family Papers
James Keyte Collection
Liliburn A. Kingsbury Collection
Natalie Wagner Kuemmel Notebook
Jacob Lanius Diary
Thomas C. Lannan Letters
Lenoir Family Letters
Walter R. Lenoir Letter
Ethelbert Lewis Letters
Fannie Blair Long Papers
David Manchester Letters
Mamie J. McCormick Papers
John D. McKown Papers
Jessie Mellon Letter
Missouri Collection
Payne-Broadwell Family Papers
Justus Post Letter
Justus Post Letters
William Powell Letters
William A. Richards Letters
Samuel L. Sawyer Letters
Ernestine Selter Collection
John A. Stauder Diary
Frederick Steines Letters
Pauline H. Stratton Papers
James A. Tate Diary
George F. and Ursula Terry Letters
Typescript Collection, State Historical Society of Missouri
James Alexander Ward Memoir
William Waye Papers
Sam S. Wilson Letter
Winston Family Papers
Woods-Holman Family Papers

T. S. Yates Account Books
William Yates Diary

Missouri History Museum Archives, St. Louis

Cooper County Collection
Newton G. Elliott Papers
Goddard Family Papers
Hockaday Family Papers
Thomas Keyes Humphreys Diary
Journals and Diaries Collection
Mauthe's Store Account Book
Missouri History Collection
Missouri History Envelope
Missouri History Papers
William Nash Diary
Justus Post Letters
St. Charles Collection
St. Louis History Collection
Switzler Family Papers
C. Corwith Wagner Collection
Western Travel Collection
Christian Wilt Papers
Jacob Wyan Collection

Government Documents

1860 Population Census
1860 Slave Census

NEWSPAPERS AND PERIODICALS

Albany (N.Y.) *Cultivator*
Boonville *Weekly Observer*
California (Mo.) *Weekly California News*
Columbia *Missouri Intelligencer*

Columbia *Patriot*
Fayette *Missouri Intelligencer*
Fayette *Boon's Lick Times*
Franklin *Missouri Intelligencer*
Hunt's Merchant Magazine and Commercial Review
Liberty *Far Western*
Liberty *Weekly Tribune*
Michigan Farmer
Springfield *Mirror*
St. Louis *Daily Missouri Republican*
Westport *Weekly Border State*

PUBLISHED PRIMARY SOURCES

Agriculture of the United States in 1860: Compiled From The Original Returns of the Eighth Census. Washington, D.C.: Government Printing Office, 1864.

Allen, Michael, ed. "Reminiscences of a Common Boatman (1849–1851)." *Gateway Heritage* 5, no. 2 (Fall 1984): 36–49.

Atherton, Lewis E., ed. "Life, Labor and Society in Boone County, Missouri, 1834–1852, As Revealed in the Correspondence of an Immigrant Slave Owning Family from North Carolina." Part 1. *Missouri Historical Review* 38, no. 3 (April 1944): 275–302.

———. "Life, Labor and Society in Boone County, Missouri, 1834–1852, As Revealed in the Correspondence of an Immigrant Slave Owning Family from North Carolina." Part 2. *Missouri Historical Review* 38, no. 4 (July 1944): 408–429.

Audubon, John James. *The Life of John James Audubon, The Naturalist*. New York: G. P. Putnam's Sons, 1873.

Audubon, Maria R., ed. *Audubon and His Journals*. Vol. 2. New York: Charles Scribner's Sons, 1897.

Babcock, Rufus, ed. *Forty Years of Pioneer Life: The Memoir of John Mason Peck*. 1864. Reprint, Carbondale: Southern Illinois University Press, 1965.

Baird, Robert. *View of the Valley of the Mississippi, Or the Emigrant's and Traveller's Guide To The West. Containing A General Description of That Entire Country: And Also Notices of the Soil, Productions, Rivers, and Other Channels of Intercourse and Trade: And Likewise of the Cities and Towns,*

Progress of Education, &c. of Each State and Territory. Philadelphia: H. S. Tanner, 1834.

Barry, Louise, ed. "Overland to the Gold Fields of California in 1852: The Journal of John Hawkins Clark." *Kansas Historical Quarterly* 11, no. 3 (August 1942): 227–292.

Bek, William G., ed. "The Followers of Duden: The American as Neighbor." *Missouri Historical Review* 16, no. 3 (April 1922): 343–383.

———. "The Followers of Duden: Gert Goebel." *Missouri Historical Review* 16, no. 2 (January 1922): 289–307.

———. "The Followers of Duden: Nicholas Hesse, German Visitor to Missouri, 1835–1837, Part One." *Missouri Historical Review* 41, no. 1 (October 1946): 19–44.

Bidwell, John. "The First Emigrant Train to California." *Century Illustrated Monthly Magazine* 41, no. 1 (November 1890): 106–130.

Birkbeck, Morris. *Notes On A Journey In America, From the Coast of Virginia to the Territory of Illinois*. London: Severa, 1818.

Bode, Edward, ed. "Charles Kleinsorge: Missouri to California in 1854." *Missouri Historical Review* 76, no. 4 (July 1982): 421–446.

Brackenridge, Henry Marie. *Views of Louisiana: Together with a Journal of a Voyage up the Missouri River, in 1811*. 1814. Reprint, Chicago: Quadrangle Books, 1962.

Bronaugh, J. H. "Western Missouri in 1837." *Missouri Historical Review* 20, no. 3 (April 1926): 388–392.

Brown, John Evans. *Memoirs of a Forty-Niner*. New Haven, Conn.: Associated Publishers of American Records, 1907.

Bryan, Charles W., Jr., ed. "From Marthasville to Marysville in 1850." *Missouri Historical Society Bulletin* 19, no. 2 (January 1963): 115–126.

Bryant, Edwin. *What I Saw in California: Being the Journal of A Tour By the Emigrant Route And South Pass of the Rocky Mountains, Across the Continent of North America, The Great Desert Basin And Through California, In the Years 1846, 1847*. New York: D. Appleton, 1849.

Burnett, Peter Hardeman. *Recollections and Opinions of an Old Pioneer*. New York: D. Appleton, 1880.

De Finiels, Nicolas. *An Account of Upper Louisiana*. 1803. Ed. Carl J. Ekberg and William E. Foley. Reprint, Columbia: University of Missouri Press, 1989.

De Tocqueville, Alexis. *Democracy in America*. 1840. Reprint, New York: Perennial Classics, 2000.

Drake, Charles D., ed. *Pioneer Life in Kentucky: A Series of Reminiscential Letters From Daniel Drake, M.D., of Cincinnati, to His Children.* Cincinnati: Robert Clarke, 1870.

Draper, Arthur G., ed. "Farming on the Missouri Frontier: Essays by Philander Draper." *Missouri Historical Review* 87, no. 1 (October 1992): 18–35.

Duden, Gottfried. *Report on a Journey to the Western States of North America and A Stay of Several Years Along the Missouri (During the Years 1824, '25, '26 and 1827).* 1829. Ed. James W. Goodrich. Reprint, Columbia: University of Missouri Press, 1980.

Duncan, Lucy Routt Bradford. "Early Days in Phelps County." *Missouri Historical Review* 19, no. 1 (October 1924): 99–104.

Ekberg, Carl J., ed. *A French Aristocrat in the American West: The Shattered Dreams of De Lassus de Luzieres.* Columbia: University of Missouri Press, 2010.

Flagg, Edmund. *The Far West, Or A Tour Beyond the Mountains, Embracing Outlines of Western Life and Society: Sketches of the Prairies, Rivers, Ancient Mounds, Early Settlements of the French, Etc., Etc.* New York: Harper and Brothers, 1838.

Flint, Timothy. *Biographical Memoir of Daniel Boone, The First Settler of Kentucky: Interspersed With Incidents In the Early Annals of the Country.* Cincinnati: George Conclin, 1845.

———. *The History and Geography of the Mississippi Valley. To Which Is Appended A Condensed Physical Geography of the Atlantic United States, And the Whole American Continent.* Vol. 1. Cincinnati: E. H. Flint, 1833.

———. *Recollections of the Last Ten Years, Passed in Occasional Residences and Journeyings in the Valley of the Mississippi.* 1826. Reprint, New York: DeCapo Press, 1968.

Goebel, Gert. *Longer Than a Lifetime in Missouri.* 1877. Ed. Martin W. Heinrichsmeyer. Reprint, St. Louis: Missouri Historical Society, 1956.

Goodrich, James W., and Lynn Wolf Gentzler, eds. "'I Well Remember': David Holms Conrad's Recollections of St. Louis, 1819–1823." *Missouri Historical Review* 90, no. 1 (October 1995): 1–37.

Graham, Margaret Baker, ed. "Stories of Everyday Living: The Life and Letters of Margaret Bruin Machette." *Missouri Historical Review* 93, no. 4 (July 1999): 367–385.

Gregg, Joseph. *The Commerce of the Prairies*. 1844. Ed. Milo Milton Quaife. Reprint, Lincoln: University of Nebraska Press, 1967.

Gregory, Ralph, ed. "The Autobiography of Henry Wellenkamp, 1822–1907." *Missouri Historical Society Bulletin* 19, no. 4 (July 1963): 311–327.

Gregory, Sarah J., ed. "Pioneer Housewife: The Autobiography of Sally Dodge Morris." *Gateway Heritage* 3, no. 4 (Spring 1983): 25–33.

Gustorf, Fred, ed. *The Uncorrupted Heart: Journal and Letters of Frederick Gustorf, 1800–1845*. Columbia: University of Missouri Press, 1969.

Hall, Basil. *Travels in North America, in the Years 1827, 1828*. Vol. 3. Edinburgh: Simpkin and Marshall, 1830.

Hall, James. *The West: Its Commerce and Navigation*. Cincinnati: H. W. Derby, 1848.

Hammon, Neal O., ed. *My Father, Daniel Boone: The Draper Interviews with Nathan Boone*. Lexington: University Press of Kentucky, 1999.

Houck, Louis, ed. *The Spanish Regime in Missouri: A Collection Of Papers And Documents Relating To Upper Louisiana Principally Within The Present Limits of Missouri During The Dominion of Spain From The Archives Of the Indies At Seville, Etc., Translated From The Original Spanish Into English, And Including Also Some Papers Concerning The Supposed Grant To Colonel Morgan At The Mouth Of The Ohio, Found In The Congressional Library*. Vol. 2. Chicago: R. R. Donnelley and Sons, 1909.

Hoyt, William D., Jr., ed. "A Clay Countian's Letters of 1834." *Missouri Historical Review* 45, no. 4 (July 1951): 349–353.

Irving, Washington. *The Works of Washington Irving*. Vol. 8, *Astoria: Or Anecdotes Of An Enterprise Beyond the Rocky Mountains*. New York: G. P. Putnam, 1861.

Isely, Elise Dubach. *Sunbonnet Days, by Elise Dubach Isely, as Told to Her Son, Bliss Isely*. Caldwell, Idaho: Caxton Printers, 1935.

Jervey, Edward D., and James E. Moss, eds. "From Virginia to Missouri in 1846: The Journal of Elizabeth Ann Cooley." *Missouri Historical Review* 60, no. 2 (January 1966): 162–206.

Johnston, William Graham. *Experiences of A Forty-Niner*. Pittsburgh: n.p., 1892.

Kelly, William. *An Excursion to California Over The Prairie, Rocky Mountains, And Great Sierra Nevada. With A Stroll Through The Diggings And Ranches Of That Country*. Vol. 1. London: Chapman and Hall, 1851.

Klein, Frederick S., ed. "Letters of a Young Surveyor, 1828–1829." *Missouri*

Historical Review 23, no. 1 (October 1928): 61–84.

Kronenberg, Kenneth, ed. *Lives and Letters of an Immigrant Family: The van Dreveldts' Experiences along the Missouri, 1844–1866*. Lincoln: University of Nebraska Press, 1998.

Latrobe, Charles Joseph. *The Rambler in North America, 1832–1833*. London: R. G. Seeley and W. Burnside, 1835.

Laws of the State of Missouri, Passed at the First Session of the Twentieth General Assembly. Jefferson City, Mo.: C. J. Corwin, Public Printer, 1859.

Lester, W. W. *Decisions of the Interior Department In Public Land Cases and Land Laws Passed By The Congress of the United States; Together With The Regulations Of the General Land Office*. Philadelphia: H. P. & R. H. Small, 1860.

MacKay, Charles. *Life and Liberty in America: Sketches of a Tour in the United States and Canada in 1857–1858*. New York: Harper and Brothers, 1859.

McConnel, John Ludlum. *Western Characters: Or, Types of Border Life in Western States*. New York: Redfield, 1853.

McCormack, Thomas J., ed. *Memoirs of Gustave Koerner, 1809–1896: Life Sketches Written at the Suggestion of His Children*. Vol. 1. Cedar Rapids, Iowa: Torch Press, 1909.

Overdyke, W. Darrell, ed. "A Southern Family on the Missouri Frontier: Letters from Independence, 1843–1855." *Journal of Southern History* 17, no. 2 (May 1951): 216–237.

Palmer, Joel. *Journal of Travels Over the Rocky Mountains, to the Mouth of the Columbia River; Made During the Years 1845 and 1846: Containing Mining Descriptions of the Valleys of the Willamette, Umpqua, And Clamet: A General Description of the Oregon Territory; Its Inhabitants, Climate, Soil, Productions, Etc., Etc.; A List of Necessary Outfits For Emigrants; And A Table of Distances from Camp to Camp on the Platte*. 1847. Reprint, Fairfield, Wash.: Ye Galleon Press, 1983.

Parkman, Francis. *The Oregon Trail*. 1849. Reprint, New York: Library of America/Viking Press, 1991.

Peck, John Mason, and Nicholas Patterson. "The Boon's Lick Country: Two Gospel Preachers Explore a New Settlement." *Missouri Historical Society Bulletin* 6, no. 4 (July 1950): 442–490.

Peyton, John Lewis. *Over the Alleghanies and Across the Prairies: Personal Recollections of the Far West, One and Twenty Years Ago*. London: Simpkin, Marshall, 1869.

Phillips, Christopher, and Jason C. Pendleton, eds. *The Union on Trial: The Political Journals of Judge William Barclay Napton, 1829–1883*. Columbia: University of Missouri Press, 2005.

Prentiss, George Lewis, ed. *A Memoir of S. S. Prentiss*. New York: Charles Scribner, 1856.

Pritchard, J. A. "Diary of a Journey from Kentucky to California in 1849." *Missouri Historical Review* 18, no. 4 (July 1924): 535–545.

Report of the Commissioner of Patents For the Year 1853: Agriculture. Washington, D.C.: A. O. P. Nicholson Printer, 1854.

Report on the Productions of Agriculture As Reported In The Tenth Census. Washington, D.C.: Government Printing Office, 1883.

Schoolcraft, Henry R. *A Journal of A Tour Into the Interior of Missouri and Arkansaw From Potosi, or Mine a Breton, in Missouri Territory, in a Southwest Direction, toward The Rocky Mountains; Performed in the Years 1818 and 1819*. London: Sir Richard Phillips, 1821.

Schroeder, Adolf E., and Carla Schulz-Geisberg, eds. *Hold Dear, As Always, Jette: A German Immigrant Life in Letters*. Columbia: University of Missouri Press, 1988.

Schultz, Christian. *Travels On an Inland Voyage Through the States of New York, Pennsylvania, Virginia, Ohio, Kentucky and Tennessee, And Through the Territories of Indiana, Louisiana, Mississippi and New-Orleans: Performed In the Years 1807 and 1808; Including A tour of Nearly Six Thousand Miles*. Vol. 1. New York: Isaac Riley, 1810.

Sedgley, Joseph. *Overland to California in 1849*. Oakland, Calif.: Butler and Bowman, 1877.

Seventh Census of the United States, 1850. Washington, D.C.: Robert Armstrong, Public Printer, 1853.

Shortfield, Luke. *The Western Merchant, A Narrative, Containing Useful Instruction for the Western Man of Business Who Makes His Purchases in the East; Also, Information for the Eastern Man Whose Customers Are In the West; Likewise, Hints For Those Who Design Emigration to the West. Deduced From Actual Experience*. Philadelphia: Gregg, Elliot, 1849.

Stephens, F. F., ed. "Major Alphonso Wetmore's Diary of a Journey to Santa Fe, 1828." *Missouri Historical Review* 8, no. 4 (July 1914): 177–197.

Stoddard, Amos. *Sketches, Historical and Descriptive, of Louisiana*. Philadelphia: Matthew Carey, 1812.

Stokes, Durward T. "The Wilson Letters, 1835–1849." *Missouri Historical Review* 60, no. 4 (July 1966): 495–517.

Thwaites, Ruben Gold, ed. *Early Western Travels, 1748–1846*. Vols 4, 5, 14, and 21. Cleveland: Arthur H. Clark, 1904–1907.

Webb, James Josiah. *Adventures in the Santa Fe Trade, 1844–1847*. 1931. Reprint, Lincoln: University of Nebraska Press, 1995.

Wetmore, Alphonso, ed. *Gazetteer of the State of Missouri: With a map of the state. From the Office of the Surveyor-General, Including the Latest Additions and Surveys to Which Is Added An Appendix, Containing Frontier Sketches, and Illustrations of Indian Character*. St. Louis: C. Keemle, Harper and Brothers, Printers, 1837.

Williams, James. *75 Years on the Border*. Kansas City, Mo.: Press of Standard Printing, 1912.

Williams, Sara Lockwood. "Pioneer Days in 'Old Sparta.'" *Missouri Historical Review* 25, no. 4 (July 1931): 550–555.

Windell, Marie George, ed. "The Road West in 1818, The Diary of Henry Vest Bingham, Part II." *Missouri Historical Review* 40, no. 2 (January 1946): 174–204.

Woods, John. *Two Years Residence In The Settlement On The English Prairie In the Illinois Country, United States. With An Account Of Its Animal And Vegetable Productions, Agriculture, &c. &c. A Description Of the Principal Towns, Villages, &c. &c. With The Habits And Customs Of The Back-Woodsmen*. London: Longman, Hurst, Rees, Orme, and Brown, 1822.

Wyman, Walker, ed. "California Emigrant Letters." *California Historical Society Quarterly* 24, no. 1 (March 1945): 17–46.

Zimmerman, Eduard. "Travel into Missouri in October, 1838." *Missouri Historical Review* 9, no. 1 (October 1914): 33–42.

SECONDARY SOURCES

Allen, Michael. *Western Rivermen, 1763–1861: Ohio and Mississippi Boatmen and the Myth of the Alligator Horse*. Baton Rouge: Louisiana State University Press, 1990.

Anderson, Hattie. "Frontier Economic Problems in Missouri, 1815–1828." *Missouri Historical Review* 34, no. 1 (October 1939): 38–70.

Ankli, Robert E. "Farm-Making Costs in the 1850s." *Agricultural History* 48, no. 1 (January 1974): 51–70.

Appleby, Joyce Oldham. *Inheriting the Revolution: The First Generation of Americans.* Cambridge, Mass.: Harvard University Press, 2001.

———. "The Vexed Story of Capitalism Told by American Historians." *Journal of the Early Republic* 21, no. 1 (Spring 2001): 1–18.

Aron, Stephen. *American Confluence: The Missouri Frontier from Borderland to Border State.* Bloomington: Indiana University Press, 2006.

———. *How the West Was Lost: The Transformation of Kentucky from Daniel Boone to Henry Clay.* Baltimore: Johns Hopkins University Press, 1996.

Atack, Jeremy, and Fred Bateman. "Marketable Farm Surpluses: Northeastern and Midwestern United States, 1859 and 1860." *Social Science History* 8, no. 4 (August 1984): 371–393.

———. *To Their Own Soil: Agriculture in the Antebellum North.* Ames: Iowa State University Press, 1987.

Atack, Jeremy, and Peter Passell. *A New Economic View of American History: From Colonial Times to 1940.* New York: W. W. Norton, 1994.

Atherton, Lewis E. *The Frontier Merchant in Mid-America.* Columbia: University of Missouri Press, 1971.

———. "James and Robert Aull: A Frontier Missouri Mercantile Firm." *Missouri Historical Review* 93, no. 1 (October 1998): 27–47.

———. "The Santa Fe Trader as Mercantile Capitalist." *Missouri Historical Review* 77, no. 1 (October 1982): 1–12.

———. "The Services of the Frontier Merchant." *Mississippi Valley Historical Review* 24, no. 2 (September 1937): 153–170.

Bailyn, Bernard. *Voyagers to the West: A Passage in the Peopling of America on the Eve of the Revolution.* New York: Vintage Books, 1986.

Baker, Andrew H., and Holly V. Izard. "New England Farms and the Marketplace, 1780–1865." *Agricultural History* 65, no. 3 (Summer 1991): 29–52.

Baptist, Edward E. "The Migration of Planters to Antebellum Florida: Kinship and Power." *Journal of Southern History* 62, no. 3 (August 1996): 527–554.

Barney, William L. *The Passage of the Republic: An Interdisciplinary History of Nineteenth-Century America.* Lexington, Mass.: D. C. Heath, 1987.

Barron, Hal S. "Rediscovering the Majority: The New Rural History of the Nineteenth-Century North." *Historical Methods* 19, no. 4 (Fall 1986): 141–152.

———. *Those Who Stayed Behind: Rural Society in Nineteenth Century New*

England. New York: Cambridge University Press, 1984.

Bartlett, Richard A. *The New Country: A Social History of the American Frontier, 1776–1890*. Oxford: Oxford University Press, 1974.

Bell, Ovid. "Pioneer Life in Callaway County." *Missouri Historical Review* 21, no. 2 (January 1927): 156–165.

Beneria, Lourdes, and Catherine R. Stimpson, eds. *Women, Households and the Economy*. New Brunswick, N.J.: Rutgers University Press, 1987.

Bernstein, William J. *A Splendid Exchange: How Trade Shaped the World*. New York: Grove Press, 2008.

Bidwell, Percy W., and John I. Falconer. *History of Agriculture in the Northern United States, 1620–1860*. New York: Peter Smith, 1941.

Billingsley, Carolyn Earle. *Communities of Kinship: Antebellum Families and the Settlement of the Cotton Frontier*. Athens: University of Georgia Press, 2004.

Billington, Ray Allen. *Westward Expansion: A History of the American Frontier*. New York: MacMillan, 1960.

Blanke, David. *Sowing the American Dream: How Consumer Culture Took Root in the Rural Midwest*. Athens: Ohio State University Press, 2000.

Bogue, Allan G. *From Prairie to Corn-Belt: Farming on the Illinois and Iowa Prairies in the Nineteenth Century*. Chicago: University of Chicago Press, 1963.

Bolton, S. Charles. *Arkansas, 1800–1860: Remote and Restless*. Fayetteville: University of Arkansas Press, 1998.

Boydston, Jeanne. *Home and Work: Housework, Wages, and the Ideology of Labor in the Early Republic*. Oxford: Oxford University Press, 1990.

———. "The Woman Who Wasn't There: Women's Market Labor and the Transition to Capitalism in the United States." *Journal of the Early Republic* 16, no. 2 (Summer 1996): 183–206.

Britton, Wiley. "Pioneer Life in Southwest Missouri." *Missouri Historical Review* 16, no. 1 (October 1921): 42–85.

Bruchey, Stuart. *Enterprise: The Dynamic Economy of a Free People*. Cambridge, Mass.: Harvard University Press, 1990.

Bruegel, Martin. *Farm, Shop, Landing: The Rise of a Market Society in the Hudson Valley, 1780–1860*. Durham, N.C.: Duke University Press, 2002.

Bryant, William S., and Robert Rose. *A History Of The Pioneer Families Of Missouri, With Numerous Sketches, Anecdotes, Adventures, Etc., Relating To Early Days In Missouri. Also The Lives Of Daniel Boone And The Celebrated*

Indian Chief Black Hawk, With Numerous Biographies And Histories Of Primitive Institutions. St. Louis: Bryan, Brand, 1876.

Burke, Diane Mutti. *On Slavery's Border: Missouri's Small Slaveholding Households, 1815–1865*. Athens: University of Georgia Press, 2010.

Burnett, Robin, and Ken Luebbering. *German Settlement in Missouri: New Land, Old Ways*. Columbia: University of Missouri Press, 1996.

Bushman, Richard Lyman. "Markets and Composite Farms in Early America." *William and Mary Quarterly*, 3rd Series, 55, no. 3 (July 1998): 351–374.

Calloway, Calvin. *One Vast Winter Count: The Native American West before Lewis And Clark*. Lincoln: University of Nebraska Press, 2003.

Carpenter, Clifford D. "The Early Cattle Industry in Missouri." *Missouri Historical Review* 47, no. 3 (April 1953): 201–215.

Carr, Jacqueline Barbara. *After the Siege: A Social History of Boston, 1775–1800*. Boston: Northeastern University Press, 2005.

Cashin, Joan. *A Family Venture: Men and Women on the Southern Frontier*. Baltimore: Johns Hopkins University Press, 1991.

Cayton, Andrew R. L. *Frontier Indiana*. Bloomington: Indiana University Press, 1998.

Cayton, Andrew R. L., and Peter S. Onuf. *The Midwest and the Nation: Rethinking the History of an American Region*. Bloomington: Indiana University Press, 1990.

Chittenden, Hiram Martin. *The American Fur Trade of the Far West: A History of the Pioneer Trading Posts and Early Fur Companies of the Missouri Valley and the Rocky Mountains and of the Overland Commerce with Santa Fe*. Vol. 1. New York: Francis P. Harper, 1902.

Clark, Christopher. "Household Economy, Market Exchange and the Rise of Capitalism in the Connecticut Valley, 1800–1860." *Journal of Social History* 13, no. 2 (Winter 1979): 169–189.

———. *The Roots of Rural Capitalism: Western Massachusetts, 1780–1860*. Ithaca, N.Y.: Cornell University Press, 1990.

———. *Social Change in America: From the Revolution to the Civil War*. New York: Ivan R. Dee, 2007.

Clark, John G. "The Antebellum Grain Trade of New Orleans: The Changing Patterns in the Relationship of New Orleans with the Old Northwest." *Agricultural History* 38, no. 3 (July 1964): 131–142.

———. *New Orleans, 1718–1812: An Economic History*. Baton Rouge: Louisiana

State University Press, 1970.

Clark, Thomas D. "Manners and Humors of the American Frontier." *Missouri Historical Review* 35, no. 1 (October 1940): 3–24.

Clark, Thomas D., and John D. W. Guice. *Frontiers in Conflict: The Old Southwest, 1795–1830*. Albuquerque: University of New Mexico Press, 1989.

Coburn, Carol K. *Life at Four Corners: Religion, Gender and Education in a German-Lutheran Community, 1868–1948*. Lawrence: University Press of Kansas, 1992.

Cott, Nancy. *The Bonds of Womanhood: "Women's Sphere" in New England, 1780–1835*. New Haven, Conn.: Yale University Press, 1997.

Craig, Beatrice. *Backwoods Consumers and Homespun Capitalists: The Rise of a Market Culture in Eastern Canada*. Toronto: University of Toronto Press, 2009.

Craven, Avery Odelle. *Soil Exhaustion as a Factor in the Agricultural History of Virginia and Maryland, 1606–1860*. 1925. Reprint, Columbia: University of South Carolina Press, 2006.

Dains, Mary K. "Missouri Women in Historical Writing." *Missouri Historical Review* 83, no. 4 (July 1989): 417–428.

Danbom, David B. *Born in the Country: A History of Rural America*. Baltimore: Johns Hopkins University Press, 1995.

Danhof, Clarence H. *Change in Agriculture: The Northern United States, 1820–1870*. Cambridge, Mass.: Harvard University Press, 1969.

Daniels, Bruce C. "Economic Development in Colonial and Revolutionary Connecticut: An Overview." *William and Mary Quarterly*, 3rd Series, 37, no. 3 (July 1980): 438–454.

Dary, David. *The Oregon Trail: An American Saga*. New York: Oxford University Press, 2004.

———. *The Santa Fe Trail: Its History, Legends and Lore*. New York: Penguin Books, 2000.

Davis, James E. *Frontier Illinois*. Bloomington: Indiana University Press, 1998.

Diamond, Jared. *Guns, Germs and Steel: The Fates of Human Societies*. New York: W. W. Norton, 1999.

Dick, Everett. *The Dixie Frontier: A Social History*. Norman: University of Oklahoma Press, 1993.

Din, Gilbert. "Spain's Immigration Policy in Louisiana and the American Penetration, 1792–1803." *Southwestern Historical Quarterly* 76, no. 3 (January

1973): 255–276.

Dorsey, Dorothy B. "The Panic and Depression of 1837–1843 in Missouri." *Missouri Historical Review* 30, no. 2 (January 1936): 132–161.

———. "The Panic of 1819 in Missouri." *Missouri Historical Review* 29, no. 2 (January 1935): 79–91.

Dunaway, Wilma A. *The First American Frontier: The Transition to Capitalism in Southern Appalachia, 1700–1860*. Chapel Hill: University of North Carolina Press, 1996.

Dunlop, M. H. *Sixty Miles from Contentment: Traveling the Nineteenth-Century American Interior*. Boulder, Colo.: Westview Press, 1998.

Dunn, Susan. *Dominion of Memories: Jefferson, Madison and the Decline of Virginia*. New York: Basic Books, 2007.

Dupre, Daniel. "Ambivalent Capitalists on the Cotton Frontier: Settlement and Development in the Tennessee Valley of Alabama." *Journal of Southern History* 56, no. 2 (May 1990): 215–240.

DuVal, Kathleen. *The Native Ground: Indians and Colonists in the Heart of the Continent*. Philadelphia: University of Pennsylvania Press, 2006.

Easterlin, Richard A. "Population Change and Farm Settlement in the Northern United States." *Journal of Economic History* 36, no. 1 (March 1976): 45–75.

Eaton, Miles W. "The Development and Later Decline of the Hemp Industry in Missouri." *Missouri Historical Review* 43, no. 4 (July 1949): 344–359.

Eckhert, Allan W. *The Silent Sky: The Incredible Extinction of the Passenger Pigeon*. Lincoln, Neb.: iUniverse.com, 2000.

Ekberg, Carl. *French Roots in the Illinois Country: The Mississippi Frontier in Colonial Times*. Chicago and Urbana: University of Illinois Press, 1998.

Ellis, David M. *The Frontier in American Development: Essays in Honor of Paul Wallace Gates*. Ithaca, N.Y.: Cornell University Press, 1969.

Ellis, Joseph J. *His Excellency: George Washington*. New York: Vintage Books, 2004.

Faragher, John Mack. *Daniel Boone: The Life and Legend of an American Pioneer*. New York: Henry Holt, 1993.

———. *Sugar Creek: Life on the Illinois Prairie*. New Haven, Conn.: Yale University Press, 1986.

———. *Women and Men on the Overland Trail*. New Haven, Conn.: Yale University Press, 2000.

Farmer, Charles J. *In the Absence of Towns: Settlement and Country Trade in*

Southside Virginia, 1730–1800. Lanham, Md.: Rowman and Littlefield, 1993.

Feldman, Jay. *When the Mississippi Ran Backwards: Empire, Intrigue, Murder and the New Madrid Earthquakes*. New York: Free Press, 2005.

Ferleger, Lou, ed. *Agriculture and National Development: Views on the Nineteenth Century*. Ames: Iowa State University Press, 1990.

Fickle, James E. *Mississippi Forests and Forestry*. Jackson: University Press of Mississippi, 2001.

Finger, John R. *Tennessee Frontiers: Three Regions in Transition*. Bloomington: Indiana University Press, 2001.

Foley, William E. *The Genesis of Missouri: From Wilderness Outpost to Statehood*. Columbia: University of Missouri Press, 1989.

———. *A History of Missouri*. Vol. 1, *1673 to 1820*. Columbia: University of Missouri Press, 1999.

———. "Justus Post: Portrait of a Frontier Land Speculator." *Missouri Historical Society Bulletin* 36, no. 1 (October 1979): 18–25.

Foley, William E., and C. David Rice. *The First Chouteaus: River Barons of Early St. Louis*. Chicago: University of Illinois Press, 1983.

Ford, Lacy K. "Yeoman Farmers in the South Carolina Upcountry: Changing Production Patterns in the Late Antebellum Era." *Agricultural History* 60, no. 4 (Fall 1986): 17–37.

Friend, Craig T. *Along the Maysville Road: The Early American Republic in the Trans-Appalachian West*. Knoxville: University of Tennessee Press, 2005.

———. *Kentucke's Frontiers*. Bloomington: Indiana University Press, 2010.

———. "Merchants and Markethouses: Reflections on Moral Economy in Early Kentucky." *Journal of the Early Republic* 17, no. 4 (Winter 1997): 553–574.

Frizzell, Robert W. *Independent Immigrants: A Settlement of Hanoverian Germans in Western Missouri*. Columbia: University of Missouri Press, 2007.

———. "Marie Dierking Herd Neuhaus: Lafayette County German Farm Wife and Proto-Feminist." *Missouri Historical Review* 102, no. 1 (October 2007): 1–13.

Gates, Paul Wallace. *The Farmer's Age: Agriculture, 1815–1860*. New York: Holt, Rinehart and Winston, 1960.

———. *Frontier Landlords and Pioneer Tenants*. Ithaca, N.Y.: Cornell University Press, 1945.

———. "The Railroads of Missouri, 1850–1870." *Missouri Historical Review* 26, no. 2 (January 1932): 126–141.

Gerlach, Russell L. "Population Origins in Rural Missouri." *Missouri Historical Review* 71, no. 1 (October 1976): 1–21.

Gitlin, Jay. *The Bourgeois Frontier: French Towns, French Traders and American Expansion*. New Haven, Conn.: Yale University Press, 2010.

Gray, Lewis Cecil. *History of Agriculture in the Southern United States to 1860*. Vol. 2. Gloucester, Mass.: Peter Smith, 1958.

Gregg, Kate L. "Boonslickers in the Gold Rush to California." *Missouri Historical Review* 41, no. 4 (July 1947): 345–360.

Grob, Gerald. *The Deadly Truth: A History of Disease in America*. Cambridge, Mass.: Harvard University Press, 2002.

Gross, Robert A. "Culture and Cultivation: Agriculture and Society in Thoreau's Concord." *Journal of American History* 69, no. 1 (June 1982): 42–61.

Gruenwald, Kim M. *River of Enterprise: The Commercial Origins of Regional Identity in the Ohio Valley, 1790–1860*. Bloomington: Indiana University Press, 2002.

Hahn, Steven. *The Roots of Southern Populism: Yeoman Farmers and the Transformation of the Georgia Upcountry, 1850–1890*. New York: Oxford University Press, 1983.

Haites, Erik F., and James Mak. "Steamboating on the Mississippi, 1810–1860: A Purely Competitive Industry." *Business History Review* 45, no. 1 (Spring 1971): 52–78.

Haites, Erik F., James Mak, and Gary M. Walton. *Western River Transportation: The Era of Early Internal Development, 1810–1860*. Baltimore: Johns Hopkins University Press, 1975.

Hammond, George P., ed. *New Spain and the Anglo-American West: Historical Contributions Presented to Herbert Eugene Bolton*. Vol. 1. New York: Kraus Reprint, 1969.

Hansen, Karen V. *A Very Social Time: Crafting Community in Antebellum New England*. Berkeley: University of California Press, 1994.

Hansen, Mary Eschelbach. "Land Ownership, Farm Size, and Tenancy after the Civil War." *Journal of Economic History* 58, no. 3 (September 1998): 822–829.

Hattervig, Eldon. "Jefferson Landing: A Commercial Center of the Steamboat Era." *Missouri Historical Review* 74, no. 3 (April 1980): 277–299.

Henretta, James A. *The Origins of American Capitalism: Collected Essays*. Boston: Northeastern University Press, 1991.

———. "The 'Market' in the Early Republic." *Journal of the Early Republic* 18, no. 2 (Summer 1998): 289–304.

Henretta, James A., and Gregory H. Nobles. *Evolution and Revolution: American Society, 1600–1820*. Lexington, Mass.: D. C. Heath, 1987.

Herscovici, Steven. "Migration and Economic Mobility: Wealth Accumulation and Occupational Change among Antebellum Migrants and Persisters." *Journal of Economic History* 58, no. 4 (December 1998): 927–956.

Hine, Robert V. *Community on the American Frontier: Separate But Not Alone*. Norman: University of Oklahoma Press, 1980.

Hofstra, Warren R., and Robert D. Mitchell. "Town and Country in Backcountry Virginia: Winchester and the Shenandoah Valley, 1730–1800." *Journal of Southern History* 59, no. 4 (November 1993): 619–646.

Holliday, J. S. *The World Rushed In: The California Gold Rush Experience*. Norman: University of Oklahoma Press, 2002.

Horsman, Reginald. *Feast or Famine: Food and Drink in American Westward Expansion*. Columbia: University of Missouri Press, 2008.

Houck, Louis. *A History of Missouri: From the Earliest Explorations and Settlements until the Admission of the State into the Union*. 3 vols. Chicago: R. R. Donnelley and Sons, 1908.

Howe, Daniel Walker. *What Hath God Wrought: The Transformation of America, 1815–1848*. New York: Oxford University Press, 2007.

Hudson, John C. *Making the Corn Belt: A Geographical History of Middle-Western Agriculture*. Bloomington: Indiana University Press, 1994.

Hunter, Louis C. *Steamboats on Western Rivers: An Economic and Technological History*. New York: Octagon Books, 1969.

Hurley, Andrew, ed. *Common Fields: An Environmental History of St. Louis*. St. Louis: Missouri Historical Society, 1997.

Hurt, R. Douglas. *Agriculture and Slavery in Missouri's Little Dixie*. Columbia: University of Missouri Press, 1992.

———. *American Agriculture: A Brief History*. West Lafayette, Ind.: Purdue University Press, 2002.

———. *Nathan Boone and the American Frontier*. Columbia: University of Missouri Press, 1998.

———. *The Ohio Frontier: Crucible of the Old Northwest, 1720–1830*. Bloomington: Indiana University Press, 1996.

———. "Planters and Slavery in Little Dixie." *Missouri Historical Review* 88, no. 4 (July 1994): 397–415.

———. "Seeking Fortune in the Promised Land: Settling in the Boon's Lick Country, 1808–1825." *Gateway Heritage* 13, no. 1 (Summer 1992): 4–19.

Hyde, Anne F. *Empires, Nations, and Families: A History of the North American West*. Lincoln: University of Nebraska Press, 2011.

Hyslop, Stephen G. *Bound for Santa Fe: The Road to New Mexico and the American Conquest, 1806–1848*. Norman: University of Oklahoma Press, 2002.

Inman, Ethel Grant. "Pioneer Days in Northwest Missouri—Harrison County, 1837–1873." *Missouri Historical Review* 22, no. 3 (April 1928): 307–330.

Innes, Stephen. *Creating the Commonwealth: The Economic Culture of Puritan New England*. New York: W. W. Norton, 1995.

Inscoe, John. *Mountain Masters, Slavery, and the Sectional Crisis in Western North Carolina*. Knoxville: University of Tennessee Press, 1989.

Jensen, Joan M. *Loosening the Bonds: Mid-Atlantic Farm Women, 1750–1850*. New Haven, Conn.: Yale University Press, 1986.

Johnson, Paul E. *The Early American Republic, 1789–1829*. New York: Oxford University Press, 2007.

Jones, Robert Leslie. *History of Agriculture in Ohio to 1880*. Kent, Ohio: Kent State University Press, 1983.

Jordan, Terry G., and Matt Kaups. *The American Backwoods Frontier: An Ethnic and Ecological Interpretation*. Baltimore: Johns Hopkins University Press, 1989.

Kamphoefner, Walter D. *The Westfalians: From Germany to Missouri*. Princeton, N.J.: Princeton University Press, 1987.

Kane, Adam I. *The Western River Steamboat*. College Station: Texas A&M Press, 2004.

Klingman, David C., and Richard Vedder. *Essays on the Economy of the Old Northwest*. Athens: Ohio University Press, 1987.

Kulikoff, Allan. *The Agrarian Origins of American Capitalism*. Charlottesville: University Press of Virginia, 1992.

———. "Households and Markets: Toward a New Synthesis of American Agricultural History." *William and Mary Quarterly*, 3rd Series, 50, no. 2 (April 1993): 342–355.

Lamoreaux, Naomi. "Rethinking the Transition to Capitalism in the Early American Northeast." *Journal of American History* 90, no. 2 (September 2003): 437–461.

Larkin, Jack. *The Reshaping of Everyday Life, 1790–1840*. New York: Harper and Row, 1986.

Larson, John Lauritz. *The Market Revolution in America: Liberty, Ambition, and the Eclipse of the Common Good*. New York: Cambridge University Press, 2010.

Lass, William E. *Navigating the Missouri: Steamboating on Nature's Highway, 1819–1935*. Norman: University of Oklahoma Press, 2007.

———. "Tourists' Impressions of St. Louis, 1763–1859, Part II." *Missouri Historical Review* 53, no. 1 (October 1958): 10–21.

Limerick, Patricia Nelson. *The Legacy of Conquest: The Unbroken Past of the American West*. New York: W. W. Norton, 1987.

Mahoney, Timothy R. *River Towns in the Great West: The Structure of Provincial Urbanization in the American Midwest, 1820–1870*. Cambridge: Cambridge University Press, 1990.

Majewski, John. *A House Dividing: Economic Development in Pennsylvania and Virginia before the Civil War*. New York: Cambridge University Press, 2000.

Mak, James, and Gary M. Walton. "Steamboats and the Great Productivity Surge in River Transportation." *Journal of Economic History* 32, no. 3 (September 1972): 619–640.

Martin, Ann Smart. *Buying into the World of Goods: Early Consumers in Backcountry Virginia*. Baltimore: Johns Hopkins University Press, 2008.

Martin, Scott C., ed. *Cultural Change and the Market Revolution in America, 1789–1860*. Lanham, Md.: Rowman and Littlefield, 2005.

McCandless, Perry. *A History of Missouri*. Vol. 2, *1820–1860*. Columbia: University of Missouri Press, 2000.

McCurry, Stephanie. *Masters of Small Worlds: Yeoman Households, Gender Relations and the Political Culture of the Antebellum South Carolina Low Country*. New York: Oxford University Press, 1997.

McDermott, John Francis, ed. *The Spanish in the Mississippi Valley, 1762–1804*. Urbana and Chicago: University of Illinois Press, 1974.

McDougall, Walter A. *Freedom Just Around the Corner: A New American History, 1585–1828*. New York: Harper Collins Press, 2004.

McGettigan, James William, Jr. "Boone County Slaves: Sales, Estate Divisions and Families, 1820–1865, Part 1." *Missouri Historical Review* 72, no. 2 (January 1978): 176–197.

McKinley, Daniel. "White Man's Fly on the Frontier." *Missouri Historical Review* 58, no. 4 (July 1964): 442–451.

McLear, Patrick. "The St. Louis Cholera Epidemic of 1849." *Missouri Historical*

Review 63, no. 2 (January 1969): 171–181.

Meinig, D. W. *The Shaping of America*. Vol. 1, *Atlantic America, 1492–1800*. New Haven, Conn.: Yale University Press, 1986.

———. *The Shaping of America*. Vol. 2, *Continental America, 1800–1867*. New Haven, Conn.: Yale University Press, 1993.

Merrill, Michael. "Cash Is Good to Eat: Self-Sufficiency and Exchange in the Rural Economy of the United States." *Radical History Review* 4, no. 1 (1977): 42–71.

Miller, James. *South by Southwest: Planter Emigration and Identity in the Slave South*. Charlottesville: University of Virginia Press, 2002.

Morgan, M. J. *Land of Big Rivers: French and Indian Illinois, 1699–1778*. Carbondale: Southern Illinois University Press, 2010.

Morris, Christopher. *Becoming Southern: The Evolution of a Way of Life, Warren County and Vicksburg, Mississippi, 1770–1860*. New York: Oxford University Press, 1995.

Morris, Richard B. *Forging of the Union, 1781–1789*. New York: Harper and Row, 1987.

Morrow, Lynn. "Dr. John Sappington: Southern Patriarch in the New West." *Missouri Historical Review* 90, no. 1 (October 1995): 38–60.

Nagel, Paul C. *The German Migration to Missouri: My Family's Story*. Kansas City, Mo.: Kansas City Star Books, 2002.

———. *Missouri: A History*. Lawrence: University Press of Kansas, 1988.

Nobles, Gregory H. *American Frontiers: Cultural Encounter and Continental Conquest*. New York: Hill and Wang, 1997.

———. "Commerce and Community: A Case Study of the Rural Broom-making Business in Antebellum Massachusetts." *Journal of the Early Republic* 4, no. 3 (Autumn 1984): 287–305.

———. "The Rise of Merchants in Rural Market Towns: A Case Study of Eighteenth-Century Northampton, Massachusetts." *Journal of Social History* 24, no. 1 (Fall 1990): 5–23.

North, Douglass C. *The Economic Growth of the United States, 1790–1860*. New York: W. W. Norton, 1966.

Oakes, James. *The Ruling Race: A History of American Slaveholders*. New York: W. W. Norton, 1982.

O'Brien, Michael J. *Grassland, Forest and Historical Settlement: An Analysis of Dynamics in Northeast Missouri*. Lincoln: University of Nebraska Press, 1984.

Osterud, Nancy Grey. *Bonds of Community: The Lives of Farmwomen in Nineteenth Century New York*. Ithaca, N.Y.: Cornell University Press, 1991.

———. "Gender and the Transition to Capitalism in Rural America." *Agricultural History* 67, no. 2 (Spring 1993): 14–29.

Otto, James Solomon. "The Migration of the Southern Plain Folk: An Interdisciplinary Synthesis." *Journal of Southern History* 51, no. 2 (May 1985): 183–200.

Owsley, Frank Lawrence. *Plain Folk of the Old South*. Chicago: Quadrangle Books, 1965.

Parrish, William E. *A History of Missouri*. Vol. 3, *1860 to 1875*. Columbia: University of Missouri Press, 1975.

Paxton, William McClurg. *Annals of Platte County, Missouri, From Its Exploration Down To June 1, 1897: With Genealogies of Its Noted Families and Sketches of Its Pioneer and Distinguished People*. Kansas City, Mo.: Hudson-Kimberly, 1897.

Perkins, Elizabeth A. "The Consumer Frontier: Household Consumption in Early Kentucky." *Journal of American History* 78, no. 2 (September 1991): 486–508.

Phillips, Authorene Wilson. *Arrow Rock: The Story of a Missouri Village*. Columbia: University of Missouri Press, 2005.

Pickle, Linda Schelbitzki. *Contented among Strangers: Rural German-Speaking Women and Their Families in the Nineteenth-Century Midwest*. Urbana: University of Illinois Press, 1996.

Popplewell, Frank S. "St. Joseph, Missouri, as a Center of the Cattle Trade." *Missouri Historical Review* 32, no. 4 (Spring 1938): 443–457.

Potts, Louis W. "From Speculator to Gentleman: Waltus L. Watkins and the Case for Land Speculation on the Missouri Frontier." *Gateway Heritage* 13, no. 1 (Fall 1992): 46–55.

Primm, James Neal. *Lion of the Valley: St. Louis, Missouri, 1764–1980*. St. Louis: Missouri Historical Society Press and University of Missouri Press, 1998.

Pruitt, Bettye Hobbs. "Self-Sufficiency and the Agricultural Economy of Eighteenth-Century Massachusetts." *William and Mary Quarterly*, 3rd Series, 41, no. 3 (July 1984): 331–350.

Rafferty, Milton D. "Agricultural Change in the Western Ozarks." *Missouri Historical Review* 69, no. 3 (April 1975): 299–322.

Ramage, John. *John Wesley Hunt: Pioneer Merchant, Manufacturer and Finan-*

cier. Lexington: University Press of Kentucky, 1974.

Ransom, Roger L., and Richard Sutch. *One Kind of Freedom: The Economic Consequences of Emancipation*. London: Cambridge University Press, 1977.

Rezneck, Sam. "The Depression of 1819–1822: A Social History." *American Historical Review* 39, no. 1 (October 1933): 28–47.

Richardson, Lemont. "Private Land Claims in Missouri, Part I." *Missouri Historical Review* 50, no. 2 (January 1956): 132–144.

Riley, Glenda. *The Female Frontier: A Comparative View of Women on the Prairie and the Plains*. Lawrence: University Press of Kansas, 1988.

———. *Frontierswomen: The Iowa Experience*. Ames: Iowa State University Press, 1994.

Rollings, Willard H. *The Osage: An Ethnohistorical Survey of Hegemony on the Prairie-Plains*. Columbia: University of Missouri Press, 1992.

Rohrbough, Malcolm J. *Days of Gold: The California Gold Rush and the American Nation*. Berkeley: University of California Press, 1997.

———. *The Land Office Business: The Settlement and Administration of American Public Lands, 1789–1837*. New York: Oxford University Press, 1968.

———. *The Trans-Appalachian Frontier: Peoples, Societies, and Institutions, 1775–1850*. Bloomington: Indiana University Press, 2008.

Rorabaugh, W. J. *The Alcoholic Republic: An American Tradition*. New York: Oxford University Press, 1979.

Rothenberg, Winifred B. "The Market and Massachusetts Farmers, 1750–1855." *Journal of Economic History* 41, no. 2 (June 1981): 283–314.

Rothman, Adam. *Slave Country: American Expansion and the Origins of the Deep South*. Cambridge, Mass.: Harvard University Press, 2005.

Rugh, Susan Sessions. *Our Common Country: Family Farms, Culture, and Community in the Nineteenth Century Midwest*. Bloomington: Indiana University Press, 2001.

Rutkow, Eric. *American Canopy: Trees, Forests and the Making of a Nation*. New York: Scribner, 2012.

Ryle, Walter H. "A Study of Early Days in Randolph County, 1818–1860." *Missouri Historical Review* 24, no. 2 (January 1930): 214–237.

Salstrom, Paul. *From Pioneering to Persevering: Family Farming in Indiana to 1880*. West Lafayette, Ind.: Purdue University Press, 2007.

Sampson, F. A. "Washington Irving: Travels in Missouri and the South." *Missouri Historical Review* 5, no. 1 (October 1910): 15–33.

Scarpino, Phillip. "Slavery in Callaway County, Missouri: 1845–1855." *Missouri Historical Review* 71, no. 1 (October 1976): 23–43.

Schlebecker, John T. *Whereby We Thrive: A History of American Farming, 1607–1972*. Ames: Iowa State University Press, 1975.

Schroeder, Walter A. "The Spread of Settlement in Howard County, Missouri, 1810–1859." *Missouri Historical Review* 63, no. 1 (October 1968): 1–37.

Schutt, William A., Jr. *Dark Banquet: Blood and the Curious Lives of Blood-Feeding Creatures*. New York: Harmony Books, 2008.

Sellers, Charles. *The Market Revolution: America, 1815–1846*. New York: Oxford University Press, 1991.

Shah, Sonia. *The Fever: How Malaria Has Ruled Humankind for 500,000 Years*. New York: Farrar, Strauss and Giroux, 2010.

Shammas, Carole. "How Self-Sufficient Was Early America?" *Journal of Interdisciplinary History* 13, no. 2 (Autumn 1982): 245–268.

Shirley, Michael. "The Market and Community Culture in Antebellum North Carolina." *Journal of the Early Republic* 11, no. 2 (Summer 1991): 219–248.

Shortridge, James R. "The Expansion of the Settlement Frontier in Missouri." *Missouri Historical Review* 75, no. 1 (October 1980): 64–90.

———. *The Middle West: Its Meaning in American Culture*. Lawrence: University Press of Kansas, 1989.

Stephens, F. F. "Missouri and the Santa Fe Trade." *Missouri Historical Review* 11, nos. 3–4 (April–July 1917): 289–313.

Stokes, Melvyn, and Stephen Conway, eds. *The Market Revolution in America: Social, Political and Religious Expressions, 1800–1880*. Charlottesville: University of Virginia Press, 1996.

Swan, Alonzo M. *Canton: Its Pioneers and History. A Contribution to the History of Fulton County*. Peoria, Ill.: N. C. Mason, 1871.

Swierenga, Robert P. *Pioneers and Profits: Land Speculation on the Iowa Frontier*. Ames: Iowa State University Press, 1968.

Taylor, Alan. *Liberty Men and Great Proprietors: The Revolutionary Settlement on the Maine Frontier, 1760–1820*. Chapel Hill: University of North Carolina Press, 1990.

Taylor, George Rogers. *The Transportation Revolution, 1815–1860*. New York: Harper and Row, 1951.

Thelen, David. *Paths of Resistance: Tradition and Dignity in Industrializing Missouri*. New York: Oxford University Press, 1986.

Thomas, Raymond D. "Missouri Valley Settlement: St. Louis to Independence." *Missouri Historical Review* 21, no. 1 (October 1926): 19–40.

Thorne, Tanis C. *The Many Hands of My Relations: French and Indians on the Lower Missouri*. Columbia: University of Missouri Press, 1996.

Transportation and the Early Nation. Indianapolis: Indiana Historical Society, 1982.

Ulrich, Laurel Thatcher. *A Midwife's Tale: The Life of Martha Ballard, Based on Her Diary, 1785–1812*. New York: Vintage Books, 1990.

Unruh, John D., Jr. *The Plains Across: The Overland Emigrants and the Trans-Mississippi West, 1840–1860*. Urbana: University of Illinois Press, 1979.

Uselding, Paul J. "Peddling in the Antebellum Economy: Precursor of Mass-Marketing or a Start in Life?" *American Journal of Economics and Sociology* 34, no. 1 (January 1975): 55–66.

Valencius, Conevery Bolton. *The Health of the Country: How American Settlers Understood Themselves and Their Land*. New York: Basic Books, 2002.

Vickers, Daniel. "Competency and Competition: Economic Culture in Early America." *William and Mary Quarterly*, 3rd Series, 47, no. 1 (January 1990): 3–29.

Viles, Jonas. "Old Franklin: A Frontier Town of the Twenties." *Mississippi Valley Historical Review* 9, no. 4 (March 1923): 269–282.

Voss, Stuart F. "Town Growth in Central Missouri, 1815–1860: An Urban Chaparral, Part I." *Missouri Historical Review* 64, no. 1 (October 1969): 64–80.

———. "Town Growth in Central Missouri, 1815–1860: An Urban Chaparral, Part III." *Missouri Historical Review* 64, no. 3 (April 1970): 322–350.

Waal, Carla, and Barbara Oliver Korner, eds. *Hardship and Hope: Missouri Women Writing About Their Lives, 1820–1920*. Columbia: University of Missouri Press, 1997.

Walz, Robert B. "Migration into Arkansas, 1820–1880: Incentives and Means of Travel." *Arkansas Historical Quarterly* 17, no. 4 (Winter 1958): 309–324.

Weber, David J. *The Mexican Frontier, 1821–1846: The American Southwest under Mexico*. Albuquerque: University of New Mexico Press, 1982.

West, Elliott. *The Contested Plains: Indians, Goldseekers, and the Rush to Colorado*. Lawrence: University Press of Kansas, 1998.

———. *Growing Up with the Country: Childhood on the Far Western Frontier*. Albuquerque: University of New Mexico Press, 1989.

Wettstaed, James R. "A Look at Early Nineteenth Century Life in an Ozarks

Mining Town: The View from the Company Store." *Plains Anthropologist* 45, no. 171 (February 2000): 85–112.

White, John Barber. "The Missouri Merchant One Hundred Years Ago." *Missouri Historical Review* 13, no. 2 (January 1919): 91–111.

Whites, LeeAnn, Mary C. Neth, and Gary R Kremer. *Women in Missouri History: In Search of Power and Influence.* Columbia: University of Missouri Press, 2004.

Winters, Donald L. *Tennessee Farming, Tennessee Farmers: Antebellum Agriculture in the Upper South.* Knoxville: University of Tennessee Press, 1994.

Wood, Gordon S. *Empire of Liberty: A History of the Early Republic, 1789–1815.* New York: Oxford University Press, 2009.

———. *The Radicalism of the American Revolution.* New York: Vintage Books, 1993.

———. "The Significance of the Early Republic." *Journal of the Early Republic* 8, no. 1 (Spring 1988): 3–20.

Wyman, Mark. *The Wisconsin Frontier.* Bloomington: Indiana University Press, 1998.

Wyman, Walker D. "The Outfitting Posts." *Pacific Historical Review* 18, no. 1 (February 1949): 14–23.

UNPUBLISHED THESES AND DISSERTATIONS

Combs, Jason H. "Early Settlement of a Frontier Community: The Platte Purchase, 1836–1850." Ph.D. diss., University of Nebraska, 2000.

Johnson, Ella. "The Economic Development of the Boonslick Country as Reflected in the *Missouri Intelligencer.*" Master's thesis, University of Missouri, 1931.

Kennedy, Mary Alice. "The Business Career of Moses U. Payne, 1828–1870." Master's thesis, University of Missouri, 1944.

Mergenthal, Rebekah Myfanwy Kirstin. "Border Lines: The People of the Lower Missouri River Valley and the Expansion of the United States, 1803–1855." Ph.D. diss., University of Chicago, 2008.

Pope, James Sterling. "A History of Steamboating on the Lower Missouri: 1838–1849, St. Louis to Council Bluffs, Iowa Territory." Ph.D. diss., St. Louis University, 1984.

INDEX

IOWA AND THE MIDWEST EXPERIENCE

On Behalf of the Family Farm: Iowa Farm Women's Activism since 1945
by Jenny Barker Devine

What Happens Next? Essays on Matters of Life and Death
by Douglas Bauer

A Store Almost in Sight: The Economic Transformation of Missouri from the Louisiana Purchase to the Civil War
by Jeff Bremer

The Lost Region: Toward a Revival of Midwestern History
by Jon K. Lauck

The Drake Relays: America's Athletic Classic
by David Peterson

Iowa Past to Present: The People and the Prairie, Revised Third Edition
by Dorothy Schwieder, Thomas Morain, and Lynn Nielsen

Necessary Courage: Iowa's Underground Railroad in the Struggle against Slavery
by Lowell Soike

Transcendental Meditation in America: How a New Age Movement Remade a Small Town in Iowa
by Joseph Weber

Main Street Public Library: Community Places and Reading Spaces in the Rural Heartland, 1876–1956
by Wayne A. Wiegand